Time Out Guides Ltd
4th Floor
125 Shaftesbury Avenue
London WC2H 8AD
United Kingdom
Tel: +44 (0)20 7813 3000
Fax: +44 (0)20 7813 6001
Email: guides@timeout.com
www.timeout.com

Contributors Jessica Ablitt Sudbury, Dominic Addison, Sharif Ahmed, Edoardo Albert, Ashleigh Arnott, Simone Baird, Alex Barlow, Daisy Bowie-Sell, Paul Burston, David Clack, Rachael Claye, Clare Considine, Simon Coppock, William Crow, Annie Dare, Keith Davidson, Patrick Davis, Amy Ellis, Anna Faherty, Mike Flynn, Grant Gillespie, Charlie Godfrey-Faussett, Hugh Graham, Sarah Guy, Derek Hammond, Ronnie Haydon, Kate Hutchinson, Serena Kutchinsky, Ben Lerwill, Jon Levene, Cathy Limb, Emily Mahon, Katie McLady, Megha Mohan, Jenni Muir, Julie Pallot, Tristan Parker, Toby Pearce, Cath Phillips, Natasha Polyviou, Kate Riordan, Alan Rutter, Robin Saikia, Cyrus Shahrad, Andrew Shields, Bella Todd, Helen Walasek, Peter Watts, Patrick Welch, Sonia Zhuravlyova.

Front and back cover Andrew Brackenbury, Luana Failla, Rob Greig, Britta Jaschinski, Ed Marshall, Jonathan Perugia, Kris Piotrowski, Ming Tang-Evans, Alys Tomlinson, Celia Topping, Marzena Zoladz, and courtesy Ham Yard Hotel, London

Photography pages 3, 5 (bottom left), 7 (bottom middle and bottom right), 13 (left), 25, 74, 103, 115, 121, 141 (left), 161, 188, 208, 209 (middle and bottom left), 250/251, 261, 262 Britta Jaschinski; 5 (top left), 89, 124, 236/237, 257, 284, 309 Jonathan Perugia; 5 (top middle and bottom middle), 9 (top), 53, 106, 107, 143, 230/231, 233, 275 Jitka Hynkova; 5 (top right), 28/29, 30/31, 37, 38, 90/91, 123, 130/131, 194 (top and bottom left), 195, 210/211 Olivia Rutherford; 5 (bottom right), 240, 285 Heloise Bergman; 7 (left), 105 (right), 141 (right) Haris Artemis; 7 (top right), 73 (bottom right), 120, 175 Andrew Brackenbury; 9 (middle) Michelle Grant; 9 (bottom), 183, 278 (bottom) Scott Wishart; 10/11 © simo bogdanovic/Alamy; 13 (top right and bottom right) Wellcome images; 18, 19, 26, 41, 185, 266, 276 Ben Rowe; 24 Stephen Morris; 27 Eric Bobrie; 33 National Maritime Museum; 42 siobhandoran.com; 46 (left) cristapper; 46 (right) Georgios Kollidas; 48, 67, 81 (top), 164, 165, 273, 274, 279 (bottom) Rob Greig; 50/51 Alastair Muir; 57 ONLY BY NGHT; 58 (right) Hannah Goodwin; 61 Libby Mor; 62, 63, 239 Tove K Breitstein; 64 Bikeworldtravel/Shutterstock.com; 69 (right) Stephen White; 70/71, 264, 265, 303 Marzena Zoladz; 73 (top left) Dean and Chapter of Westminster; 73 (top right), 169 r.nagy; 76 (top) Nick Hawkes/ Shutterstock.com; 76 (bottom) chrisdorney/Shutterstock.com; 78 RideLondon; 79 Will Pryce/www.willpryce.com; 81 (bottom left), 278 (top and middle) Ed Marshall; 81 (bottom right), 105 (left), 108, 113, 127, 209 (top right), 301 Ming Tang-Evans; 93 Katri Salonen; 95 Sarah Thorowgood; 96 (top) Kirsanov; 96 (bottom) WWT London Wetland/Selena Sherid; 97 The Royal Parks; 99 ariadna de raadt/Shutterstock. com; 100 Dan Afshar; 104 The Foundling Museum; 110/111 Peter Macdiarmid/Getty Images; 129, 167, 267 (bottom left) Alys Tomlinson; 133, 244 Chris Jenner/Shutterstock.com; 144, 197, 198, 207 Elisabeth Blanchet; 147 www.gorminator.com; 148 © PCL/Alamy; 158 Simon Goss; 159 Suzi Corker; 162 Jean Goldsmith; 170/171 Tim Hunkin; 173 (top) Peter Garner; 173 (middle) Sophie Lee; 173 (bottom) Fung Wah-Man; 178 Kleon3/Wikimedia Commons; 179 Kiev.Victor/Shutterstock.com; 187 Mirren Rosie; 190/191 QQ7/Shutterstock.com; 193 Dan Breckwoldt/Shutterstock.com; 194 (bottom right) Layton Thompson; 200 (top) Frantzesco Kangaris; 200 (bottom) Margaret Kelly; 203 Adrian Pancucci; 204, 279 (top) David Axelbank; 205 Tim Crocker; 206 Brian David Stevens; 209 (top left and bottom right) Rogan Macdonald; 214 Richard Bryant/arcaid.co.uk; 216 © Andy Carver 2015; 220 Stephen Cummiskey; 221 John Rankin and Nicola; 222 Chris Pippard/WWT; 225 (top left) Damian Griffiths; 225 (top right and bottom) © Kate Elliott Courtesy of The Photographers' Gallery; 226 © 2013 Luke Hayes; 229 Michael Cockerham; 243 Diana Jarvis; 245 Ron Ellis/Shutterstock.com; 246 Charlie McKay; 247 Ewan Munro/ Wikimedia Commons; 254 fasphotographic/Shutterstock.com; 267 (top and bottom right) Gemma Day; 268 Nick Ballon; 269 Anthony Webb; 270/271 James Perry; 280 The Players of St Peter; 282 Nick Cobbing; 283 Justin David; 286/287 Damian O'Hara; 288 Royal Collection Trust/© Her Majesty Queen Elizabeth II 2015; 290/291 James O Jenkins; 294 Kemptonsteam.org; 295 Julia Gavin/Alamy Stock Photo; 297 Philip Mould Ltd; 299 Michal Bednarek/Shutterstock.com; 306 Thomas Skovsende

The following images were supplied by the featured establishments/artists: 40, 43, 47, 58 (left), 69 (left), 77, 83, 109, 122, 134, 135, 150/151, 153, 157, 160, 174, 176, 217, 219, 228, 234, 242, 248, 249, 289, 293, 298

Contents

A PICTURE PERECT DAY OUT

Explore magnificent interiors and discover world-famous paintings by Rembrandt, Gainsborough and Vermeer.

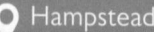 Hampstead

ENGLISH HERITAGE
KENWOOD

Step into England's story

About the guide

Telephone numbers

All phone numbers listed in this guide assume that you are calling from within London. From elsewhere within the UK, prefix each number with 020. From abroad, dial your international access code, then 44 for the UK, and then 20 for London.

Disclaimer

While every effort has been made to ensure the accuracy of information within this guide, the publishers cannot accept responsibility for any errors it may contain. Businesses can change their arrangements at any time, so, before you go out of your way, we strongly advise you to phone ahead to check opening times, prices and other particulars.

Advertisers

The recommendations in *1000 Things to do in London for under £10* are based on the experiences of Time Out journalists. No payment or PR invitation of any kind has secured inclusion or influenced content. The editors select which venues and activities are listed in this guide, and the list of 1,000 was compiled before any advertising space was sold. Advertising has no effect on editorial content.

Let us know what you think

Did we miss anything? We welcome tips for 'things' you consider we should include in future editions and take note of your criticism of our choices. You can email us at guides@timeout.com.

Introduction

London is a famously – some might even say reassuringly – expensive city. A place that consistently tops highest cost of living charts and which people from out of town save up to visit. There's no denying the fact that a martini at Claridge's or a box at the Royal Opera House will set you back considerably more than £10 – and that's probably the way it should be. Some things are worth paying a lot for. Yet despite the high rents and other costly living expenses, there is also a wealth of entertainment on offer in the city that's free – or at least attainable for less than a tenner.

When we set about compiling a list of ideas, it soon became clear that we were not going to be short of suggestions. For starters, since the great national museums threw open their doors for free after the millennium, it's been possible to spend days wandering the capital soaking up culture without paying a penny – once you've bought your Travelcard. But even travelling through the city can be part of the floor show – head upstairs on a double decker bus with Peter Watts (*see p84*) and you'll see what we mean, and happy is the child that bags the front seat on a driverless DLR train (*see p240*). Then there are the hundreds of other art galleries and museums to visit, walks to take, performances to see (including opera in Covent Garden), bargains to buy, food to eat and even cocktails to sip – all for less than £10. You can use the thematic index (*see p315*) for inspiration and the A-Z one (*see p310*) if you are looking for something specific.

It's true that sometimes a little ingenuity – and occasionally a little blagging – is required to keep things ticking along for less than a tenner, and there are some things in this book that would not be here if it weren't for the generosity of the people that run them. But, as you'll quickly discover with the help of this guide, London is full to bursting with gloriously cheap thrills. Grab a crisp ten pound note and start exploring.

1

Refresh yourself in Battersea Park

Here's hoping for a succession of glorious summer days, in which London's fountains become more than just decorative attractions. If a heatwave comes, you'll be relieved to know that the fountains in Battersea Park – the largest of any London park – spring into life at least once every hour.

2

Take tea in the British Museum

You could have a cuppa in one of the museum's various cafés, but if you have some spare time why not enjoy the free 'Way of Tea' session instead? This demonstration of the Japanese tea ceremony takes place in Room 92 roughly once a fortnight.

There's also a terrific programme of free gallery talks, all linked to the vast museum collection in some way, ranging from 'The sculptures of the Parthenon' to 'The Indian Ocean – trade and transport'. Many of them are also timed just right (at 45 minutes) for a lunch break.

Some other events, particularly family ones (such as Medieval Animation workshops) are also free. Check the website for specific dates and details of all events.
British Museum *Great Russell Street, WC1B 3DG (7323 8299, www.britishmuseum.org).*

3

Buy Chinese food in Chinatown

Head to New Loon Moon (9A Gerrard Street, W1D 5PL, 7734 3887) – a labyrinth of foodie delights – for an unrivalled range of products from different countries, including China, Thailand, Vietnam, Korea, India, Japan, Indonesia, the Philippines, Malaysia and even Burma. Try fresh gai lan (Chinese broccoli), Thai pea aubergines or huge, spiky jackfruit sold by the slice (in season, otherwise tinned). Loon Fung (42-44 Gerrard Street, W1D 5QG, 7437 7332, www.loonfung.com) is one of the only oriental supermarkets in this part of town to have a butcher's counter – pork shin bones and chicken feet are offered alongside more traditional cuts. See Woo (18-20 Lisle Street, WC2H 7BE, 7439 8325, www.seewoo.com) is good for fresh vegetables and cured Chinese meats.

4

Go falcon-watching on the South Bank

The Royal Society for the Protection of Birds (RSPB) isn't just about red kites, golden eagles and puffins – all high-profile species living in remote sanctuaries. From July to September, you'll find Society volunteers toting telescopes next to the Millennium Bridge just outside Tate Modern. The RSPB's Richard Bashford told us that their plan is 'to approach people and say "would you like to see a falcon", then give them binoculars and information, and point them up to where they're perched on top of the Tate Modern chimney, post breeding.' Find out more at www.rspb.org.uk.

5

See a free film

Free outdoor film screenings take place in interesting public spaces in south-east London, thanks to an enterprising community group. Previous events have included *Battleship Potemkin* (with a live music soundtrack), shown on the roof of Peckham multi-storey car park, and *Breaking Away* (a bike-powered screening) at Herne Hill Velodrome. There are also workshops, talks and walks. See www.freefilmfestivals.org for details.

6

Drink to George Orwell in the Fitzroy Tavern

This lively West End boozer first secured its reputation as a literary salon in the 1920s, when it provided a bolt- and watering-hole for Fitzrovia's more outré residents, including Augustus John, Jacob Epstein and Aleister Crowley. Queen of bohemia Nina Hamnett could also be found sprawled over the bar here, trading anecdotes of her numerous adventures with Picasso in exchange for drinks. In the '50s, regulars included Dylan Thomas, George Orwell and Soho raconteur Julian McLaren-Ross.

The Sam Smith pub still wears its history with pride – head downstairs to the Writers' and Artists' Bar, find yourself a cosy wooden booth and toast London's former literary glories.
Fitzroy Tavern *16A Charlotte Street, W1T 2LY (7580 3714).*

7

Be grateful for modern medicine...

The Wellcome Collection explores the connections between medicine and art through its three spaces. Upstairs, exhibits drawn from 19th-century explorer Sir Henry Wellcome's findings include a 14th-century Peruvian mummy, a used guillotine blade, Napoleon's toothbrush and a wickedly bladed torture chair. Next door is 'Medicine Now', which contains some startling modern art on medical themes (a realistic sculpture of a man disappearing into the folds of his own obese stomach, for example). Downstairs, the series of temporary exhibitions, such as 'Forensics – the anatomy of crime', gets better and better.

A revamp in 2014 added a fascinating reading room, where, alongside medical and scientific books, there are extraordinary artefacts (a 'Smoky Sue Smokes for Two' health-warning doll, for example). One especially fascinating addition is the 'Virtual Autopsy' table – effectively a giant tablet where you can swipe cuts through and otherwise manipulate a variety of cadavers in 3D, including Egyptian and Aztec mummies. The replica of Freud's couch comes complete with Rorschach tests you can have a go at.

Wellcome Collection *183 Euston Road, NW1 2BE (7611 2222, www.wellcomecollection.org). Free*

8

...and learn in your lunch hour, at the Wellcome Collection

There are many interesting ways to pass an hour in the Wellcome Collection's galleries, but when it comes to maximising your lunch hour the free Packed Lunch talks can't be beaten. Bring along your sandwiches and tuck in while scientists present a 45-minute talk on their specialist subject. Previous topics have included baby laughter, synaesthesia, gambling and germs in the city. Which hopefully didn't put anyone off their food.

Wellcome Collection

On this day...

In 2012 time was everything, today you can take things a little slower

A walk in Queen Elizabeth Olympic Park
Less than 10 minutes from central London

See the place where it all happened. And where it's all happening still. Queen Elizabeth Olympic Park is not just an unmissable venue for sports enthusiasts, but the perfect place to relax, cycle, stroll and play. There's so much to see, do and explore! It's more than your average walk in the park, so come and enjoy it for free today!

Visit QueenElizabethOlympicPark.co.uk
Making memories since 2012

QUEEN ELIZABETH OLYMPIC PARK

9-13

Support a community café

Bonnington Café

This vegetarian and vegan restaurant in Vauxhall started life in the 1980s as a squat café, and is now run co-operatively, serving cheap meals at lunch and dinner, seven days a week. A varied roster of cooks take it in turns to devise the menu, but the quality is always good. Just make sure to take advantage of the BYO policy, so that you have a glass of wine ready for when the service is that bit more laid-back than you're used to. Cash only.
11 Vauxhall Grove, SW8 1TD (www.bonningtoncafe.co.uk).

Gallery Café

Once upon a time, the Gallery Café was about the only place to have lunch near Bethnal Green tube – and it's still a great one. A tasty vegan menu, local beers, great coffee and a pretty garden make it a lovely place to relax for a few hours. Profits go to St Margaret's House, a charity that provides the local community with support, funding and arts events that range from folk music to spoken-word performances.
St Margaret's House, 21 Old Ford Road, E2 9PL (office 8980 2092, www.stmargaretshouse.org.uk/ thegallerycafe).

Hornbeam Café

Staffed by volunteers, this friendly, colourful hub in the centre of Walthamstow dishes out vegetarian and vegan food. Much of the veg is locally grown by workers co-op Organiclea, while bread comes from the Hornbeam Bakers' Collective. It's a busy place: regular classes include Italian for beginners, guitar tuition and knitting, and numerous community groups use the upstairs meeting rooms.
458 Hoe Street, E17 9AH (8558 6880, www.hornbeam.org.uk).

Paper & Cup

Supporting recovering addicts by offering training and ongoing career advice, the Spitalfields Crypt Trust runs this cute little daytime café in Shoreditch. Its charming staff, locally made food, decent coffee and top-notch second-hand book selection will have you wishing it was your local. It's open daily (the trust's other café, in Poplar, is closed on Sunday).
18 Calvert Avenue, E2 7JP (7739 5358, www. paperandcup.co.uk).

Skylight Café

This Shoreditch coffee shop does a mean line in fixing lives. Run by homelessness charity Crisis, it trains around 100 people a year, many of whom are ex-offenders who've been referred by local charity Switchback. They're standing strong against newer, trendier competition with healthy lunch options (aubergine and chickpea tagine, perhaps, or meatballs and spaghetti) and excellent coffee.
64 Commercial Street, E1 6LT (7426 3867, www.crisis.org.uk/cafelondon).

14

Take pleasure in the Palace on Bankside

As recently as the 1960s, the Bishop of Winchester's Palace on Bankside was little more than a rumour, hidden away behind Victorian warehouse walls. But now its tumbledown walls and high rose window once again add some spiritual frisson, as well as some 13th-century gravitas, to Clink Street. In the 15th and 16th centuries, Bankside was the focal point for fun in London – and who better to control the theatrical shenanigans, the dog-tossers, bear-baiters and prostitutes (aka 'Winchester geese', *see p264*) than the right honourable bishop himself? Oh, for the days when this 'private retreat from the pressures of medieval governance' featured not only 'a prison, a brewhouse and a butchery' but also the more wholesome delights of a 'tennis court, bowling alley and pleasure gardens'. No wonder the area was known as the 'Liberty of the Clink'.
Winchester Palace *www.englishheritage.org.uk.*

Path to glory

Cath Phillips packs some plasters and walks the Thames Path – all the way from the Thames Barrier to Hampton Court Palace.

The pain set in just past County Hall. The sunlight was bouncing off the water, the Houses of Parliament were resplendent in the afternoon sun, and the riverside café did a mean cappuccino. But my feet were suffering: the blisters on my ankles had started to bleed, my toes were red and raw, and a strange puffy swelling had appeared on the underside of one foot. Perhaps we could call it a day, nip round the corner to Waterloo station and get the tube home? Fat chance. We were on a mission: to walk the Thames Path through London, all 36 miles of it from the Thames Barrier to Hampton Court Palace, over one weekend, and no way was the little matter of bleeding blisters going to stop us. At least I'd got some plasters and a spare pair of socks. And it was only another 23 miles to go. It was a bright Saturday morning at the beginning of October. We'd started at 9am, meeting at North Greenwich tube station at the top of the desolate Greenwich

Peninsula, next to the O2 Centre. From there it was a bus ride to the Thames Barrier, the official 'end' of the Thames Path, which starts 184 miles away at the river's source in the Cotswolds. For us it was the beginning, however, because we were walking east to west. You can do it in either direction, of course, but we had an overnight stop in Barnes and, anyway, it somehow seemed more appropriate to walk west – away from the city into the countryside, the sunset and the glories of a splendid palace.

Few people walk great distances in London. Walks tend to be short and practical: to and from the tube station or bus stop, to the shops, perhaps a Sunday stroll around a park if you're lucky. There are other long-distance paths within the capital (the Capital Ring, the London Loop, the Green Chain Walk), but the Thames Path takes you through the heart of London, not the outskirts; it reveals the ever-changing nature of the city, from the industrial east through the seats of power in the built-up centre to the increasingly rural west; and it's a brilliant way to reclaim the Thames, that great thoroughfare that defines the city yet is often ignored by its inhabitants.

You don't need a map as there are signposts all along the route, but it's worth taking the three (free) mini guides to the London stretch of the Thames Path National Trail. You can download them from the Transport for London website (www.tfl.gov.uk/modes/walking). The brochures are written west to east, but they're just as useful in the opposite direction if you want sights pointed out to you, historical information and, crucially, for helping you decide which side of the river to walk on. You have no choice at the extremities, but from Greenwich to Teddington Lock the path straddles both sides of the river and it's possible to zigzag via the numerous bridges. Swapping sides gives a different perspective, but there are also lengthy and irritating detours that are best avoided, when the path is forced away from the water's edge and goes all round the houses (literally, in some instances) before getting back on course. Other essential equipment should include proper hiking boots and thick socks for cushioning, plasters, water and raingear. Binoculars are useful too.

The first ten miles, to Tower Bridge, were easy. From the shiny silver pods of the Thames Barrier to genteel Greenwich, it's a bleak but thrilling landscape of industrial decay, the path hugging the shoreline past scrapyards, derelict wharves, heaps of aggregate and mysterious metal structures dangling over the water. Rusting shopping trolleys are visible in the mud at low tide, and signs of life are few, bar the solitary Anchor & Hope pub and the occasional dog walker. In the 17th century, pirates' corpses were hung in cages at the tip of the peninsula as a deterrent to other pirates; later, it became an industrial stronghold, dominated by works for guns, ships, steel, metal, cement and gas, and therefore heavily polluted. Nowadays, the Greenwich Ecology Park and rows of colourful new apartment blocks signal the area's transformation – but it's still got a long way to go.

Just past the O2 Centre is Antony Gormley's sculpture *Quantum Cloud*, a tangle of metal rods that gradually reveals the outline of a human figure. A sweet, heavy stench hangs in the air: Tate & Lyle's refinery still processes a million tonnes of sugar a year here. The brick towers of the Greenwich Power Station loom dramatically over the diminutive Trinity Hospital almshouses, founded in 1613; beyond lies the stately Royal Naval College and tourist shops of Greenwich, an ideal place for a coffee break.

> '*The path reveals the ever-changing nature of the city: from the industrial east, through the seats of power, to the increasingly rural west.*'

At Greenwich, you can continue along the south bank, through Deptford and Rotherhithe, or traverse the Thames via the Greenwich Foot Tunnel and walk through the Isle of Dogs and Wapping. It's one or the other: there's no alternative river crossing until you reach Tower Bridge. We chose the southern route, ducking and diving around historic Rotherhithe, with changing views, as the river bends around the Isle of Dogs, of the higgledy-piggledy apartment blocks and gleaming high-rises of Canary Wharf opposite.

There's an awkward detour at Pepys Park in Deptford (look out for the Thames Path signs or you'll get lost). Then comes Deptford Strand, site of Henry VIII's Royal Dockyards – Drake's Steps mark the point where Francis Drake was knighted by Elizabeth after his circumnavigation of the globe in the *Golden Hinde*. The docks here, once the heart of Britain's seafaring ambitions – whalers left for the Arctic from Greenland Dock – are now used by watersports enthusiasts and yachting types. Occasional danger signs warn of 'Slippery Steps. Sudden Drop. Deep Water.' Surrey Docks Farm, a ramshackle oasis with its goats, pigs, donkeys and café, is another handy refreshment stop. As the river bends to the west, you get your first glimpse of Tower Bridge.

Perhaps surprisingly, the section from Tower Bridge through the heart of the city and the tourist hotspots of the Tower of London, HMS *Belfast*, Shakespeare's Globe, Tate Modern, the Southbank Centre and the London Eye is the least interesting for the purposes of this mission. Inevitably, this is the most crowded part of the walk; it was hard to retain a sense of purpose and an air of adventure as we struggled through hordes of sightseers and office workers on their lunch break. (The northern bank, along the edge of the City, Victoria Embankment and Charing Cross, is quieter.) Eventually, the throngs petered out beyond Westminster Bridge.

We crossed to the north at Lambeth Bridge (to avoid lengthy detours in Vauxhall and around the dilapidated hulk of Battersea Power Station), then crossed back again at Chelsea Bridge to take in leafy Battersea Park. We then yo-yoed once more to the north over Albert Bridge and wandered past assorted houseboats and gleaming yachts at Chelsea Harbour, followed by a seemingly endless array of swanky new riverside apartment blocks to get to Wandsworth Bridge. By now, it was getting dark and we were dog-tired; which is perhaps the reason that we made the mistake of continuing on the north side and had to endure a tedious longcut around the grounds of Fulham's Hurlingham Club, before hitting Putney Bridge.

We crossed the Thames once more. From here, the most direct route to Barnes was a couple of miles, but we were walking next to the river and at this point it does one of its great meandering loops up to Hammersmith Bridge and then south again. At least the hard, foot-grinding tarmac turned to gravel after the boathouses of Putney, and the tree-lined path was tranquil and increasingly pretty as we headed behind the London Wetland Centre, past playing fields and the Leg o' Mutton nature reserve. Finally, the humps of Barnes Bridge signalled the end of day one. A stiff drink, a hot bath and an early night swiftly followed. We weren't up early the following morning.

Day two started well. The stretch from Barnes to Richmond on the south bank is particularly idyllic. (It also avoids a rambling detour through the backstreets of uninteresting Brentford and, if you're counting miles – which of course we were – the southern route is more than two miles shorter than the northern one.) Trees line the gravel path, which hugs the water's edge, curving past cottages, various pubs, the Budweiser brewery at Mortlake (the smell of hops in the west countering the sugar in the east) and a glitzy, glassy housing development just before Kew Pier and Bridge.

The weather was bright and sunny, and ducks and swans paddled by on the water, keeping out

of the way of the heaving rowers. Then a lovely green vista opened up as the path skirted the edge of the Royal Botanic Gardens and the Old Deer Park. It was low tide, and foxes were playing on the foreshore opposite; beyond, we could see lion-topped Syon House amid the grassy expanse of Syon Park. Then came pretty Richmond Lock, Twickenham Bridge and, shortly afterwards, the White Cross pub and the smart riverside frontage of Richmond. We stopped for coffee, cake and a breather at the café nestled under the bridge.

Just after Richmond lies one of the most picturesque parts of the Thames. The buildings disappear and there's the long sweep of Petersham Meadows (where cows still graze) and a little island midstream. Handsome 17th-century Ham House on the south bank faces off against 18th-century Marble Hill House on the north (a foot ferry runs between the two). Himalayan balsam has colonised the riverbank here; it's an invasive exotic, but it's hard to resist squeezing the seedcases – which pop satisfyingly, as if alive – thus spreading it further. Then comes a series of playing fields, nature reserves and, finally, Teddington Lock.

As well as the lock (which is crammed with pleasure boats in summer), there's a weir, a summer café and footbridges to Teddington

proper. The lock marks the end of the tidal Thames; from this point, the river takes on a placid and unhurried air, very different from the turbulent highs and lows Londoners are used to. This is also where the path loses its doublesided character. It runs on the south bank through a grassy hinterland as far as Kingston, then you have to cross to the northern bank, following the sweeping edge of Hampton Court Park to Henry VIII's glorious Tudor palace.

Just three miles to go. Trees and bushes dangled in the water, swans floated gently past a marina; the houses of Thames Ditton across the water the only reminder that we weren't in the heart of the country. But the light was fading, and an autumnal chill had descended, making our legs feel heavy and stiff. Even the gravel towpath was getting too hard underfoot, so we hobbled, staggered and stumbled on the grassy verge until the long brick wall and ornate gates of Hampton Court Palace came into view. The sense of achievement was profound and – not capable of much more – we fell into the nearest pub for a celebratory pint.

On the train home (Hampton Court station is 30 minutes from Waterloo), despite aching limbs and bleeding feet, we were already planning to do it all again, this time from west to east, filling in the gaps we'd missed this time.

GLOBE THEATRE

@HELLO_HICCUP
"Get there early and you'll be able to stand right by the stage, amazing!! =)"

@__TARBS
"it's great. feels like you're at a festival."

GET THE BEST VIEW THIS SUMMER AND BE A PART OF THE ACTION BY STANDING @THE__GLOBE

@ELIZABETHMOYA
"Being a groundling is the BEST. It's MAGIC, I always get standing tix."

700 £5 TICKETS
FOR EVERY PERFORMANCE

@LADESU
"Worth every £. You won't have another experience like it!"

@ROODAVEY
"It's the only way to see a show at the Globe in my eyes. Such a great experience."

@JAMES910CR
"Actors often walk amongst you, which is fun."

JOIN THE CONVERSATION  #groundling @The_Globe
f /ShakespearesGlobe

@JAMIECDIXON
"Really feel like you become a part of the show."

BOOK NOW 020 7401 9919
SHAKESPEARESGLOBE.COM

16-19

Decode Da Vinci

'In London lies a knight a Pope interred...' reads the clue in Dan Brown's *The Da Vinci Code* that leads our heroes to the 'Pantheonically pagan' round nave at the 12th-century Temple Church off Fleet Street (Temple, EC4Y 7BB). There are spooky, lifelike memorial effigies of knights arrayed in the Round, where the order once held their secret initiation rites. But the hunt swiftly moves on to Westminster Abbey (20 Dean's Yard, SW1P 3NY), where fans will find Isaac Newton's tomb, complete with the orb mentioned in the next part of the clue; although on a quiet day, the Chapter House may feature a distinct lack of flying cryptex cylinders, gunplay and/or damsels in distress. It turns out that Alexander Pope ('A Pope', geddit?) read Newton's funeral eulogy.

Code devotees will also enjoy the crucifixion mural by Jean Cocteau (like Da Vinci, allegedly Grand Master of the Priory of Sion) in the Notre Dame de France church, off Leicester Square (5 Leicester Place, WC2H 7BX). The surreal 1950s mural features much occult symbolism, from disguised pentagrams through John the Baptist hand-signs to a black sun casting black rays into the sky.

But top of the hit list has to be the hulking art deco Freemasons Hall (60 Great Queen Street, WC2B 5AZ, 7831 9811, www.ugle.org.uk), in Covent Garden – especially as it isn't common knowledge that tours are freely available. Highlights at the hall include a wealth of magickal, inexplicable regalia, walls and paraphernalia strewn with Egyptian, Hebrew and esoteric symbolism – and the 2,000-seat Grand Temple. It's stacked with zodiacal signs, a depiction of Solomon's architect Hiram, and symbols for Faith, Hope, Charity and Jacob's Ladder. There are also celestial and terrestrial globes, all-seeing eyes, charioteers and 'five-pointed stars'. Other items in the collection include the various belongings of notable masons such as Winston Churchill and Edward VII.

20
Get behind the scenes at London Transport Museum's depot

London Transport Museum has a secret hoard at its depot in Acton. Normally, this is closed to the public but the trove of unused exhibits opens for a themed weekend twice a year (spring and autumn) so that the public can have a peek – a treat that includes its working model layouts of London's transport network. You can ride on the depot's miniature railway – there are steam as well as electric trains – or take a trip on full-size heritage vehicles, including the 1950s prototype of the Routemaster bus (the RM1).

London Transport Museum Depot *2 Museum Way, 118-120 Gunnersbury Lane, W3 9BQ (7565 7298, www.ltmuseum.co.uk). £10, free under-16s.*

21
Taste Trinidad at Roti Joupa

This ordinary-looking takeaway opposite Clapham North tube station has raised the bar for roti in London. This Trinidadian staple of a wholewheat flatbread wrapped around fillings originates in India but Trinidad has taken it as its own. It's also worth a trip across town for the doubles (roti stuffed with curried chick peas). There's also macaroni pie, tamarind balls, fresh coconut and other treats for homesick Trinis. It's almost impossible to spend more than £10, however hungry you are.

Roti Joupa *12 Clapham High Street, SW4 7UT (7627 8637).*

22
Make space in your diary for Open House weekend

Block out the third weekend of September and spend it visiting some of the more than 700 places – buildings of every conceivable size and type – that you can't visit the rest of the year. And, what's more, they are all free. See www.openhouselondon.org.uk for details.

23-31
Head for the hills

Alexandra Palace, N22
Alexandra Palace is famous for its splendid Victorian architecture and ice-skating rink, but the view is a similarly big draw. Framed by a low brick wall and ornamental railings, and dotted with pay-per-view machines, the prospect encompasses everything from the leafy Victorian terraces of Crouch End and Wood Green to the City glitter of the Gherkin. The view from below, looking back at the flamboyant 'Ally Pally', is equally majestic.

Brockwell Park, SW2
A short walk from the streets of Brixton, leafy Brockwell Park is worlds away in feel. Wandering amid the ancient trees, postcard lakes and gentle hills, you may feel like you're in the shires, but turn northwards and take in the vista – the Gherkin, the London Eye, the Shard – and suddenly the city meets the country.

Denmark Hill, SE5
Formerly Dulwich Hill, Denmark Hill was rechristened in honour of Queen Anne, wife of Prince George of Denmark, who lived on the east side. The Fox on the Hill pub stands on the site of the 'Fox under the Hill', the only building in the area shown on John Cary's 1786 map.

Forest Hill, SE23
This sleepy southern suburb is best-known for the eccentric Horniman Museum. It's a gem, to be sure, but the view from the park behind will leave an equally lasting impression – the City shimmering in the distance, rising above a canopy of leafy green.

Greenwich Park, SE10
It's quite a steep hike up to the summit of Greenwich Park from the river but it's worth it. As well as the genteel views of the Royal Park spread out before you, there's a host of graceful structures to take in on the way: from Wren and Hawksmoor's Baroque Old Royal Naval College through to Inigo Jones's Queen's House and on up to the Royal Observatory. The view from the top looking back across the river is breathtaking (*see p190*).

Muswell Hill, N10
The site of a spring named 'Mossy Well' that was thought to have healing properties, Muswell Hill was a place of medieval pilgrimage. Later on, its impressive views over the Thames and Lea valleys made it a popular rural retreat until – back in 1896 – key estates were bought by developer James Edmondson. He built new houses and shopping arcades, effectively creating a London suburb from scratch.

Parliament Hill, NW3
At the top of wild and woody Hampstead Heath, you are a long way from the urban grit, but Parliament Hill offers a true natural high within the city. The extraordinary view provides a medley of London's greatest landmarks – the Gherkin, the London Eye, the Houses of Parliament, St Paul's – and many harder-to-spot highlights.

Primrose Hill, NW3
The name sounds incredibly romantic, and the view from the top of Primrose Hill is just that. On a warm summer evening, this spot is a magnet for loved-up couples – it's the perfect cheap date in a neighbourhood of millionaires. London is laid out before you and its buildings are helpfully identified on a plaque. Visual highlights include Regent's Park and its zoo, the London Eye, and a couple of modernist icons: the BT Tower and Centrepoint.

Shooters Hill, SE18
At 433 feet, Shooters Hill is the highest point in south London. During the Middle Ages, the lofty position was a favourite with archers; much later, highwaymen took it to their hearts in the 17th century (because it was on the route of the mail coaches that ran between London and Dover). There was a gallows at the bottom of the hill, and the bodies of the hanged were displayed on a gibbet at the summit, close to where the Victorian Gothic water tower now stands.

32-33

Ring church bells

If you thought bell-ringing was just a simple matter of pulling on a rope, think again. It's an art form, one that requires precision, a degree of physical exertion and team work. The current technique, known as change ringing, was developed in the 17th century. Don't expect to be able to ring perfectly straight away; there are plenty of practice sessions around London that welcome beginners. For more details, check out www.mcaldg.org.uk. We particularly recommend St John at Hackney (Lower Clapton Road, E5 0PD, www.stjohnat hackney.org.uk, Mondays) and St Mary Abbots Kensington (Kensington High Street, W8 4HN, www.stmaryabbots church.org, Thursdays).

34-43 Take your time in London's bookshops

For some, there are few retail joys more unalloyed than an afternoon spent in a bookshop. And, with many now offering seating, and in some cases, cafés, it's become one of the capital's classic budget activities. Here are just a few of our favourite browsing haunts.

Big Green Bookshop

A community bookshop, run with a love and enthusiasm for books that's hard to find these days – and it has a sofa. As well as the expected local bookstore stock, it's strong on children's titles and multicultural books, and also has a second-hand department. The events programme is worth a look too; there are author events, children's storytelling sessions, a writers' group and a book group.
Unit 1, Brampton Park Road, N22 6BG (8881 6767, www.biggreenbookshop.com).

Books for Cooks

If the range of cookery books spanning many cuisines, plus culinary history, and food-related fiction and biographies doesn't make you hungry, then the aromatic smells coming from the tiny café at the back of the shop will. An essential browsing experience for any foodie.
4 Blenheim Crescent, W11 1NN (7221 1992, www.booksforcooks.com).

Daunt Books

A wonderful place to while away a few hours, Daunt Books is housed in a beautiful Edwardian building, complete with oak balconies, viridian walls, conservatory ceiling and a stained-glass window. The back room boasts a travel section extraordinaire but Daunt is also a good all-round bookshop: staff are well-read and dedicated, and their carefully curated picks – the best literary fiction, biography, and children's, design and cookery books – are dotted throughout the rest of the store.
83-84 Marylebone High Street, W1U 4QW (7224 2295, www.dauntbooks.co.uk).

Foyles

The big daddy of independent bookshops, Foyles is a London legend and a browser's best friend. Size does matter here: over 200,000 different titles on four miles (6.5km) of shelves. Fiction is a forte, as are music, sport, film and gay interest. Enhancing the contemplative mood is the Café at Foyles.
107 Charing Cross Road, WC2H 0DT (7437 5660, www.foyles.co.uk).

Hatchards

London's oldest bookshop has a refined air, but it's not too stuffy for browsing. On the contrary, the old-school charm is particularly conducive to drifting off into a literary reverie. Biography, politics, travel and fiction are strengths. Keep your eyes peeled for famous authors – the shop regularly gets in bigwigs for signings.
187 Piccadilly, W1J 9LE (7439 9921, www.hatchards.co.uk).

John Sandoe

This independent bookshop, founded in 1957, has a loyal clientele, professional staff and an enviably broad stock. New and classic releases

Foyles

Daunt Books

rub shoulders with more unusual items (books that have been privately printed, for example). There's a high proportion of quality hardbacks, a good travel section, and children's books in the basement. Wherever you look, the tottering piles of reading matter are a book-lover's dream.
10 Blacklands Terrace, SW3 2SR (7589 9473, www.johnsandoe.com).

London Review Bookshop

In the heart of Bloomsbury, the London Review Bookshop oozes intellectual gravitas, as you'd expect from a shop owned by the esteemed periodical. If you need inspiration, you'll find it here: the impeccable selection includes politics, current affairs, history, philosophy and poetry, and the tables are piled high with cleverly chosen tomes. Walk through an archway into the adjoining London Review Cake Shop, a charming café adorned with original art.
14 Bury Place, WC1A 2JL (7269 9030, www.lrbshop.co.uk).

Magma

In some ways, design books are the ideal genre for browsing – lots of eye candy and minimal reading required. Magma is the motherlode of look-at-me coffee-table books and glossy style magazines,

featuring cutting-edge design, architecture and graphics. In fact, the shop's objective is to blur the boundary between bookshop and exhibition space, so quiet contemplation is highly appropriate.
117-119 Clerkenwell Road, EC1R 5BY (7242 9503, www.magmabooks.com).

Skoob

At Skoob you'll stumble across out-of-print gems, cult classics, obscure biographies and forgotten best-sellers. There are some 70,000 titles spread across 2,500 square feet and every subject under the sun is represented: from philosophy, biography, maths and science to languages, literature and criticism, art, history, economics and politics.
Unit 66, Brunswick Centre, WC1N 1AE (7278 8760, www.skoob.com).

Stanfords

If Daunt whets your appetite for travel, Stanfords will trigger a case of full-blown wanderlust. The shelves are bursting with books on every country, city, highway and byway. Pick up a book, a map and a latte and get planning your dream trip in the small ground-floor café.
12-14 Long Acre, WC2E 9LP (7836 1321, www.stanfords.co.uk).

44-51

Look for John Soane (and find him in a telephone box)

One of Britain's greatest and most innovative architects, Sir John Soane (1753-1837) was a national treasure by the time of his death; his wonderfully idiosyncratic home, now the Sir John Soane's Museum (13 Lincoln's Inn Fields, WC2A 3BP, 7405 2107, www.soane.org), was bequeathed to the nation by an Act of Parliament.

Soane believed in 'the poetry of architecture' and used his house as a testing ground for his ideas on light and space. He was a great collector, so the house is full of ingenious space-saving touches – such as the panels hung with paintings that unfold from the walls. The downstairs is packed with antiquities, architectural models and art; above ground, in airy contrast, light streams through top-lit ceilings and is reflected off mirrored inserts.

But there's more to Soane than his museum – London is still full of his architectural influences. His most important commission (and the building he was most proud of) was the Bank of England. An established architectural masterpiece, it's all the more shocking that most of it was torn down

after World War I. But Soane's powerful perimeter wall remains and his first major work, the Bank Stock Office, has been reconstructed inside the bank's museum (Threadneedle Street, EC2R 8AH, 7601 4878, www.bankofengland.co.uk).

Purchased as Soane's country retreat in 1800, Pitzhanger Manor (Walpole Park, Mattock Lane, W5 5EQ, 8567 1227, www.pitzhanger.org.uk) was soon remodelled according to the architect's ideas of design and decoration, and features his trademark curved ceilings and inset mirrors. Acquired by Ealing Council in 1900, the house became a library. Today, the library has gone and the building has been restored to showcase Soane's work. Set in lovely Walpole Park, its extension houses a contemporary art gallery.

Dulwich Picture Gallery (Gallery Road, SE21 7AD, 8693 5254, www.dulwichpicturegallery. org.uk) was an unlikely outcome of 18th-century European politics. Art dealers François Bourgeois and Noel Desenfans spent years gathering a spectacular assemblage of art for the King of Poland. But by 1795, Poland was partitioned; the King was kingdomless and so had no need of a royal collection. With no takers for the pictures, Bourgeois willed them to Dulwich College in 1811, stipulating that his friend Sir John Soane design a building to display them and that it be open to the public. What Soane built has been described as the most beautiful art gallery in the world and has been an inspiration for countless later architects.

Set in a little Regency enclave, St Peter's Walworth (76 Tatum Road, SE17 1QR, 7703 3139) is the best preserved of Soane's three London churches, with its slim dome-topped tower, austere brick façade and Ionic portico. Its crypt is a masterful example of 19th-century brickwork. Soane's Holy Trinity Church, opposite Great Portland Street station (Marylebone Road, NW1 4DU, www.one-events.co.uk), is now only open for events, but the exterior is eye-catching; St John's Bethnal Green (Cambridge Heath Road, E2 9PA, www.stjohnbethnalgreen.org) has been remodelled following damage in 1870 and World War II, but for Soane groupies, it's still worth a visit.

A final must-see is Soane's tomb in the atmospheric setting of St Pancras Gardens, behind St Pancras station. Originally erected by Soane for his wife, the monument inspired the design of one of Britain's most iconic structures: Giles Gilbert Scott's K6 series of red telephone boxes.

52-53 *Spend peanuts at the cinema*

Genesis Cinema (93-95 Mile End Road, E1 4UJ, 7780 2000, www.genesiscinema.co.uk) shows a mix of arthouse movies and blockbusters in restored Victorian premises, currently incorporating five screens. The smallest, Studio 5, only has 40 seats but they're all sofas and armchairs with table service; additional attractions include Bar Paragon for drinks, the Grindhouse Café and the Kitchen for eats. Entry to headline movies at peak times in Studio 5 comes at a premium; virtually all other ticket prices are under a tenner though – often way under (£4 on Monday and Wednesday).

The PeckhamPlex (95A Rye Lane, SE15 4ST, 0844 567 2742, www.peckhamplex.com) has stayed the course in Peckham for more than 20 years. It may not be London's swankiest cinema – some would say that's an understatement – but what it lacks in finesse, it makes up for in economy. 'All tickets all day £4.99' is the credo, although 3D showings cost a little extra. It's an informal, independent multiplex – with staff who will chat about the films if prompted – the opposite of the usual bland, branded multi-screen experience.

54 *Swing dance*

Learn to swing dance (£8 a class) or attend a social (£4, or free if you've attended a class beforehand) at one of Swing Patrol's (www.swingpatrol.co.uk) many locations.

55

Play skittles at the Freemasons Arms...

No, don't even mention ten-pin bowling in the same breath. That commercial, sanitised version has little to do with the ancient game and its descendant, London Skittles, which is not so much played as venerated by the Hampstead Lawn Billiard & Skittle Club. The game uses nine pins and a cheese – the wooden discus players use to knock down the pins – and involves such intricacies as the 'flying fornicator' (a cheese with bad spin) and the dreaded 'Gates of Hell' pin formation, which takes expert felling. Few skittle alleys remain in London, but it's still being played, much as it has been since 1934, in the cellar at the Freemasons Arms in Hampstead. Come along on club night or book the alley for a group of friends – an experienced club member will provide help and equipment. To arrange a game, contact the club at www.londonskittles.co.uk.
32 Downshire Hill, NW3 1NT (7433 6811, www.freemasonsarms.co.uk).

56-59

...or throw things at a 'piglet'

The Balls Brothers wine bar (Hay's Galleria, Tooley Street, SE1 2HD, 7407 4301, www.balls brothers.co.uk) runs a free pétanque pitch in the middle of the shopping arcade near London Bridge and this essential French pastime has proved such a success that there's now an annual lunchtime tournament in summer. Games are played at the Surprise pub (16 Southville, SW8 2PP, 7622 4623), on a pitch near the Chevening Road entrance to Queen's Park in north-west London (8969 5661) and, occasionally, in the square outside the Prince of Wales pub (48 Cleaver Square, SE11 4EA, 7735 9916).

The game requires no prior experience and can be played on equal terms by young and old, male and female, drunk and sober. Each of three teams or individuals has two 'boules', which they must throw in turns as near as possible to the golf ball-sized 'cochonnet' (literally 'piglet'). The player or team whose boule is closest to the cochonnet wins. *Voilà*!

60

Get around town on a Clipper

When you look at the river these days, it's full of traffic – and we don't just mean day-tripping cruisers. The speedy and sleek catamaran service Thames Clippers (7001 2222, www. thamesclippers.com), largely designed for commuters, is still going strong since its launch in 1999.

61 Play table tennis...

Check out the Ping London website (www.ping london.co.uk) to find your nearest table. There are lots about – Broadgate in the City has six ping-pong tables, there are some near the British Library, and there's one at Leon in Spitalfields Market.

62 ...or tennis for free

Thanks to the Tennis for Free organisation (55 Thornhill Square, N1 1BE, 7609 9026, www.tennis forfree.com), there's no excuse for not becoming the next Andy Murray. Visit the website for a list of council courts at which you can play for free.

63

Enter the Great Spitalfields Pancake Race

The pancake race is said to date back 500 years, to the time when a woman, cooking at home, heard the church bells calling people to confession and ran out of her hovel, still holding her frying pan. Fast forward to the present, and there are a number of races held in London every Shrove Tuesday to mark this historic (and quite possibly entirely fabricated) event. Among the best is the Great Spitalfields race: teams of four, often in fancy dress (anything from Captain Jack Sparrow to a giant bright-green squid) toss pancakes as they run. Phone in advance if you want to take part (it's all done for the charity London Air Ambulance), and you'll have to bring your own frying pan (pancakes are provided). Alternatively, just show up if all you're after is the sight of daft costumes darting down the streets and pancakes hitting the pavement. There are engraved pans not only for the race winners but also for the best dressed tosser, so come imaginatively attired.
Great Spitalfields Pancake Race
www.alternativearts.co.uk.

64

Discover the Guildhall Art Gallery

In 1885, the City of London Corporation decided it was time to create a venue where its impressive collection could be put on display. The original Guildhall Art Gallery opened that year, adjacent to the Guildhall, and for more than half a century acted as a cultural node for the Square Mile. Some of the collection was moved out of London during World War II, but not all, and disaster struck on 10 May 1941 when fire caused by a German bombing raid largely destroyed the gallery and its remaining contents.

A temporary structure was built on site in 1946, which served as a home for the corporation's annual exhibitions and for loan exhibitions, but it wasn't until the 1980s that a plan was put in place to properly replace the original. Also in the 1980s – as an added historical bonus – archaeological investigations at the site revealed the remains of a Roman amphitheatre dating to the first century AD.

The wheels of archaeology, architecture and art turn slowly but by 1999 the all-new Guildhall Art Gallery was open to the public. Space in its basement, telling the tale of the amphitheatre, followed in 2002. It incorporates part of the fabric of the actual Roman amphitheatre from nearly two millennia ago. In the main hall you see the corporation's Victorian collection, including works by Millais and Rossetti, while galleries downstairs have notable paintings of London dating from the 16th century.

Entry to the gallery's permanent collection and to the amphitheatre is free. A charge is sometimes made for special exhibitions.
Guildhall Art Gallery *Guildhall Yard, off Gresham Street, EC2V 5AE (7332 3700, www.cityoflondon.gov.uk).*

65

Explore Mars, or launch your own space probe

The Royal Observatory houses London's only public planetarium. Designed by architects Allies & Morrison, the RIBA-award winning concrete cone of the planetarium is clad with almost 250 bronze plates. Positioning of the planetarium is minutely precise: the sloping southern side of the cone points towards the north celestial pole and pole star, the angle of the slope is the same as the degree latitude of the Royal Observatory (51° 28' 4") and the reflective glass top of the cone is sliced at an angle parallel to the celestial equator. Inside, thanks to digital laser technology, you can see Mars, Jupiter and Saturn with the untrained eye in *The Sky Tonight* show.

Royal Observatory & Planetarium *Blackheath Avenue, Greenwich Park, SE10 8XJ (8312 6565, www.nmm.ac.uk). Planetarium £8.50.*

66

Visit a 'Happy Café'

The Canvas is a café and creative venue that was launched in early spring 2015. It's a not-for-profit venture set up in association with Action for Happiness (www.actionforhappiness.org), an outfit that wants to build a happier and more caring society; the Canvas is officially a 'Happy Café'. Here, you'll find free comedy nights, lunchtime yoga (£10 per drop-in session, cheaper for block bookings), creative storytelling workshops (£5), free Wi-Fi, charity events and much more. There's a garden too. The café menu, meanwhile, ranges over breakfast, lunch, sharing boards and weekend brunch – none of which will break the bank.

Canvas Café *42 Hanbury Street, E1 5JL (7018 1020, http://thecanvascafe.org).*

Royal Observatory & Planetarium

Markets to visit at The Old Truman Brewery

THE OLDTRUMAN BREWERY

Home to East London's creative community, housing designers, illustrators and food artisans from all platforms offering an exciting array of work and culinary delights. Come along and experience the charm of Brick Lane's most diverse and exciting markets.

Thursday, Friday and Saturday 11am - 6pm & Sunday 10am - 5pm

Backyard Mark[E]t

Boiler House

The TEA rooms

sunday up market

VINTAGE MARKET

67-75 *Seek out 20th-century sculptures*

Two great Dames of 20th-century sculpture – abstract Barbara Hepworth and figurative Elisabeth Frink – have various works sited all over the city; link them together and you've got a great day's sculpture stroll. Start your trail at Kenwood House on Hampstead Heath. After a cuppa and a scone in the tea room, in the grounds you'll find Hepworth's *Monolith (Empyrean)* from 1953, still standing proud.

Then head south-east to find Dame Elisabeth's first major public commission, *Blind Man and his Dog* (1957), at the Bethnal Green end of Roman Road. Next, it's a short hop on the Central line to St Paul's to see her *Shepherd and Sheep* (1975) in Paternoster Square, a naked man herding four Attic-looking ovine forms. Further along the Central line, near Oxford Circus, Hepworth's *Winged Figure* (1963) adorns the Holles Street façade of John Lewis on Oxford Street.

A quick walk through Mayfair to Grosvenor Square is rewarded by Frink's winged bronze bald American eagle (1986), which sits atop the World War II Eagle Squadron memorial. Head on south to find her *Horse and Rider* (1975), inspired by the stallions of the Camargue, now surrounded by the tables and chairs of Caffè Nero on Dover Street. Next, hop on a bus to Knightsbridge to see the beaten copper panels, entitled the *Four Seasons* (Frink, 1961), adorning the Jumeirah Carlton Tower Hotel on Cadogan Place.

From here, head south-west to Battersea Park, for Hepworth's lakeside *Single Form* (1961). It's a smaller version (about 10 feet tall) of her monumental piece for the United Nations in New York. One sad end note: *Two Forms (Divided Circle)*, commissioned in 1970 by the Greater London Council, was stolen from Dulwich Park in December 2011.

A different league

Andrew Shields gets his kicks with some cheap footie thrills.

Why pay through the nose to sit behind a pillar at White Hart Lane? Or to be shoehorned into a plastic seat at Stamford Bridge designed for a six-year-old? Professional football clubs know they have a near-stranglehold over the emotions of their fans, but control of their wallets is less secure. It's no surprise that, with cash tight but the pull of live football as strong as ever, more and more supporters are acquainting themselves with London's non-league scene.

If you're used to the Barclays Premier and are contemplating getting your fix at a lower level, you'll need to be prepared. The crowds are small – typically a couple of hundred through to a couple of thousand – and any atmosphere has to be self-generated in grounds that may be short on creature comforts. The standard of football varies too. Even though what's known officially as 'level seven' of the game – encompassing the Ryman Premier – has its share of ex-pros, never-quite-made-its and young prospects, don't expect Arsenal-like wizardry.

There are, however, compensations. You will generally find camaraderie rather than antagonism among the opposing fans, and a warmth from clubs to whom your payment at the turnstile really matters. Merchandise, too, is rarely a rip-off. Games still kick off at the familiar time of 3pm on a Saturday afternoon and are not arbitrarily moved to suit TV schedules. You'll be up close to the action and, with none of the spectator health and safety restrictions that are imposed on big clubs' stadiums, you'll have the chance to stand rather than sit if you prefer. If you hang around afterwards, you can also probably share a pint with the big number nine you've spent 90 minutes roundly abusing.

Here are nine great non-league destinations offering history, tradition, pride, passion and a determination not merely to survive, but to thrive. With admission costing £10 or less at every one, you might discover that after all these years you're ditching that Spurs scarf and cheering for Enfield Town FC instead.

Dulwich Hamlet FC

Dulwich Hamlet FC

Hampton & Richmond Borough FC

Steptoe and Son scriptwriter Alan Simpson is club president and has a stand named after him at the tree-fringed Beveree Stadium in the heart of salubrious Hampton village. Former West Ham hero Alan Devonshire was manager here for a number of years – another claim to fame – but left in 2011; that role now falls to Alan Dowson. The team, currently in the Ryman Premier, are saddled with one of the game's worst nicknames though: the Beavers. Fans like to think of themselves as, ahem, the Beaver Patrol...
8979 2456, www.hamptonfc.net.

Enfield Town FC

Until 1999, the former Enfield FC were one of England's top amateur clubs and once close to gaining admission to the Football League. Then they sold their stadium and began a series of catastrophic ground-shares, which alienated most fans and led (like the well-known example of AFC Wimbledon) to the formation of fan-owned Enfield Town FC. Marking their move to the new Queen Elizabeth II stadium in late 2011

with a win against Harefield United, the Towners are making solid progress and currently play in the Ryman Premier. The old Enfield club was liquidated in 2007, having rebuffed a suggestion by the Enfield Town chairman that if the two clubs pooled their resources and fan base they could 'take Enfield back to the top of non-league football'. The entirely separate Enfield 1893 FC was then formed – they play in the Essex Senior League.
07787 875650, www.enfieldtown football club.co.uk.

Carshalton Athletic FC

Surrey's oldest club, founded in 1903, and now one of the county's most active in terms of community football development, the Robins are on a mission 'to become the most friendly football club in the league pyramid'. They play in the Ryman Division 1 South.
8642 2551, www.carshaltonathletic.co.uk.

Clapton FC

Founder members of the Southern League along with Luton, Millwall, Reading and Southampton (Tottenham Hotspur's application

was rejected), the Tons are five-time winners of the FA Amateur Cup. They became the first English team to play in Europe when they beat a Belgian XI in Antwerp way back in 1892 and then, in 1956, were the first amateur club to play under floodlights. Clapton are still based at the famous (well, slightly famous) Old Spotted Dog Ground in Forest Gate, but times are hard and they're currently in the Essex Senior League.
3652 2951, http://claptonfc.com.

Dulwich Hamlet FC

They sport pink and navy striped shirts, they were giants of the amateur game between the two world wars and they have one of the great football addresses: Champion Hill Stadium, Dog Kennel Hill, SE22. What's not to like? When the Hamlet are playing away (they're in the Ryman Premier), you can watch tenants Fisher FC tussling in the Southern Counties East League.
7274 8707, www.dulwichhamletfc.co.uk.

Hoddesdon Town FC

Inaugural winners of the FA Vase back in 1975, the Lilywhites – yet another club with that nickname – play in the Spartan South Midlands Premier, covering the north-west fringes of London and nearby counties. Their programme and pitch are both award-winning, while former Spurs legend Ossie Ardiles is club patron.
01992 463133, www.hoddesdontownfc.co.uk.

AFC Hornchurch

The Urchins emerged from the ruins of Hornchurch FC, who collapsed in 2004-05 when their backers went bankrupt. Grandiose plans to reach the Football League were abandoned and a roster of ex-pros on big wages proved unsustainable. However, the reconstituted club have shown that they can endure even with more cautious financial management, although the team slipped from the Ryman Premier to Division 1 North in 2015.
01708 220 080, www.afchornchurch.com.

Corinthian-Casuals FC

This is the story of a club that has survived more than 125 years with its ideals intact. The Corinthians were founded in 1882 (Casuals FC were established in 1878; the pair merged in 1939) as a reaction against the tide of professionalism sweeping through football in the late 19th century. They had no home ground and at first refused to enter anything as vulgar as the FA Cup. Training was outlawed and only challenge matches played. The team would refuse to take a penalty if awarded one, and would remove their goalkeeper if a spot kick was conceded, on the basis that the foul must have been serious enough to warrant a goal.

All this may sound somewhat sickly given today's style of play, but the players were genuinely talented. They inflicted Manchester United's record defeat, twice fielded the entire England side and scored 12 goals in a game against the Belgian national team.

The club spread the gospel of good sportsmanship as a globe-trotting equivalent of rugby union's Barbarians. A tour of Brazil in 1910 inspired the formation of SC Corinthians Paulista and, when they returned nearly 80 years later, the Brazilian legend Socrates donned their kit for one game. Real Madrid even adopted the Corinthians' strip for one season in 1925-26.

Social change brought an end to the club's sporting superiority, though Corinthian-Casuals are battling on in Division 1 South of the Ryman League. Despite securing their first-ever home ground (King George's Field in Tolworth) in 1988, players are still picked off by wealthier teams.

Some things never change, though, such as their spectacular chocolate and pink halved shirts. That, and the first rule of the club: 'to promote fair play and sportsmanship, to play competitive football at the highest level possible whilst remaining strictly amateur and retaining the ideals of the Corinthian and the Casuals football clubs.' The greatest English amateur football club ever? No contest.
8397 3368, www.corinthian-casuals.com.

Tooting & Mitcham United FC

Tooting were founded in 1887, Mitcham in 1912, and the amalgamation of the mighty south London duo happened in 1932. They now play in Morden at the grandly named Imperial Fields (also known as the KNK Stadium), a neat ground with space for 3,500. The 1970s were quite a heyday with Surrey Senior Cup wins and runs in the FA Cup and FA Trophy; in 2007 and 2008, there was more silverware (the Surrey Senior Cup again and the London Senior Cup twice). Now they play in the Ryman Division 1 South.
8685 6193, http://tmu-fc.co.uk.

85 Take up orienteering

A sport that's been likened to tackling *The Times* crossword while enjoying a jog, orienteering is the art of navigating a course in the shortest possible time, using a map and compass. The British Orienteering Federation (01629 583037, www.britishorienteering.org.uk) has a list of clubs and courses, and you can also buy a map of the permanent courses in London. It's a sociable sport, with regular club events (colour-coded to suit different skill levels), and it's an easy and family-friendly way to get some real exercise that feels just like messing about outdoors.

86 Meditate at the London Buddhist Centre

Opened in 1978 in a building that was once a Victorian fire station, this is one of the largest urban Buddhist centres in Europe. The London Buddhist Centre (51 Roman Road, E2 0HU, 8981 1225, www.lbc.org.uk) offers lunchtime and evening drop-in meditation classes (free-£10), as well as creative writing and poetry events, retreats on site and in the Suffolk countryside, and works in the wider community through outreach projects.

87 Follow a riverside sculpture tour

The Line (http://the-line.org) is a walking/cycling trail that takes in some little-known sites beside the Thames and some of the biggest names in contemporary British art, including a giant sweat-gland sculpture by Damien Hirst. Starting in North Greenwich – site of the O2 and a road sign by artists Thomson & Craighead that shows the distance you'd need to travel around the world until you returned to 'Here' – the route includes a ride in the Emirates cable car, a meander through Cody Dock and a visit to an old tidal mill before ending up in the Queen Elizabeth Olympic Park in Stratford. It takes about three hours on foot. Along the way, you'll encounter works by Eduardo Paolozzi, Richard Wilson, Bill Viola and others – we're particularly fond of Abigail Fallis's 22 shopping trolleys stacked in the shape of a double helix. Feeling extra adventurous? The sculptures are illuminated at night, so you could even schedule yourself an after-hours tour.

88

See London by gaslight

Tired of the neon glare of the West End? Do you yearn for some of ye olde city charm on your evening strolls? If so, then you'll find it, free of charge, in the parts of London still lit by gaslight. Some of the earliest street lighting in the city was established in the Royal Parks, where oil lamps were hung from the trees, but gas lighting soon followed, installed along Rotten Row in Hyde Park.

A green plaque at 100 Pall Mall commemorates Frederick Winsor, who put up London's first gas street lamps in Pall Mall in 1807 and became one of the pioneers of gas lighting in the UK and France. Born in 1763 in Brunswick, Germany, Winsor went to Paris in 1802 to investigate the 'thermo-lamp' that French engineer Phillipe Lebon had patented three years earlier. Over the next two decades, about 50,000 gaslights were installed across the city's streets.

Today, around 1,600 gaslights still illuminate central London every night. Keep your eyes peeled and in many parts of town you'll see the tell-tale bars sticking out of lampposts – before the process became automated, these used to support the lamplighter's ladder. Ignore the orange glare of the city's many sodium lamps – London's standard example of street light – and head for the capital's grander postcodes.

Fine examples of ornate lights can be seen outside Buckingham Palace, along Queen's Walk in Green Park, in St James's Park and at St James's Palace, around the Palace of Westminster and Westminster Abbey, along the Mall, in Horse Guards Parade and at Covent Garden. Several tiny and picturesque alleys off the Strand are also still lit by gas (Bull Inn Court, Lumley Court), and there's even a gaslight in Carting Lane that is run by sewage gas. Heading east into the City, the Temple is famously still gaslit, as is Charterhouse Square and the Guildhall.

89-90

Boost your vitamin intake at a Middle Eastern juice bar

Alongside simple orange, carrot, grapefruit and melon juices, you can sample a mixed fruit cocktail at the Lebanese Ranoush Juice (43 Edgware Road, W2 2JE, 7723 5929, www.maroush.com) for £3.50. And if juices aren't exotic enough, try jellab – a sweet, red-wine coloured drink with pine nuts and raisins. It's made by combining the pulp of raisins with some grape molasses, rose water and sugar, then smoking the mixture and, finally, adding the pine nuts and raisins, which float in the glass. The best time to call in at Ranoush is late on a summer night: it's an Arab London institution and the place is buzzing until closing time at 3am. There's more creative treatment of fruit over at Fresco (31 Paddington Street, W1U 4HD, 7486 6113, www.frescojuices.co.uk), where a menu of super-healthy vegetable juices featuring the likes of cabbage, cucumber and broccoli is complemented by a huge range of fruit juices – served singly or as combos (such as mango, banana and strawberry, £3.25) – and fruity milkshakes, all served in large glasses.

Fresco

91 Attend a preview screening for free

Sites such as www.showfilmfirst.com offer the chance to see previews of new releases, without paying a penny. Sign up for a chance to catch movies such as *Inside Out* and *Southpaw*.

92 Visit the Charles Dickens Museum

After the success of *The Pickwick Papers* in 1836, Dickens left his cramped chambers in Holborn and moved to a Georgian terraced house in Doughty Street for three years; *Oliver Twist*

Charles Dickens Museum

and *A Christmas Carol* were written here. The building, the author's only surviving London residence, is crammed with memorabilia and artefacts, including his reading and writing desks. The museum recently underwent a £3 million redevelopment project, which has opened the attic and kitchen for the first time and created a café and visitor centre in the adjacent building. **Charles Dickens Museum** *48 Doughty Street, WC1N 2LX (7405 2127, www.dickensmuseum.com). £8 (£4-£6 reductions).*

93 Drive dodgems on the South Bank

If you're put off by the queues or the prices – or both – for the London Eye, why not nip into its neighbour, Namco Funscape (County Hall, Westminster Bridge Road, SE1 7PB, 7967 1067, www.namcofunscape-londonevents.co.uk, free admission) and drive dodgems instead. Everything at this indoor entertainment centre is token-operated, so you just pay as you go (£2.50 for the bumper cars; 1.4m height restriction applies). There are also 12 bowling lanes (£5.95-£7.95 per person per game), US pool tables and 150 arcade games, simulators and dance machines (tokens cost 50p), plus karaoke. Namco Funscape is open until midnight, and has a pub-priced bar.

94 Marvel at the boat that made it to South Georgia

Tucked away in a corridor of grand Dulwich School in south London, the James Caird might look like any old boat, but this 26-foot whaler is the one in which Sir Ernest Shackleton and five companions sailed over 800 miles to South Georgia during the Antarctic winter of 1916 in a bid to rescue their men from Elephant Island. They took stores to last one month, reckoning that if it took longer they would be dead anyway. In fact they reached their destination after 16 days – a voyage 'of supreme strife among heaving waters', Shackleton recalled. Amazingly, all members of the expedition were saved. To view this piece of history at Shackleton's old school, get a visitor's pass from reception. **Dulwich College** *Dulwich Common, SE21 7LD (8693 3601, www.dulwich.org.uk). Free.*

95-100

Bash Redford,
Director, Forza Win

My brother and I share a love of noodles, so we often go to Viet Restaurant (113 Deptford High Street, SE8 4NS, 8692 8475, www.viet-restaurant.co.uk). It has a weird-out of perspective pictures all over the walls, a disco room you can hire and, in my opinion, the best pho in London (and I've eaten a lot of pho). The lotus root salad is also delicious. At Sunday lunchtimes, it's packed with Vietnamese families who create a wall of noise; that, coupled with the broth, can get you through any hangover.
The Creekside Education Trust (14 Creekside, SE8 4SA, 8692 9922, www.creeksidecentre.org.uk), which works to sustain and promote the regeneration of Deptford Creek, runs monthly low-tide walks along the muddy riverbed for £10. It's a great way to spend a sunny Sunday morning. The guides know loads about nature and conservation, and you'll meet lots of people with beards – not the trendy kind. Afterwards, go and have a pint in the Royal Albert (460 New Cross Road, SE14 6TJ, 8692 3737, http://royalalbertpub.com). It's an absolute banger of a pub, with interesting guest taps and battered sausages on the menu.
Next door to Peckham's Ali Baba juice bar (12B Rye Lane, SE15 4ST) is Asian Takeaway, who make the most delicious food that £3.50 can get you anywhere. While we were building Forza Win, we lived on their rice and dahl and

tikka wraps with green sauce. They make the naan while you wait, and the guy on the till has a smile to lift the heaviest of hearts. There are all sorts of people to chat to while you wait for your little bundle of edible joy – businessmen, locals with great taste in kebabs, and Afghani families who come for the authentic food. Use the change from your tenner to buy a healthy, refreshing juice from their neighbour.
Best Mangal (107-109 Great Eastern Street, EC2A 3JD, 7250 1188, www.thebestmangal.com) in Shoreditch is my most recent discovery. It's pretty unassuming, so it took me a while to venture in. Their lamb doner is made from leg and breast meat, and I'd happily eat it for the rest of my days. The chef is insanely confident and wants you to try everything; luckily, his pride is well placed. The only downside is that the other customers are drunk and loud. Avoid going late on a weekend evening or you'll risk the cheesy-chips brigade breathing booze all over your meal.
I have to mention the £10 deal at Forza Win (133 Copeland Road, SE15 3SN, 7732 9012, www.forzawin.com). At weekends, we serve big, Italian, wood-fired banquets, but on Wednesdays it's 'Awesome Sauce'. You get a bowl of pasta and a glass of wine for a tenner. The fact it's affordable means we pull in a really great blend of customers. It gets very busy early on, so come around 9pm – and look out for me eating my body weight in bolognese.
I had driven, cycled, skated and walked past Egi's Restaurant (395A Queen's Road, SE14 5HD, 7732 0292) about a trillion times and had always admired the sign; any place that labels itself 'licenced to grill' is surely wor a visit. When I finally went in with frien? from work late on a Saturday night, i*s been closed for an hour, but Egi s*kes chefs, took pity on us, and ten r*ce. we had perfectly cooked ste* and three different dippin? simple food really well *on for under £10 **43**

101-110

Pick a perfect place to picnic

There's no need to leave town to picnic in the fresh air, surrounded by trees and flowers. Concrete jungle it may be, but London is also one of the world's greenest capitals. We've rounded up ten of the city's most perfect spots, from Tudor gardens to space-age parks.

Battersea Park

Once marshland and also a notorious duelling spot, the 200 acres of greenery that constitute Battersea Park (8871 7530, www.battersea park. org, free) are a far more salubrious place these days (and have also been given an £11 million Lottery-funded boost). We recommend the calming Peace Pagoda.

Fulham Palace Gardens

If you fancy sipping a crisp chablis on the shady lawn of a lovely formal garden, head to Fulham Palace's (7736 3233, www.fulham palace.org, free) tranquil Thames-side grounds by Bishops Park. The palace and its gardens, a country retreat for centuries for the medieval bishops of London, are a well-kept local picnicking secret. Full of unusual plant species, the 12 acres offer plenty to explore: as well as the lawns, there's woodland, an 18th-century walled garden full of herbs, an orchard and a wisteria-clad pergola.

Ham House Gardens

Ensconce yourself on the lawns of Ham House's garden (8940 1950, www.nationaltrust.org.uk, entrance to garden only £4). These glorious 17th-century grounds have both formal splendour in their lavender, box and yew parterres as well as a so-called wilderness of maze-like hornbeam.

Hampstead Heath

Hampstead Heath is, of course, full of great picnic spots – and stunning views – but we especially love the slope above Highgate Pond, where you can hide out in the long grass and gaze across to the City and Canary Wharf.

Holland Park

With its charmingly secluded hideaways, Holland Park has loads of great private picnic spots. If you want to make more

of a splash, though, there's the Japanese garden or the lawns just north of Holland House. Just make sure you don't leave food lying around for the curious resident peacocks.

Horniman Museum Gardens
There are many good reasons to visit the Horniman Museum (8699 1872, www.horniman. ac.uk, free), but the gardens – with their roses, woodland, exotic shrubs and wild flowers – are as enchanting a reason as any. If you are planning a trip to the museum anyway, don't forget to pack a picnic.

Regent's Park
Regent's Park (www.royalparks.org.uk, 0300 061 2000, free) can get pretty busy if the weather's good and during the holidays, but for dreamy, summer perfection, head to its northern reaches and lay out your rug near the colourful blossoms and luscious scents in the Rose Garden.

Springfield Park
Hackney's Springfield Park (www.hackney. gov.uk/cp-parks-springfield.htm) is a good spot for a picnic with a view: nibble cucumber sandwiches while looking out over the River Lee, with its narrow boat marina, and the Hackney Marshes beyond.

Thames Barrier Park
A masterpiece of contemporary landscape gardening, the Thames Barrier Park (7476 3741, www.london.gov.uk, free) is worth making the effort to get to. Plonk yourself in the middle of 22 acres of lawns, trees and surreal yew and maygreen topiary and look out over the mighty silver shells of the Thames Barrier.

Waterlow Park
Try the lawns of Highgate's Waterlow Park (www.waterlowpark.org.uk, free) for more exhilarating views of London as well as three spring-fed ponds. Sweeping down the steep face of Highgate Hill, the scene is dotted with elegant, mature trees framing a fabulous view of the City's skyscrapers.

111 Hunt for Admiral Lord Nelson

At least we know where to start: Horatio Nelson stands three-times life size (but then he was only five and a half feet tall), 145 feet up in the centre of Trafalgar Square, so named after his final, fatal victory over Napoleon's fleet in 1805. Even so, the most popular military hero in British history didn't rise to this distinction until almost 40 years after his death, when his statue was finally placed on his column in 1843. He faces south-west, into the prevailing winds, and towards the fleet at Portsmouth. Visit the National Portrait Gallery for a fine view of the back of his tricorn hat from the eighth-floor bar; alternatively, go and look at one or more of its ten portraits of him in the primary collection (they have at least 57 more in the archives), which is bound to be on display somewhere in the gallery.

From here, head towards Mayfair via Soho and 33A Dean Street (now Gino's barbershop), which, as Walker's Hotel, was where Nelson spent his last night in London before heading off for Trafalgar. He set up home at 5 Cavendish Square, with his new,

and soon to be long-suffering, wife Frances. Although they only lived here for four years, much was made of the fact that his address was to be used as a YMCA for US officers towards the end of World War I.

After this, make your way to the Royal Arcade, at 28 Old Bond Street, once the first premises of Dollond & Aitchison, the firm from which Nelson bought a telescope after losing an eye attacking Corsica in 1793. He also lodged nearby in New Bond Street on his return from the Battle of Cape St Vincent in 1797. (In the same year, he lost his right arm at the Battle of Santa Cruz, off Tenerife.) The Goat Tavern, at 3 Stafford Street, was a favourite haunt, which he later used for shenanigans with his mistress, Lady Hamilton.

Trade in Nelson memorabilia was huge after his death, and a trail of his personal effects can be tracked down around town: the shoe buckles that he wore at Trafalgar are on the wax effigy in the Westminster Abbey Museum (20 Dean's Yard, SW1P 3PA, 7222 5152, www.westminster-abbey.org),

as well as some of his clothes; his razor is in the Wellcome Museum of the History of Medicine at the Science Museum; and his solid gold combined knife and fork, made for a left-hander and given to him by Countess Spencer, is in the Lloyd's building's Nelson collection. (You can see this on Open House weekend.) The collection also includes Nelson's favourite breakfast plate, his collar for the Order of the Bath and Lady Hamilton's toothpick box. The jewel-encrusted sword, also designed for a left-hander, presented to him with the Freedom of the City in 1800, is on display in the Expanding City gallery at the Museum of London.

Nearby, you can find a fine statue of our hero, sculpted in 1810 by James Smith, in the Guildhall Art Gallery, but then it's high time you made tracks to Greenwich, the official home of Horatio worship. The Nelson Gallery at the National Maritime Museum (Romney Road, SE10 9NF, 8858 4422, www.rmg.co.uk/national-maritime-museum, free) houses the clothes he was wearing at Trafalgar (see the musket-ball hole in the shoulder) among other fantastic artefacts. Then there's the Coade stone Nelson Pediment above the King William Block of the Old Royal Naval College, inspired by the Elgin Marbles, and showing Neptune bringing the admiral's body to Britannia.

Real devotees should also visit Southside House (Woodhayes Road, SW19 4RJ, 8946 7643, www.southsidehouse.com), which he enjoyed visiting with Emma Hamilton when she was living nearby at Merton Place. Also check out the Marine Society & Sea Cadets headquarters (202 Lambeth Road, SE1 7JW, 7654 7000, www.ms-sc.org), where one of Nelson's flags is kept.

Finally, no hunt for Horatio would be complete without visiting his tomb in St Paul's Cathedral. His black marble sarcophagus was originally designed for Cardinal Wolsey, who had died over 200 years earlier.

112
Meet the author

You can listen to, and perhaps even meet, your favourite writers at book signings, author readings and in-store discussions. All bookshops, from tiny local ones to giant chains, hold these events as a way of encouraging sales. Waterstones, for example, has details of 'an evening with…' events on its website (www.waterstones.com). The Piccadilly flagship branch has seen names ranging from Scandinavian crime writer Håkan Nesser to Prue Leith (tickets free-£7). With six branches in London, Daunt Books (www.dauntbooks.co.uk) has regular (often free) events with authors such as William Boyd and Alexander McCall Smith.

113

Eat pie and mash at Manze's

You only need to glance briefly at the seedier burger joints around town to understand that cheap food often also means cheap decor. We know London's got loads of good-value places to eat, but it's rare that you'll be spending less than a fiver on food in as lovely surroundings as those at Manze's on Tower Bridge Road. London's oldest pie and mash shop (eels – jellied and stewed – also available, of course) was established in 1902 by the present owner's grandfather, Michele Manze, of Ravello in southern Italy, and the same art nouveau-style green and cream tiles grace the walls as did back then. Those solid wooden benches also look like they've done decades' worth of service propping up hungry folk.

M Manze *87 Tower Bridge Road, SE1 4TW (7407 2985, www.manze.co.uk).*

114-116

Tour the capital's breweries...

Mass-produced lagers are not only a burden on your taste buds but on your wallet as well. By way of therapy, we recommend a visit to one of London's breweries to get you in the mood for cheaper and tastier ales. Fullers' Griffin brewery (Chiswick Lane South, W4 2QB, 8996 2000, www. fullers.co.uk) is open for two-hour guided tours, weekdays only, at £10 a pop. At the other end of the scale, Brodie's Beers (816A High Road Leyton, E10 6AE, 07976 122853, www.brodiesbeers.com) is a tiny operation run by brother and sister team James and Lizzie Brodie, who concoct a variety of beers in all sorts of styles. Tours are free. Sambrook's Brewery in Battersea (Yelverton Road, SW11 3QG, 7228 0598) runs an open evening on the third Wednesday of the month (7pm, free), as well as private tours for groups.

117-119

...or drink craft beer from the source at an open day

The new-found popularity of American-style IPAs, Belgian *saisons*, rich chocolate porters and many other flavoursome brews has meant the bubble of microbreweries can now be heard in railway arches, industrial estates and other nooks and crannies all over town. Their wares can be found all over the place, too, but you'll get rare and small-batch beers at low prices on brewery open days. Beavertown Brewery (www.beavertown brewery.co.uk) is open every Saturday, serving their usuals alongside some more experimental flavours from a warehouse in Tottenham Hale. There's usually food and ping pong on offer too. Less regular but more accessible is Hammerton Brewery (www.hammertonbrewery.co.uk), who open their premises neighbouring Pentonville Prison for lively evening drinking sessions on the last Friday and Saturday of every month.

The ambitious beer enthusiast will want to attempt the Bermondsey Beer Mile – a challenge that sees drinkers start at Four Pure in South Bermondsey and finish at Southwark Brewing Company on Druid Street, stopping at Partizan, Kernel, Brew By Numbers, Bottle Shop and

Anspach & Hobday along the way. Timing it so that you can grab lunch from the impressive selection of food stalls at the nearby Ropewalk market is recommended, as is ordering halves.

120

Spot a stenchpipe

Stenchpipes, aka stinkpipes, can be spotted all over London. They're Victorian, built at the same time as the city's sewerage system, to allow noxious gases to escape (well above head height). Once you've noticed one, you'll see them everywhere – if you don't believe us, just check out http://stinkpipes.blogspot.com. Try finding the one in Addison Square, Camberwell, or the fine crowned one on Kennington Road. Some are even listed, such as the one near Parliament Fields Lido, at the entrance to the park off Gordon House Road.

121

People-watch at the National Portrait Gallery...

Possibly your best bet for celebrity spotting – on canvas and film – this is one of our favourite London galleries. The prestigious BP Portrait Award and the Taylor Wessing Photographic Portrait Prize are both annual highlights. The permanent collection is free and has more than enough to keep visitors entranced. Some of the temporary exhibitions carry an entrance fee. **National Portrait Gallery** *St Martin's Place, WC2H 0HE (7312 2463, www.npg.org.uk).*

122

...or draw a portrait

The National Portrait Gallery isn't just a stellar collection of portraiture – it runs events such as Drop-in Drawing from 6.30pm to 8.30pm every Friday. Like the gallery, this is free; all materials are provided and there's a professional artist on hand to lead the session. It kicks off with a short introduction but informality is the order of the day – so you can come along for the whole two hours, or just pop by for 30 minutes.

123

See the world at the Greenwich & Docklands International Festival

Billed not unreasonably as 'London's most spectacular free festival', the Greenwich & Docklands International Festival (8305 1818, www.festival.org) throws up all the eccentricities of urban multiculturalism. A host of different venues – from the O2 and Cutty Sark Gardens to the Royal Observatory – have welcomed giant French caterpillars, tango demonstrations and a South Asian dance/football fusion. A June slot makes it a colourful portal into the summer.

124
Hear voices at the British Library Sound Archive

There are 3.5 million recordings in the British Library's Sound Archive, which is one of the most extensive facilities of its kind in the world and includes published and unpublished material dating back to the late 19th century. Founded in 1955, the collections are now divided into eight main sections: classical music, featuring many rare and unpublished recordings; drama and literature (including the voices of James Joyce, Antonin Artaud, Leo Tolstoy, William Burroughs, Kurt Schwitters and Sylvia Plath); oral history, including unpublished interviews with historic figures such as Churchill as well as commercial recordings (there's an oral history of Tesco); wildlife sounds, including the work of the RSPB; popular music; international and traditional music (published and unpublished); archived BBC Radio broadcasts; and moving images (including the complete rehearsal and performance video archive of Forced Entertainment theatre company). The easiest way to get a flavour of the extraordinary scope of the collection is to visit a SoundServer in Humanities, Floor 2, or, if you have specific requests, make a listening appointment beforehand. The Sound Archive also accepts published and unpublished recordings from the public if they are suitable (in three of the basic categories – spoken word, music, wildlife). If you are interested, send recordings to the address below.

Sound Archive Information Service *Sound Archive, British Library, 96 Euston Road, NW1 2DB (7412 7831, www.bl.uk).*

125
Catch the BP Summer Big Screens

In an attempt to bring opera out of its elite closet, the Royal Opera House is continuing its annual tradition of screening its most popular work for free in Trafalgar Square and other locations around central London. Screenings happen on various dates between May and July. Check the website for details.
www.roh.org.uk.

126
Get a handle on Handel

The Baroque composer George Frideric Handel moved from Germany to Britain in 1710, aged just 25, having secured the position of *Kappelmeister* to George, Elector of Hanover and soon to be King George I of England. He received an annual salary of £200 and by 1723 had established himself comfortably in his London home, where he lived for 36 years until his death in 1759. The house, in Mayfair, is now a museum and provides a good opportunity to get under the skin of the great man.

The interior has been lovingly restored and includes some beautiful replica instruments. The best way to get the feel for it is at the recitals of Baroque music that take place every Thursday (and occasionally on Tuesday) and regularly at the weekends (£9, £5 reductions).
Handel House Museum *25 Brook Street, W1K 4HB (7495 1685, www.handelhouse.org).*

127
Hear leather on willow at Walker Ground

Back in cricket's heyday, crowds of up to 10,000 would flock to watch United All England XI play titanic matches at Walker Ground. Established in 1855 by the seven cricket-mad Walker brothers who lived locally and who went on to found Marylebone Cricket Club (MCC) and Lord's, Walker Ground is one of the capital's oldest and perhaps most idyllic cricket fields. Today, it's the home of Southgate Cricket Club. Located as it is by pretty Southgate Green, and surrounded by tall oaks with the spire of Christ Church rising above the treetops, you can squint and imagine that you're deep in the English countryside. Post match, head for Ye Olde Cherry Tree on the Green for refreshments. The MCC play regularly at the ground, check the website for match schedules.
Southgate CC *Walker Ground, Waterfall Road, N14 7JZ (8886 8381, www.southgatecc.com).*

128 *Go bargain hunting in Bermondsey*

Up until 1995, Bermondsey Market enjoyed 'marché ouvert' status thanks to a medieval loophole law, which handily made it legal to buy and sell goods of dodgy provenance during the hours of darkness. Now, with the rise of eBay, changing fashions in antiques and the redevelopment of Bermondsey Square, the market stallholders have to work harder to earn a crust – and so do punters looking for a bargain. But Bermondsey is still a market-traders' market, where antiques change hands between traders from all over the country, and there are still some great deals to be had. If you're up at dawn, have a root around in the 'everything £1' boxes, which are full of pre-loved, worn out and eminently curious vintage knick-knackery.
Bermondsey Antiques Market *Bermondsey Square, SE1 3UN (www.bermondseysquare.co.uk).*

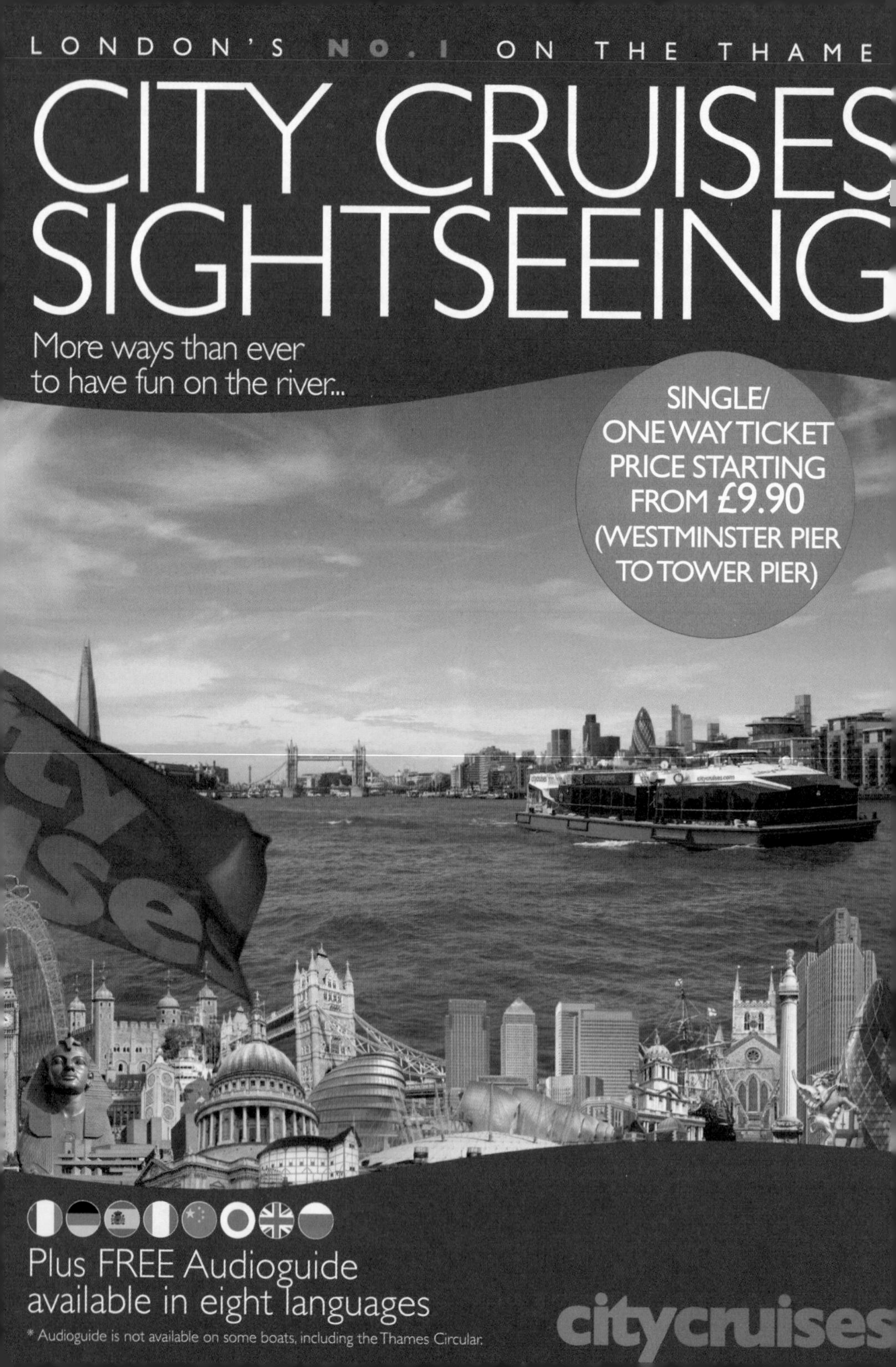
LONDON'S NO.1 ON THE THAME
CITY CRUISES
SIGHTSEEING
More ways than ever
to have fun on the river...
SINGLE/
ONE WAY TICKET
PRICE STARTING
FROM £9.90
(WESTMINSTER PIER
TO TOWER PIER)
Plus FREE Audioguide
available in eight languages
* Audioguide is not available on some boats, including the Thames Circular.
citycruises

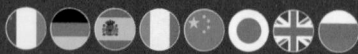

129

Have a cup of rosie with a cabbie

If you look carefully, you'll find a few curious little green huts scattered across the city. Like stray (if rather posh) garden sheds, these are Cabman's Shelters – London institutions that date back to the 1870s, when the Earl of Shaftesbury and his philanthropist chums set up a charity to provide cabbies with 'wholesome refreshments at moderate prices'. Of the 61 original shelters, only a dozen remain (among them those at Chelsea Embankment, Hanover Square, Russell Square, Temple Place, and opposite the Victoria & Albert Museum). You'll wonder how they can possibly accommodate a working kitchen plus up to ten cab drivers. Pop by for a chat and eyebrow-raising tales of recent celebrity fares. If you ask nicely, you may be served a cup of Rosie Lee (tea), for the absolutely princely sum of 50p.

130

Eat in Brixton Village

Once a rundown arcade, Brixton Village is now home to new cafés, restaurants and takeaways, and has become Brixton's culinary and cultural hub. Not all eateries here will leave you with a bill for under £10 a head, but many manage this feat, including Elephant (07715 439857), a tiny Pakistani café (own-made samosas, curries, three types of thali); Honest Burgers (7733 7963, www.honestburgers.co.uk), which uses beef from Ginger Pig; French & Grace (7274 2816, www.frenchandgrace.co.uk), where the short Mediterranean menu lists a selection of salads, wraps and the odd hot dish (such as lamb stew); and vintage-minded Relay Tea Room (www.relayboutique.blogspot.com), which specialises in tea served in mismatched crockery, and own-made bakes, open sandwiches, quiches and soups.

Brixton Village *Atlantic Road & Coldharbour Lane, SW9.*

131

Visit London's loveliest public lavatory

Featuring heavily in Joe Orton biopic *Prick up Your Ears*, the palatial Grade II-listed public loos next to the bus terminus at South End Green, NW3, were the recent benefactor of a £50,000 renovation courtesy of the National Lottery. Built in 1897 by the London & North Western Railway, it's now a positive pleasure to visit such a historic temple of convenience, all vaulted ceilings, and cream and green Doulton tiles. If you don't think it's worth trekking across town just to visit a loo, it's also conveniently located for Hampstead Heath.

132

Get shown the money at the Bank of England Museum

Attached to the Bank of England itself, this museum is housed in a replica of the original 18th-century bank's interior, designed by Sir John Soane. As part of the exhibition, you can test the weight of a real-life gold bar (28lbs). You can also discover how *Wind in the Willows* creator Kenneth Grahame foiled an armed bank robber in a permanent display on the author, who worked here for 30 years and was Secretary of the Bank from 1898 to 1908.

Bank of England Museum *Bartholomew Lane, EC2R 8AH (7601 4878, www.bankofengland.co.uk). Free.*

133

Browse on a boat

If 'there is nothing – absolutely nothing – half so much worth doing as simply messing about in boats', then shopping on one should be more fun too. For vinyl junkies, there's the Record Deck (https://therecorddeckuk.wordpress.com), a waterway-cruising barge with crates of vintage records; check its Twitter feed for the barge's current mooring. Word on the Water (Regent's Canal, Granary Square, N1, www.facebook.com/ wordonthewater), the London book barge, has taken a different tack and is now permanently moored in Granary Square; apart from a selection of books that will keep bibliophiles browsing for hours, it hosts poetry slams and live music on its roof stage.

Beats on a budget

These days, uncovering London's best nightlife is about being savvy, rather than loaded, says **Tristan Parker**.

Modern London can be a baffling prospect for clubbers. The mantra about London as a thriving hub of club culture still rings throughout the city, yet the bizarre closure of iconic and healthy venues happens with alarming regularity. The financial uncertainty of recent years still lingers and thrifty living has become fashionable, yet the cost of a night out doesn't always reflect the lack of money in people's pockets.

So it's easy to be gloomy. But read between the lines and you'll quickly see a different, more optimistic nightlife map. Because, for every highly reported venue closure, two innovative spaces will quietly open in the following weeks. For every club charging extortionate entry fees to people who don't mind paying it, a bevy of smaller, superior clubs, in fascinating nooks across the city, will be letting people in for less than the cloakroom price of a gaudier enterprise.

There's no denying that London remains expensive. But while you won't be able to tick off some of the bigger-name, headline-grabbing clubs for less than £10, you can certainly still enjoy a premium night out. Continually rising prices have created an insatiable appetite for cut-price clubbing among those who want dancefloor escapism but can't afford constant, overdraft-plunging weekends – the vast majority of Londoners, in other words.

Savvy venue owners and promoters have reacted by setting up sensibly priced nights (some cheaper than you would have found even ten years ago), and sometimes with top-level DJs. Now more than ever, you can find globally acclaimed selectors playing to seas of people in a landmark club one night, followed by a set at a hidden-away, sweaty basement the next. The two events may differ wildly in price, but energy levels are often higher in smaller venues.

The line of quirky culture that runs through modern-day London has also begun shaping budget-friendly nocturnal activity: heady variations on bingo, karaoke, quizzing and yoga

Your Mum's House

delight curious clubbers on a regular basis. These kooky experiments are often passion-projects set up in someone's spare time, with cheap admission to recoup costs rather than make a mint.

The influence of pop-up parties is also a factor. These seasonal, nomadic and incredibly popular set-ups can boast DJ line-ups that rival those of the big clubs, often with cheap or free entry. Keep your eyes peeled around Hackney Wick, Shoreditch and Dalston, and you're bound to stumble across a pop-up if you look hard enough – just follow the sound of deep disco and the aromas of pulled pork and craft beer.

The take-home message from all this? London clubbers today need to be smart. Not, thankfully, in a style sense (be wary of any London club that demands a shirt and shiny shoes to guarantee entry), but in how you think about your night out. Turn off the main road, seek out your sonics in the side streets and you'll be rewarded. London's most interesting dancing dens, set away from the main drags, are often the cheapest.

Book tickets in advance where possible, as this will almost always secure you a hefty discount. Even if you just turn up on the night, many clubs offer cheap or free entry for early arrivals – though there'll usually be queues of cash-conscious clubbers doing the same thing. Weeknight and end-of-week clubbing is often a lot cheaper – and some of London's best nights out happen from Sunday to Thursday: just because the nine-to-fivers sleep doesn't mean that London does the same.

Finally, remember that whatever your financial state – whether you've just bought a round of bubbly for everyone at the bar or whether you walked to the club because you couldn't afford the bus fare – it doesn't matter a bit when you're on the dancefloor. Once you're inside, losing yourself in the best DJ set you've heard all year was 100 per cent free last time we checked.

Pub-clubbing

London's pubs don't just quench thirsts these days – those who want beats and bass lines with their boozing are well catered for, with many drinking dens doubling up as nightlife venues. The action usually takes place in a sticky-floored side-room or basement, where you'll find DJs playing energetic sets to keep people dancing, long after they might normally have gone home. These nights are often geared towards no-frills fun, but they do still attract great DJs. Best of all, you'd be hard pushed to find many that dare charge over a fiver.

North London isn't exactly teeming with budget clubbing options, so it's a relief to glance at the wallet-friendly programming of Islington's Old Queens Head (44 Essex Road, N1 8LN, 7354 9993, www.theoldqueenshead.com). This busy boozer has an upstairs room that puts on full-fat-fun club nights featuring DJ sets from respected hip hop, funk and soul selectors such as Norman Jay and DJ Yoda, almost always for £5 or free. Look out for hugely enjoyable hip hop and R&B party No Scrubs (www.facebook.com/noscrubsclub), where you can expect '90s jams and plenty of singalongs.

Another northern star is the Lock Tavern (35 Chalk Farm Road, NW1 8AJ, 7482 7163,

www.lock-tavern.com) in Camden. Catering for north London's cooler clientele, this bohemian pub has a hip hotchpotch of free options every week, with underground DJs spinning disco, house, funk and techno in the upstairs room until late every weekend. If the weather is decent, you can cram on to the small outside terrace and watch the Camden hordes rush by.

In south London, the Dogstar (389 Coldharbour Lane, SW9 8LQ, 7733 7515, www.dogstarbrixton. com) is a huge, multi-floored beast of a pub that attracts a young crowd who wouldn't dream of heading home at closing time. Audio Sushi is a long-running favourite here, providing uptempo DJ sets geared towards house, electro and breaks, mostly spun by residents but occasionally by unannounced big-name DJs – members of Hot Chip and Massive Attack are previous guests. Arrive early for free entry and to dodge the street-snaking queues.

New Cross offers much-loved pub the Amersham Arms (388 New Cross Road, SE14 6TY, 8469 1499, www.theamershamarms.com), which has a rock and indie tint to its bargain

No Scrubs

Coffin DodgersDisco

club nights. Much like the pub itself, these are enjoyably raucous, loud and boozy affairs, fuelled by cider and students from nearby Goldsmiths University. Try free weekly Friday indie disco Whip it!

If you want to keep your finger on the pulse while you're pub-clubbing, the Shacklewell Arms (71 Shacklewell Lane, E8 2EB, 7249 0810, www.shacklewellarms.com) in Dalston is a good bet. Though it's primarily a venue for alternative live bands, this scruffy, buzzy boozer also hosts club nights, one-off parties and DJ sets (sometimes spun by band members), all taking place in its tiny back room, which is filled with hip young things.

Nearby Dalston Superstore (117 Kingsland High Street, E8 2PB, 7254 2273, www.dalston superstore.com) offers headier scenes. It's popular with gay crowds but always packed with mixed revellers, and the low-lit basement club space is constantly pulsing with edgy electro, mutant disco, Italo-house or glittery pop at nights such as Discosodoma, often for free or a few pounds. Or you can just hang and dance in the free-to-enter über-cool bar.

Though it's more of a bar than a pub, the Book Club (100-106 Leonard Street, EC2A 4RH, 7684 8618, www.wearetbc.com) in Shoreditch is a justifiably popular place to combine drinking and dancing. The downstairs space hosts various cheap-entry hip hop, disco and funk nights, including regular parties such as the (free) Request Line every Thursday, which plays 1970s grooves, and R&B-focused the Get Down.

Cutting-edge clubbing

Can you still have a night out in London at an established club and see top-level DJs for under a tenner? Absolutely. As mentioned earlier, booking tickets as far in advance as possible always helps, but if planning isn't your forte, don't fret; these venues and nights offer the kind of forward-thinking club nights that have helped build London's mighty nightlife credentials, for far less than you might expect.

Intimate, moody Elephant & Castle rave cave Corsica Studios (4-5 Elephant Road, SE17 1LB, 7703 4760, www.corsicastudios.com) is one of London's finest venues for bleeding-edge techno and house, and while many of its tickets run past £10, cheaper options remain. Sessions (www.facebook.com/sessionscorsica) is a long-running Corsica night that showcases superb selectors such as Romare and Andrés for reasonable prices.

If you fancy a jaunt into the unknown, try Tonga (www.facebook.com/tongaballoongang) at the Waiting Room (175 Stoke Newington High Street, N16 0LH, 7241 5511, www.waitingroom n16.com), the brainchild of Mike Skinner – formerly known as geezer rapper The Streets – and Manchester grime collective Murkage. Promotion verges on the non-existent, giving Tonga a covert feel, but once inside things usually get wild, with unannounced guest DJs and MCs ripping through garage, grime, house and 'party bass', as Skinner himself puts it.

Quarterly night Batukarma in Peckham's Bussey Building (133 Rye Lane, SE15 4ST, 7732 5275, www.clfartcafe.org) offers global beats, Latin-leaning breaks and Brazilian drum 'n' bass for around £5-£7, giving established DJs a chance to play something different to their usual club sets. The Bussey also offers other well-priced parties, including two furiously funky offerings in Zonk Disco and the hugely popular South London Soul Train (www.facebook.com/southlondonsoultrain), both with guest DJs.

Also in Peckham is Canavan's (www.facebook.com/canavanspeckhampoolclub), a small, old-school pool club that turns into a bustling club space at weekends. It's refreshingly rough around the edges and low on glamour, but perfect for heads-down dancing, favoured by those who focus on the music rather than the best angle at which to take a selfie (just to drill it home – really don't do this in Canavan's; it won't go down well). Entry is always pretty cheap, but queues are common. Favourite nights here include local hero Bradley Zero's eclectic deep grooves showcase Rhythm Section (www.facebook.com/wearerhythmsection).

Brixton now boasts one of London's coolest new clubs in Phonox (418 Brixton Road, SW9 7AY, 7354 9993, www.phonox.co.uk). It's underground deep house and fist-pumping techno here – led by respected DJs rather than big names – and ticket prices are set at £10 on the door, £5 advance and free for those who arrive at the club early. Savvy Scottish selector Jasper James curates Saturday nights, while impressive guest DJs such as the Bug and Gilles Peterson keep the sleek space dancing on Fridays.

Clubbing in west London – let alone budget clubbing – isn't the easiest of activities, unless you like your clubs with a strict dress code and sky-high entry fee. The Notting Hill Arts Club (21 Notting Hill Gate, W11 3JQ, 7460 4459, www.nottinghillartsclub.com) has long been an alternative, affordable haven in the area, with regular night Twisted Hearts (www. twistedheartsclub.tumblr.com) – and its soundtrack of hip hop, bass and tropical house – an ever-reliable party-starter.

As has been the case for a good few years, Dalston, Shoreditch and wider Hackney still provide enough clubbing options to floor even the hardiest of ravers. Prices have crept up, but cheaper nights out still exist. Perennially dark dance den the Nest (36 Stoke Newington Road, N16 7XJ, 7275 9336, www.ilovethenest.com) features stellar DJs and MCs – anyone from Kode9 to Aeroplane to Ms Dynamite – working through deep house, garage, dubstep and twisted disco every weekend for around £7-£9. Raucous Thursday night mash-up Your Mum's House (www.yourmumshouse.club) is a steal at £5-£7, with an achingly cool crowd losing it to R&B, hip hop and trap.

Over the road, delightfully dingy basement the Alibi (91 Kingsland High Street, E8 2PB, 7249 2733, www.thealibilondon.co.uk) is a fully free affair, with local DJs packing the small but perfectly formed dancefloor with anything from grime to trap to dubstep. Unsurprisingly, free equals popular, so head down early to beat the queues.

The Horse & Groom (28 Curtain Road, EC2A 3NZ, 7503 9421, www.thehorseandgroom.net) in Shoreditch looks like a pub, but operates as a club and is worth a look-in for its multiple floors of house, disco and techno hedonism. Entry fees at nights such as Emmanuelle's Party Bucket are kept low at around £5, plus it's open until 4am every weekend.

If you want to dodge Dalston's swarms of cool kids but still enjoy cutting-edge sounds, head to Bethnal Green and track down tucked-away Oval Space (29-32 The Oval, E2 9DT, 7183 4422, www.ovalspace.co.uk). Its one vast room has a warehouse feel with plenty of atmosphere, plus a seriously on-point schedule of techno and house nights (including London staples such as Secretsundaze, Half-Baked and the venue's own avant-leaning Oval Space Music series) and a surprisingly pretty alfresco terrace, which features free daytime events in summer months. Oval Space tickets aren't always cheap, but fast-fingered clubbers can snap up a bargain by booking ahead online.

Rock, pop and indie

If your musical tastes lie more with guitars than processed grooves, there's still plenty of brilliant budget clubbing to be had.

Soho nightlife lynchpin Gaz's Rockin' Blues (www.gazrockin.com) at St Moritz (159 Wardour Street, W1F 8WH, 7734 3324, www.stmoritzclub.co.uk), has been keeping central London skanking for over 35 years for less than a tenner, via an infectious mix of ska, rhythm 'n' blues and reggae from both live bands and DJs. Hip-shaking, wallet-friendly sounds can be found at Blow Up (www.blowupclub.com), also at St Moritz, where dapper cats cut a rug to glam rock, early Britpop and '60s soul. How Does It Feel to Be Loved? (www.howdoesitfeel.co.uk) at the Shacklewell Arms offers similar sounds at a similar price, but with a stronger indie focus. Turn the indie-ometer up to 11 for around £6 – with a dash of new wave and postpunk thrown in – at Scared to Dance (www.scaredtodance.co.uk) in Dalston's Moustache Bar (58 Stoke Newington Road, N16 7XB, 07507 152047, www.moustachebar.com).

For something psychedelic and just under a tenner, try the Cave Club in Oxford Street retreat the 100 Club (7297 3200, www.the100club.co.uk), where the walls ooze rock 'n' roll history. Run by a member of punky indie troupe the Horrors, it features far-out grooves and synth-pop weirdness. The same could be said of experimental showcase the Deep Hum at the Heart of it All, on Wednesdays at nearby bar the Social (5 Little Portland Street, W1W 7JD, 7636 4992, www.thesocial.com), where underground bands and DJs unleash alternative dancefloor-fillers. Entry is £5, free for early arrivals.

Too weird? There's pure pop paradise at gloriously silly fancy-dress party Club De Fromage (www.clubdefromage.com) at the O2 Academy in Islington (N1 Centre, 16 Parkfield Street, N1 0PS, 7288 4400). It revels in an unashamedly cheesy playlist plus a few credible tunes (think Britney and Blur) for £6.50 in advance, £8-£10 on the door.

Quirky clubbing

Not so long ago, punters decided they wanted more on a night out than traditional clubbing could provide. London obliged, sprinting through trends and devouring off-kilter ideas in its quest for all-encompassing nocturnal entertainment. The results can be seen at various venues across the city, where progressive – and in some cases, plain bizarre – parties rule the roost.

Bethnal Green Working Men's Club (42-44 Pollard Row, E2 6NB, 7739 7170, www.workers playtime.net) might look like, well, an old working men's club frozen in 1978, but the intentionally cheesy surroundings perfectly suit a kooky programme of risqué cabaret, weird club nights, drag, comedy and much more. Polysexual party crew Sink the Pink host many an outrageous, genitalia-glittering extravaganza here, and (slightly) less filthy fun can be had at various disco nights and wacky one-off parties, with almost everything priced under £10.

Set just far enough back from Oxford Street to avoid the hordes, the Phoenix (37 Cavendish Square, W1G 0PP, 7493 8003, www.phoenix cavendishsquare.co.uk) is a haven of oddball delights as far as quirky clubbing is concerned: get your grumble on at Coffin Dodgers Disco (www.coffindodgersdisco.com), a tongue-in-cheek but strictly over-28s club night (they check ID on the door) where the playlist is aimed at the slightly older clubber: think Prince, Elvis, Kate Bush and Nirvana.

Also at the Phoenix, sing your heart out at a mass-karaoke event – Friday I'm in Love presents Massaoke (www.fiilclub.co.uk) for £6-£8. Here, the audience belts out rock and pop singalong classics as a whole, backed by a live band. Lyrics are projected on to the wall for everyone to see, and if you're lucky you might end up harmonising with the likes of news journalist Jon Snow or comedian Al Murray, both of whom have popped down. Remember to bring your air guitar.

There's more singing at Gospeloke, a gospel-themed karaoke night at the Queen of Hoxton (1-5 Curtain Road, EC2A 3JX, 7422 0958, www.queenofhoxton.com). Pick your soulful song from a harmony-rich set-list and you'll be backed by a 15-piece choir, neatly sidestepping any potential problems with singing talent.

Save a little of that vocal energy for screaming 'House!' at Bogan Bingo, held on Thursdays in west London watering hole the Slug at Fulham (490 Fulham Road, SW6 5NH, 7381 5005, www.theslugatfulham.co.uk). Don't worry if you think bingo is boring – so do the foul-mouthed Australian hosts, which is why they liven it up by dressing in '80s hair-metal garb and hosting an anarchic, sweary version of the game once loved only by retirement-home residents. All for £8. You can even win – suitably silly – prizes. Who says that London never gives anything back?

163

Keep up with the cutting edge at the Free Range graduate art fair

The annual Free Range Graduate Art & Design Summer Show has become a serious event in the art world's calendar since its first show in 2001. Displaying the work of over 3,000 graduate students from some of the UK's leading art colleges, and held each year over 11 acres in Brick Lane's enormous Old Truman Brewery, it's also one of the world's largest art fairs. You'd be hard pressed to buy anything for under a tenner, admittedly, but admission to the vast display of artworks covering a multitude of different media is free and a perfect way to spot the YBAs of the future. The exhibition runs between May and July each year.
www.free-range.org.uk.

164-171

Examine the city's sick past in London's medical museums

Considering London's past record of poverty-ridden slums, overcrowding and successive immigrant influxes, it's no wonder that the city is also blessed with a rich medical history. There are nearly 30 locations listed by the London Museums of Health & Medicine website (www.medicalmuseums.org): wherever you turn, the work of early nurses, surgeons, pharmacists, anaesthetists and hospitals is being dissected and displayed.

Kick off your consultation at the atmospheric attic home of the Old Operating Theatre Museum & Herb Garret (9A St Thomas Street, SE1 9RY, 7188 2679, www.thegarret.org.uk, £6.50), tucked behind London Bridge station. Climb the steep spiral staircase to the top of the Baroque church of St Thomas's and stumble through the beautifully ramshackle apothecary store to a pre-antiseptic surgical theatre, where students once crammed in to watch amputations, gallstone removals and trepanning operations. You can still feel the grooves in the original wooden operating table: this is where unwashed saws hacked through nervous patients.

For a more clinical approach, head for the Hunterian Museum at the Royal College of Surgeons (35-43 Lincoln's Inn Fields, WC2A 3PE, 7869 6560, www.rcseng.ac.uk/museums, free).

Old Operating Theatre Museum & Herb Garret

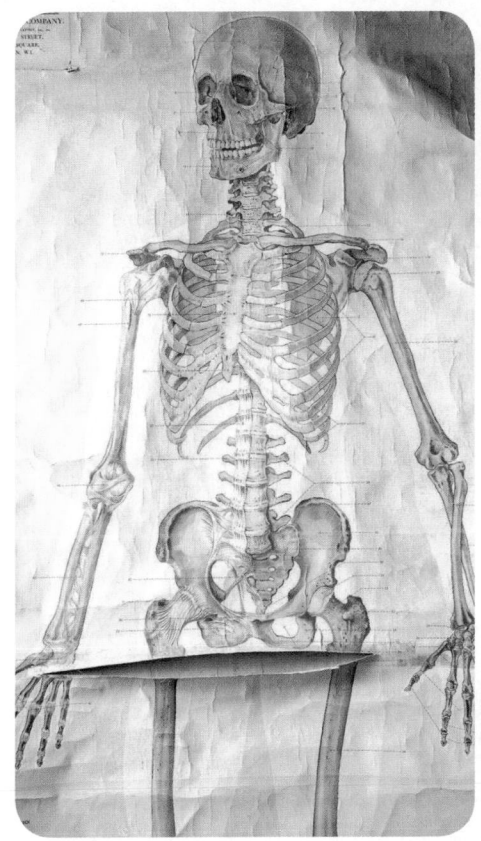

Packed with swish display cases of gruesome specimens and scary surgical instruments, the 400-year-old collection also includes distorted skeletons, 'before' and 'after' photographs of early plastic surgery and video presentations of modern operations. You can even peek at Charles Babbage's brain and Winston Churchill's dentures.

Over the river, the Florence Nightingale Museum (2 Lambeth Palace Road, SE1 7EW, 7620 0374, www.florence-nightingale.co.uk, £7.50) gives a chronological lowdown on the remarkable nurse and campaigner's life, along with some interesting mementos, including her stuffed pet owl, Athena.

If your appetite for gore hasn't been sated, there's plenty more. You can see the laboratory where Alexander Fleming discovered penicillin at St Mary's Hospital (Praed Street, W2 1NY, 3312 6528, www.imperial.nhs.uk, £4); pay homage to Joseph 'Elephant Man' Merrick

at the Royal London Hospital Museum (located in the crypt of St Augustine with St Philip's Church, Newark Street, E1 2AA, 7377 7608, www.bartsandthelondon.nhs.uk, free); follow the stories of 27,000 hospitalised 'exposed and deserted children' at the Foundling Museum (40 Brunswick Square, WC1N 1AZ, 7841 3600, www.foundlingmuseum.org.uk, £7.50); or try the museum of Bart's Hospital (West Smithfield, EC1A 7BE, 3465 5798, www.bartshealth.nhs.uk, free), founded in 1123 as part of St Bartholomew's priory, where, as well as viewing the surgical wares, you can learn about William Harvey, a physician at the hospital who discovered the circulation of blood in the 15th century.

More medical lore can also be garnered from the changing exhibitions at the Wellcome Collection (*see p13*) – but beware: any of these collections are almost guaranteed to bring on a nasty case of hypochondria.

172 Soar above the Thames in a cable car

For brilliant views of the expanses of water that make up the Royal Docks, plus the ships on the Thames, all of Docklands and the Thames Barrier, travel on the Emirates Air Line (https://tfl.gov.uk/modes/emirates-air-line, www.emiratesairline.co.uk). Designed by British architects Wilkinson Eyre, the pods, supported by elegant stanchions, travel nearly 300 feet up at a gratifying pace – but note that the cable car may not run in high winds. Tickets (£4.50 single, £2.30 children, free under-5s) are cheaper if you use an Oyster card, and you'll avoid any queues at the ticket desks.

173 Listen to the experts at Stanfords

Stanfords Travel Bookshop in Covent Garden first opened for business in 1901, and even today its three floors of maps, guides and travelogues can conjure up an almost overpowering wanderlust. Its selection of maps and guidebooks makes for pleasant browsing, but the store also provides a fitting setting for the lectures, presentations and book-readings that it hosts, which feature some of the most established figures in the travel writing world. Michael Palin, Colin Thubron and William Dalrymple, among other well-travelled luminaries, have all spoken here. Ticketed events, which usually include a glass of wine and a few nibbles, take place most weeks, either here or at the Royal Geographical Society. There's generally a Q&A session afterwards.

Stanfords *12-14 Long Acre, WC2E 9LP (7836 1321, www.stanfords.co.uk). From £3.*

174

Beautify yourself on a budget...

'It's better to be beautiful than to be good,' claimed Oscar Wilde. But he wasn't living through an economic downturn. However, mindful of the sentiment, we recommend a trip to the Esthetique salon – part of the London School of Beauty, where students (under supervision of beauty therapists) will soothe away worry lines brought on by these troubled times. Eyebrow and eyelash treatments start at £7. Booking is recommended as slots fill up fast.

London School of Beauty & Make-Up *Esthetique Student Salon, 18-19 Long Lane, EC1A 9PL (7776 9767, www.beauty-school.co.uk).*

175-176

...then get a cheap, chic haircut

There are also places in London where you can have your tresses tended to for next to nothing. Salon training schools such as Vidal Sassoon and Toni & Guy need a constant supply of models for their students to practise on, and trained stylists are always on hand to advise and deal with any

mishaps. At the Sassoon Academy, the standard haircut price is actually £12 (£5 if you're a student), but special £5 offers are often available to entice more models when there's a high volume of students – check by phoning ahead or sign up for their newsletter. Every fourth haircut is also free.

Toni & Guy *71-75 New Oxford Street, WC1A 1DG (7836 0606, www.toniandguy.com).*
Vidal Sassoon *48 Brook Street, W1K 5NE (7399 6903, www.sassoon-academy.com).*

177-178

Keep TV and radio live

See TV and radio shows for free by offering your services as an audience member (and canned laughter substitute). A quick internet search will reveal many companies offering free tickets, but we recommend the following sites for the best shows. Website www.sroaudiences.com gives away tickets for the likes of *Lorraine* and *Loose Women*, but also has places for comedy and panel shows such as *Mock the Week* and *The Last Leg*, while www.bbc.co.uk/tickets offers a huge variety of entertainment from *Strictly Come Dancing* to the surreal world of Radio 4 comedy. (Note that in order to be part of the *Question Time* audience, you have to fill in an application form.) Book early for the most popular slots (which includes almost all Radio 4 comedy shows).

179 Attend a foyer performance at RADA

The Royal Academy of Dramatic Art (7636 7076, www.rada.ac.uk) often holds performances in the bar/foyer (entrance on Malet Street), where you can see the stars of the future for a fraction of the price of a West End theatre ticket, and sometimes for free. Events include 'rehearsed readings', poetry slams, musical performances ranging from classical to folk, and comedy. Previous play readings, which have included *World Music* by Steve Waters, *The Schuman Plan* by Tim Luscombe and *Eyes Catch Fire* by Jason Hall, have gone on to be performed at the Hampstead Theatre, Donmar Warehouse and the Finborough Theatre.

180-188

Tuck into something sweet at the capital's best ice-cream parlours

Chin Chin Labs

Lab coats, liquid nitrogen and lots of 'mist' – they like to do things a bit differently at this Camden Market parlour. The four or five flavours on offer change weekly and might include the likes of mango, green tea and marshmallow, topped with a sprinkle of nigella seed powder, or melon and salted almonds. Experimental, indeed, but almost always superb. The less adventurous can opt for more conventional fare, such as Pondicherry vanilla or Valrhona chocolate. Prices start at £3.95 for one flavour.
49-50 Camden Lock Place, NW1 8AF (07885 604284, www.chinchinlabs.com).

Fortnum & Mason

David Collins-designed and delightfully dinky, Fortnum's Parlour celebrates the sweet with a coffee-and-cream colour scheme and a menu that takes ice-cream and pastries seriously. It's not cheap, but it is a treat and the postcard-perfect views over Piccadilly make it a lovely spot for meeting friends. Iced sodas, milkshakes and floats are £4.75-£10, a flight of three ice-creams £8, Austrian apple strudel served with cinnamon cream £6.50.
181 Piccadilly, W1A 1ER (7734 8040, www.fortnumandmason.com).

Gelateria Danieli

This tiny shop was a hit from the day of opening thanks to its superb own-made ice-cream. Now with several branches in London, Gelateria Danieli offers a daily changing selection of flavours drawn from over 100 recipes. Chocolate sorbet is the *specialità della casa*, one of several gorgeous dairy-free ices; if health is a concern, you'll also find options based on yoghurt. There's virtually no room to stand, let alone sit, so take your selection down to Richmond Green to enjoy. Prices start at £2.25 for a single scoop.
16 Brewers Lane, Richmond, Surrey TW9 1HH (8439 9807, www.gelateriadanieli.com).

Gelateria 3bis

Gelateria 3bis can more than hold its own among Borough Market's stellar culinary offerings. The repertoire includes Italian classics as well as creative English innovations (eton mess, anyone?). Fruit-heavy sorbets are a speciality too. There's a focus on top-notch Italian ingredients (pistachios from Sicily, hazelnuts from Piedmont, liquorice from Calabria) and the constantly churning line-up of gelato machines means everything is always super-fresh. A small cone or cup (enough for two flavours) is £3.70.
4 Park Street, SE1 9AB (7378 1977, www. gelateria3bis.co.uk).

Gelato Mio

Pesca, anguria, limone – the Italian labels reflect the heritage of this modish parlour and café in the centre of Holland Park's ritzy parade of shops, though specials may include the likes of green tea ice-cream. Prices start at £2.90 for one scoop; 500ml take-home packs are a tenner. Alternative refreshment comes in the form of frappe (Italian milkshake) and cremolata (a Sicilian drink made with ice, seasonal fruit and soda). You'll also find breakfast pastries and Illy coffee.
138 Holland Park Avenue, W11 4UE (7727 4117, www.gelatomio.co.uk).

Gelupo

Run by Jacob Kennedy and his team from the popular Bocca di Lupo restaurant, Gelupo offers own-made gelati, sorbets and granite. The flavours, many of them seasonal, will transport you to sun-saturated Italy – blood orange, mint stracciatella, ricotta with sour cherry, espresso. Can't decide? Order three in a tub or large cone, or scooped into a sugar-crusted brioche-cum-doughnut; a small scoop costs £4, a large is £6. Sit at one of the bar stools in the front or at the park bench in the rear deli section.
7 Archer Street, W1D 7AU (7287 5555, www.gelupo.com).

Oddono's

Outclassing many rivals, Oddono's gelato is not just made on the premises, but made from scratch. By using its own recipes rather than the ready-made mixes common in some cheaper establishments, this is some of the best and freshest ice-cream around. The hazelnut, coffee and chocolate (made from a unique Ecuadorian cocoa variety), and the mandarin sorbet are highly recommended, but the range changes frequently – Oddono's has developed over 140 flavours since opening in 2004 (and now has half a dozen branches). Prices start at £2.30 for a single-scoop cone or cup.
14 Bute Street, SW7 3EX (7052 0732, www.oddonos.co.uk).

Ruby Violet

Tufnell Park local Julie Fisher started out selling ice-cream on a market stall before setting up this cute parlour (named after her granny). The ices (a choice of about 20) are all made in-house from Duchy Originals organic milk, free-range eggs and British or fairtrade sugar, with occasional supplies of fruits, nuts and herbs brought in by customers. Expect plenty of fruity delights (damson and sour cream, raspberry ripple) as well as more unusual flavours (gin and tonic sorbet); we're particularly fond of the salted caramel with almond nut brittle. Fabulous hot chocolate too.
118 Fortess Road, NW5 2HL (7609 0444, www.rubyviolet.co.uk).

Scoop

Were it not for the queues snaking out of the door on sunny Friday lunchtimes, it would be easy to miss this authentic Italian gelateria discreetly tucked away in Covent Garden – but to those in the know, a shopping trip in the area is incomplete without a tub or waffle cone of its artisan-made ices. The place is wonderfully picky when it comes to the ingredients it uses – which include Piedmontese hazelnuts, Sicilian pistachios and Tuscan pine kernels – flavours that are readily discernible in the ice-cream. Prices start at £4 for a small cone or cup, and rise to £5 for a large (or £6.50 for the extravagance of an extra large with a chocolate and nut cone).
40 Shorts Gardens, WC2H 9AB (7240 7086, www.scoopgelato.com).

Scoop

189 Have a cheap and cheerful day in Sloane City

Much to the chagrin of local businesses in Chelsea, Shepherd's Bush-based shopping behemoth Westfield London has poached many of their weekend customers. The upside of this, though, is that Saturdays in Sloane City are now a much less hectic proposition.

Start at the lively food market, where over 50 speciality food producers sell a mix of hot and cold treats outside upscale food store Partridges (2-5 Duke of York Square, SW3 4LY, 7730 0651, www.partridges.co.uk). This being west London, it's the acme of polite civility and nearly all the stalls offer generous samples – artisanal breads (dipped in flavoured olive oil), rare cheeses, decorated cupcakes and spiced meats are usually all there for the tasting. Be sure to head to the Patchwork stall (0845 123 5010, www.patchwork-pate.co.uk), where you can taste a liberal splatter of rustic Cointreau and orange chicken liver pâté against the backdrop of playful tunes from the Dixie Ticklers, a street jazz band that are a King's Road fixture.

Next stop is the much-hyped Saatchi Gallery (Duke of York's HQ, King's Road, SW3 4SQ, 7811 3070, www.saatchigallery.com), which, despite its free admission, isn't quite the oversubscribed scrum of the likes of Tate Modern.

Ultra-affluent residents in the area see to it that the local charity shops are well stocked with near mint condition designer garb. Join the bargain hunters at Shawfield Street's well-hidden boutique-style Oxfam (no.123A, SW3 4PL, 7351 7979, www.oxfam.org.uk), a short walk up King's Road on the left. Further along, on Old Church Street, sits a well-organised British Red Cross (nos.69-71, SW3 5BS, 7376 7300, www.redcross. org.uk) packed with Ralph Lauren, Marc Jacobs and some vintage Gucci and Chanel. Within eyeshot is the Stockpot (273 King's Road, SW3 5EN, 7823 3175, www.stockpotchelsea.co.uk) where almost all main courses cost less than a tenner. Top the day off with a play at the Royal Court Theatre (Sloane Square, London SW1W 8AS, 7565 5000, www.royalcourttheatre.com), where day standing tickets cost 10p (only four are available, for the Downstairs space), and all tickets are £10 on Mondays. Arrive early, and there are comfortable leather sofas and free broadsheets in the downstairs bar.

Saatchi Gallery

190

Get to know your folk...
The somewhat ascetic surroundings of Cecil Sharp House, the home of the English Folk Dance and Song Society (2 Regent's Park Road, NW1 7AY, 7485 2206, www.efdss.org), play host to a variety of folk events. Check online for details of barn dances, ceilidhs and folk-dance classes, banjo and accordion lessons and gigs from a variety of traditional British musicians.

191-197
...then explore London's other folk venues

No longer relegated to back-room nights huddled round the fire, folk gigs – from lively, monthly events to intimate one-off happenings – are popping up all over town. Here are a few of the many venues with a folk focus.

The Green Note in Camden (106 Parkway, NW1 7AN, 7485 9899, www.greennote.co.uk) is a lively spot, which celebrated its tenth anniversary in 2015, and books its fair share of traditional artists, along with blues musicians and singer-songwriters. There are Sunday afternoon sessions as well as nightly gigs.

The Nest Collective (www.thenestcollective. co.uk) holds gigs at various venues, including Islington's Old Queen's Head (44 Essex Road, N1 8LN, 7354 9993, http://theoldqueenshead.com). Come Down and Meet the Folks is a session at the Apple Tree (45 Mount Pleasant, W1CX 0AE, 7837 2365, www.comedownandmeetthefolks. co.uk) on the second and last Sunday of every month. The sounds range across folk, roots, blues, country and Americana.

There's further folky fare at London's weekly folk clubs, which are dotted around the capital and scattered through the week. Among the best are the often irreverent Islington Folk Club (www.islingtonfolkclub.co.uk), held on Thursdays (except during summer) at 8pm at the Horseshoe pub in Clerkenwell (24 Clerkenwell Close, EC1R 0AG, 7253 6068); and the Cellar Upstairs (www.cellarupstairs.org.uk), which happens every Saturday at 8.15pm at either the Lucas Arms (245A Gray's Inn Road, WC1X 8QY) or the Calthorpe Arms (252 Gray's Inn Road, WC1X 8JR). It's the last word in woolly jumper-wearing folk purism, showcasing traditional British, Irish and US artists. Less beardy is the eclectic, more or less monthly the Goose is Out (www.thegooseisout.com), which operates out of two pubs in Nunhead.

Finally, there's Walthamstow Folk Club, every Sunday at 7.30pm at Ye Olde Rose & Crown Theatre Pub (53 Hoe Street, E17 4SA, 07740 612607, www.walthamstowfolk.co.uk). Line-ups are engaging and the crowd is down to earth, making this is one of London's most approachable folk clubs for newbies.

198
Prove that you're too cool for pool

The smoke-filled halls may have gone, but snooker still boasts a deliciously louche image despite (or perhaps because of?) the immense skill required to play the game. While almost anyone can sink a few balls on a pub pool table and imagine they're a real hustler, the greater dimensions of snooker's green baize and the requirement to pot in a specified order pose a far stiffer challenge. Unlike many venues that still live down to their backstreet reputation, the Hurricane Room (www.hurricaneroom.co.uk) is a plush operation. There are four locations – in King's Cross, Acton, Tooting and Colindale – open 24 hours, with full-size snooker tables, as well as American and English pool tables. Once you've became a member (£15-£20 a year), use of the tables costs less than £9 a hour.

199
Glimpse a secret Mayfair castle

Hidden away among the swank hotels and mansions of Mayfair are the elusive turrets of Berkeley Castle, built in the 1930s by artist Frederick Etchells. Inside, the mock-medieval hunting lodge reflects the leading modernist's curious passion for fixtures and fittings recycled from earlier, tumbledown castles. The best you can do, though, is catch a glimpse of the Gothic front door – through an electric portcullis, up a small alley on Mount Row between Berkeley Square and Grosvenor Square.

200
Take in tea and typography on the Strand

The Twinings shop on the Strand (no.216, WC2R 1AP, 7353 3511) is London's oldest shop still to be found in its original location. The golden lion over the doorway dates from 1787 and refers to the sign outside the original Tom's Coffee House of 1706 (before street numbers had been devised). The twin mandarins in the sign refer to the fact that tea was originally imported exclusively from China, and 'Twinings' is the world's oldest logo still in continuous use. Surely these are enough reasons to buy some tea?

201

Attend a service at Westminster Abbey...

Attending Evensong can be a calming, meditative experience, and it's also a way of seeing glorious Westminster Abbey without paying the rather steep entrance fee. Choral Evensong takes place at 5pm on Monday, Tuesday, Thursday and Friday, and at 3pm on Saturday and Sunday.
Westminster Abbey *20 Dean's Yard, SW13 3PA (7222 5152, www.westminster-abbey.org).*

202

...then explore College Garden

Visit Westminster Abbey's cloisters and wonderful College Garden, lined on one side by 14th-century walls and with a great view of the Palace of Westminster's Victoria Tower. The grounds of Westminster Abbey were once used by the monks for growing both medicinal herbs and vegetables. Extraordinarily, they have been under continuous cultivation for over 900 years. There is no charge for visiting the garden or the cloister.

203

Sing your heart out at Hot Breath Karaoke...

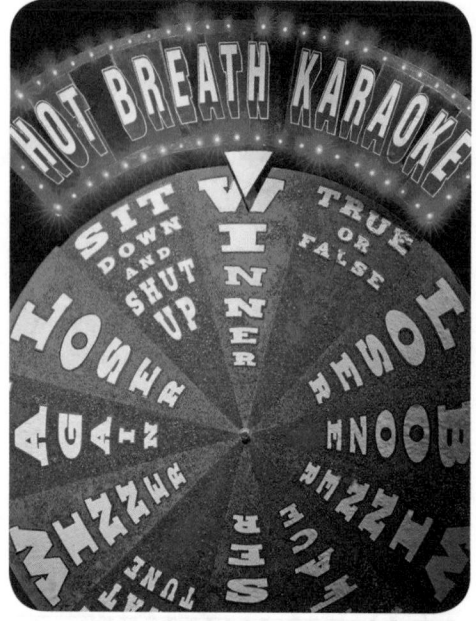

Karaoke is officially a cool pastime these days. At the *Wheel of Fortune*-style party that is Hot Breath Karaoke, wannabes can choose from a whopping 7,000 classic tracks. There are bargain-bin prizes for all who are brave, or misguided, enough to enter, and the whole evening is based on throwing your inhibitions to the wind. Check the website for the next event, and start flexing those vocal cords now.

Hot Breath Karaoke
www.thehouseofhotbreath.com.

204

...or abandon the ballads at Hip Hop Karaoke

Think karaoke is all screechy Spice Girls covers and wailing Westlife tributes? Better leave your secret pop fetish at the door, because this karaoke night's song list is less about the catchy chorus and more about the rhymes. Every Thursday, the Social's Fitzrovia basement bar becomes a shrine to hip hop, and London's fast-talking amateur rappers take to the stage to get the whole crowd bouncing. Get there early to sign up if you want to perform, but you'd best have been practising – it's likely you'll be following a tough act. Thankfully, even if you're more Weird Al than Wu-Tang Clan, the crowd won't throw you any shade; all they really want to do is 'Jump Around'.

Social *5 Little Portland Street, W1W 7JD (www.hiphopkaraoke.co.uk). £5.*

205-214

Go to a film festival

London's film festival scene is buzzing. There are dozens of them showcasing every nation, minority, niche or genre you can think of.

Try an indie-fest such as Raindance (www.raindance.co.uk, September/October) or the trendy Portobello Film Festival (8960 0996, www.portobellofilmfestival.com, September), or the London Bicycle Film Festival (www.bicyclefilmfestival.com/london), part of a growing festival that happens all over the world. Human Rights Watch International Film Festival (www.hrw.org/iff, March) aims to put a human face on threats to individual freedom and dignity.

Thrusting young festivals screening the output of up-and-coming regions such as eastern Europe and Latin America have left the traditionally dominant film-producing countries of western Europe far behind on the festival scene. The Institut Français has Mosaïques (7871 3515, www.institut-francais.org.uk, November), a celebration of cultural diversity. Among the best from eastern Europe is Kinoteka (7822 8984, www.kinoteka.org.uk,

April/May), showcasing Polish films. And there are two Latin American film festivals: Discovering Latin America (www.discovering latinamerica.com, November) offers films, docs and shorts that rarely get distribution, while the Latin American Film Festival (www.latinamericanfilmfestival.com, November) screens commercial features. The London Asian Film Festival (www.tonguesonfire.com, March) shows independent Indian films of the non-Bollywood variety, and the East End Film Festival (8981 3166, www.eastend filmfestival.com, July) explores cinema's potential to cross boundaries.

215

Celebrate Mr Punch's 'birthday'

Every year around 10 May, you can catch Punch and Judy 'professors' from all over the country celebrating the moment in 1662 when Samuel Pepys first recorded having seen an Italian Pulcinella (Punch's esteemed ancestor) puppet show on his way back home from the pub.

Covent Garden Puppet Festival *St Paul's Church Gardens, Bedford Street, WC2E 9ED (7836 5221). Free.*

216

Check out the art at Broadgate

There's a lot of art crammed into Broadgate; at the time of writing, some items were in storage because of redvelopment work, but plenty of pieces remain, such as the enormous *Fulcrum* by Richard Serra, and *Rush Hour* by George Segal, cast from real people. You can't miss the ample curves of the bronze *Broadgate Venus*, by Fernando Botero. Go after dark for the *Finsbury Avenue Lit Floor* (a striking computer-controlled light show). Download an art guide from the website (www.broadgate.co.uk) and start wandering.

217

Go boating

Spend a sunny summer afternoon messing around in a boat. It costs £10 per adult (£4 per child) to hire a rowing or pedal boat for half an hour on the Serpentine in Hyde Park. The lake is open for boating from 10am until sunset, from Easter until the end of October. Battersea Park also has a fleet of rowing and pedal boats, available in July and August, and at weekends into September as long as the weather holds (£6 adults, £3 children, for half an hour). For booking and information for both, ring 7262 1330 or visit www.solarshuttle.co.uk. Finsbury Park boating lake (07905 924282, www.finsburyparkboats.co.uk) is open seven days a week from Easter to October (weather permitting), from noon to 6pm, with extended weekend hours in high summer. All the boats are rowing boats (£8 per boat for 30 minutes).

218-228

Buffy Davis,
Actor

One part of my acting life involves playing the perspicacious Jolene Archer, landlady of the Bull in Ambridge, in Radio 4's *The Archers*. I therefore support pubs that serve pints of Shires and play live music. The Bull's Head (373 Lonsdale Road, SW13 9PY, 8876 5241, www.thebullshead.com) in Barnes doesn't do Shires – which I fear may be a fictional brewery – or, indeed, country & western, but it has an impressive pedigree as a great and influential jazz venue.

Also in Barnes, the Olympic Cinema (117-123 Church Road, W13 9HL, 8912 5161, www.olympiccinema.co.uk) is another great find. It was once a recording studio where the Stones, Beatles and Jimi Hendrix recorded. It also does great coffee and good food.
Anther fantastic pub is the Blackfriar (174 Queen Victoria Street, EC4V 4EG, 7236 5474, www.nicholsonspubs.co.uk). It's also on the river, but further east, by Blackfriars Bridge. It's an art nouveau masterpiece built in 1905 on the site of a Dominican friary. The architect and the artist who built it were both committed to the Arts and Crafts movement. It was saved from demolition by Sir John Betjeman.
It's not all about the beer (Shires or otherwise). I need to eat regularly because my work is very physical: I row, and run too when I've time. And I adore that yummy vegetarian stalwart in Soho, Mildreds (45 Lexington Street, W1F 9AN, 7494 1634,

www.mildreds.co.uk). A lot of my life is spent in Soho doing voiceovers and meetings, so it's great place to pop into – everyone loves it, even if they're confirmed carnivores.
Another source of extraordinarily tasty grub is EV Restaurant (97-99 Isabella Street, SE1 8DD, 7620 6191, www.tasrestaurants.co.uk), part of the Tas chain of Turkish restaurants. It's quite a secret place – under the arches, at the back of Waterloo. I often work in the theatres along the South Bank, and eat here regularly. Excellent house red wine too.
Which can be countered, of course, by the great coffee at the nearby Young Vic theatre (66 The Cut, SE1 8LZ, 7922 2922, www.youngvic.org). It also has a wonderful bar, and fabulous shows that I love being in.
Brixton Market is still wonderful, with so many places to explore. The Ethiopian, the Mexican, cheek by jowl with the Catholic trinket stall – and Morleys (472-488 Brixton Road, SW9 8EH, 7274 6246, www.morleysbrixton.co.uk), one of London's few independent department stores, where you can get anything.
I'm lucky to have been in two shows at the magical, atmospheric Wilton's Music Hall (Graces Alley, E1 8JB, 7702 2789, www.wiltons.org.uk) in Whitechapel. It became a music hall in the middle of the 19th century, and is said to be the first place in England where the can-can was performed. It's now a Grade II listed building. Go, and have a drink at the Mahogany Bar.
I would recommend to anyone the Wellcome Collection (183 Euston Road, NW1 2BE, 7611 2222, www.wellcomecollection.org). It's the free visitor destination for the incurably curious – what's not to love?
The same goes for the Old Operating Theatre Museum & Herb Garret (9A St Thomas Street, SE1 9RY, 7188 2679, www.thegarret.org.uk). This place is just something else; I love going there to research roles.
It's important to me to spend time outside. King Henry's Mound, next to Pembroke Lodge in Richmond Park (www.royalparks.org.uk), is one of my favourite views, all the way to St Paul's Cathedral (see p122). The view is protected: nothing is allowed to be built that would spoil it. The Mound is said to be where King Henry witnessed a rocket fired from the Tower to inform him that Anne Boleyn was now headless, which meant he could marry Lady Jane Seymour. Jolene is not responsible for killing her spouses but she is fond of variety. Henry VIII and myself both share birthdays in June, a day apart! Go figure!

229

Discover the ultimate power source at the Royal Institution

Even the most ecologically sound power stations need generators and transformers to transport electricity from source to user, and you can see the first incarnations of Michael Faraday's world-changing inventions and the lab where they were built in the basement of the 200-year-old Royal Institution, in what was formerly the Faraday Museum. There's now also a quirky video guide that enlivens other geeky contraptions and shows how other bright RI sparks (14 of whom were Nobel Prize winners) discovered ten chemical elements, explained why the sky is blue and engineered the safety lamp that revolutionised miners' working lives. Check out Faraday's digitised notebook and the singing periodic table wall before recharging your batteries at the swanky Time & Space cocktail bar.

Royal Institution *21 Albemarle Street, W1S 4BS (7409 2992, www.rigb.org). Free.*

230-238

Listen out for a gun salute

There are gun salutes on many state occasions – see the list of dates below for a complete breakdown of when the cannons roar out – as well as for state visits. A cavalry charge features in the 41-gun salutes mounted by the King's Troop Royal Horse Artillery in Hyde Park at noon (opposite the Dorchester Hotel), whereas, on the other side of town, the Honourable Artillery Company ditches the ponies and piles on the firepower with its 62-gun salutes (1pm at the Tower of London). If the dates happen to fall on a Sunday, the salute is held on the following Monday.

Dates 6 February (Accession Day); 21 April & 14 June (Queen's birthdays); 2 June (Coronation Day); 10 June (Duke of Edinburgh's birthday); 14 June (Trooping the Colour); State Opening of Parliament (usually May); Lord Mayor's Show (mid November); Remembrance Sunday (mid November); also for state visits.

239

Get on your bike

Get involved in a world-class festival of cycling with the annual RideLondon weekend (www.prudentialridelondon.co.uk) at the end of July. Roads are closed and thousands of cyclists, young and old, take to the city's streets.

240 Discover Two Temple Place

Two Temple Place opened in 2011 as a venue to showcase publicly owned art from the the UK's regional collections and museums. Previously closed to the public, the building – a late 19th-century neo-Gothic mansion built as an office for William Waldorf Astor – is owned and run by the Bulldog Trust (www.bulldogtrust.org).

The interior is ornately decorated with marble fireplaces, patterned floors, stained glass, friezes and carvings. The inaugural exhibition featured highlights from the William Morris Gallery (based in Walthamstow). The bad news is that Two Temple Place is only open when exhibitions are on, usually between January and April; the good news is that entry is free. Check the website for the latest information.

Two Temple Place *2 Temple Place, WC2R 3BD (7836 3715, www.twotempleplace.org).*

241-256 Blow your tenner in the capital's best pub jukeboxes...

Approach Tavern

Jazz, blues and R&B faves at this updated Bethnal Green boozer. At the time of writing, the jukebox was free.
47 Approach Road, E2 9LY (8980 2321).

Boogaloo

A justly famous jukebox, spinning everything from Dusty Springfield to the Pogues; three tunes for a quid.
312 Archway Road, N6 5AT (8340 2928, www.theboogaloo.co.uk).

Bradley's Spanish Bar

London's best vinyl juke, loaded with Hendrix, Presley and the Dead Kennedys (£1 for three plays).
42-44 Hanway Street, W1T 1UT (7636 0359).

Crobar

£1 for three hard and heavy tracks from the likes of Lynyrd Skynyrd, Led Zep and a lot of Iron Maiden.
17 Manette Street, W1D 4AS (7439 0831, www.crobar.co.uk).

Dublin Castle

The sweaty back-room venue hosts aspiring guitar bands; the juke in the pub out front is full of indie faves. Five songs for £1.
94 Parkway, NW1 7AN (7485 1773, www.thedublincastle.com).

Golden Heart

This trad but trendy Truman boozer is a hangout for the arty crowd. Your eyes will be drawn to the penny-chew-coloured jukebox – Three songs for £1.
110 Commercial Street, E1 6LZ (7247 2158).

Hope & Anchor

Both jukeboxes at this grizzled rock boozer are packed with punk/indie faves. £1 buys three plays, but staff often give out credits.
207 Upper Street, N1 1RL (7354 1312, www.hopeandanchor-islington.co.uk).

King Charles I

A quid buys four songs, covering all corners from reggae to country.
55-57 Northdown Street, N1 9BL (7837 7758).

Mucky Pup

Great name, great jukebox: marvellously mixed-up (Nick Drake, Jesus Lizard, Mastadon) and, best of all, free.
39 Queen's Head Street, N1 8NQ (7226 2572).

Prince George

One of Hackney's finest jukes; ranging from Sinatra to the White Stripes. Five songs, £1.
40 Parkholme Road, E8 3AG (7254 6060).

Reliance

Rock, funk, soul and blues from the 1970s to '90s. All for free.
336 Old Street, EC1V 9DR (7729 6888, www.thereliancepub.co.uk).

Royal Exchange

Trad and modern Irish plus jazz and 1960s-'90s favourites. Three songs for a nugget.
26 Sale Place, W2 1PU (7402 3468).

Shakespeare

A welcoming local where the wide-ranging jukebox plays three tunes for £1.
57 Allen Road, N16 8RY (7254 4190).

Social

New music from the Heavenly Social label plus regularly changing CDs (free).
5 Little Portland Street, W1W 7JD (7636 4992).

Swimmer at the Grafton Arms

Some 800 CD tracks that rotate every couple of months, from Elbow to Ella Fitzgerald.
13 Eburne Road, N7 6AR (7281 4632).

Three Kings

A selection of 80 vinyl seven-inches that changes each week; £1 for seven songs.
7 Clerkenwell Close, EC1R 0DY (7253 0483).

Crobar

Bradley's Spanish Bar

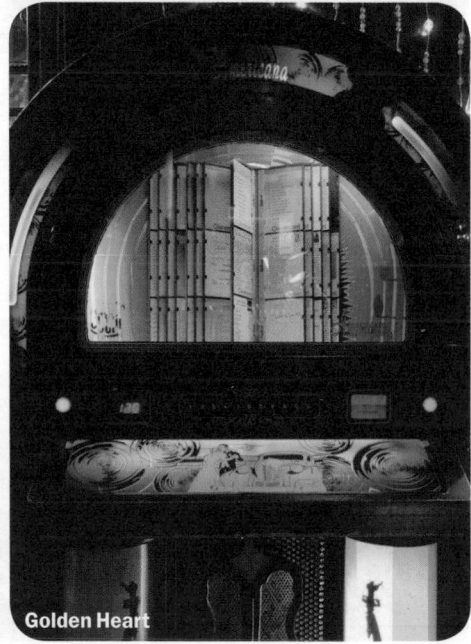

Golden Heart

257

...or go to a free gig in a record store

In-store gigs have become central to a band's marketing plan, so most of the retail giants regularly host free gigs. As do independents such as Rough Trade East (Old Truman Brewery, 91 Brick Lane, E1 6QL, 7392 7788, www.rough trade.com), which has featured top-class bands and DJs from Beirut and Boys Noize to Crystal Castles and Of Montreal. Check the website for details of performances. You may need to apply in advance for a wristband to gain entry if it's a popular band.

Transports of delight

Peter Watts *rides the buses – each and every one.*

London is unimaginable without its buses. They flow through the city's veins like little red blood cells, travelling along more than 500 different daily routes, dispensing Londoners around every limb and organ of the city. A few years ago, in a moment of recklessness, I decided to travel every single one of them, in order, end-to-end, starting with the 1 bus, Tottenham Court Road to Canada Water, and finishing with the 499, the Gallows Corner loop service via Becontree Heath. After that there are the weekday-only Red Arrow services (507, 521, 549), the school bus services (600-699) and the mobility buses (900-999) that take OAPs to local shopping centres. When you take into account all the night buses and the letter-prefixed local routes, from A10 (Heathrow Airport–Uxbridge) to X68 (West Croydon– Russell Square express service), it looks like I'll be kept on the move by the bright red behemoths until the day I die from excessive exhaust fume inhalation.

As a Londoner, I've always been a fan of buses, but I became particularly attached to them during a period of fallow employment, when I was cash poor and time rich, and therefore happy to pay £1.50 (as it then was) to take an hour to travel from A to B rather than £2.30 for the faster, more direct tube. Travelling above ground, seeing how London unfolds and how postcodes knit together, was a key part in my London education. Every Londoner carries about in their head a mental map of the city, with the unexplored bits, usually those between tube stations, left blank. The bus fills in the gaps. Cheaply.

London's routes cover plenty of ground and offer different things for different users. So if you are serious about buskateering, you need to be prepared. Start with the London Transport Museum (Covent Garden Piazza, WC2E 7BB, 7379 6344, www.ltmuseum.co.uk) or Ian Allan's transport bookshop in Waterloo (45-46 Lower Marsh, SE1 7RG, 7401 2100). Finally, crucially, get yourself an Oyster card pay-as-you-go, capped at £6.40 a day). Now you're ready to ride.

London's busy morning buses are hellish for the unprepared, but one thing we'd heartily recommend is swinging by Waterloo – there are numerous usable routes – at around 8am to see the old-fashioned British queue in all its glory. Gaze down from the top deck as commuters, fresh off the train from the sticks, line up in sober crocodiles waiting for their bus to the City. You

EMERGENCY EXIT
TO OPEN

76
MUDCHUTE

won't see neater queues outside of the Post Office and it's interesting to speculate on why they occur here of all places – the bus stations outside London Bridge and Victoria stations, by contrast, are screaming scrums of Metro-wielding ne'er-do-wells, and have none of the decorum and 1950s after-you-isms of the Waterloo brigade. Such good behaviour was clearly set in stone by commuters many years previously and has never been unbuilt by the generations that followed.

The top floor of the London bus is great for this sort of people-watching, and makes the double-decker London's answer to European café culture. Ride any of the dozen buses that shuffle along Oxford Street like scarlet pachyderms and, if you're lucky, you might see one of the great British scams in progress. It works like this: an Arthur Daley type sets up a trellis table on the pavement selling boxes of shady perfume. He starts up his patter and

Bags packed, milk cancelled, house raised on stilts.

You've packed the suntan lotion, the snorkel set, the stay-pressed shirts. Just one more thing left to do – your bit for climate change. In some of the world's poorest countries, changing weather patterns are destroying lives.

You can help people to deal with the extreme effects of climate change. Raising houses in flood-prone regions is just one life-saving solution.

**Climate change costs lives.
Give £5 and let's sort it *Here & Now***

www.oxfam.org.uk/climate-change

Be Humankind Oxfam

attracts a middle-aged woman, who, after some toing-and-froing, hands over £20 to pay for a couple of bottles of the stuff. This initial purchase then convinces a further flurry of buyers to give up their hard-earned, and between them fill Arthur's suitcase with lovely lolly. Watch from a bus backed-up in Oxford Street traffic, though, and you'll have a bird's-eye- view of the fiddle in action as you catch the initial buyer – the woman that prompted the gold rush in the first place – returning to the vendor as soon as things have quietened down. She returns the perfume and cash to her partner, and then they'll both get ready to start the process again. If the traffic is really bad, you can watch the dodgy duo work the scent scam in tandem a couple of times before the police get wind of it.

The bus is also the perfect place to see the finer, forgotten points of London architecture, such as the impeccable first-floor detailing you find in the older parts of the City. Try the 21 or 43 bus north along Moorgate and you'll see a succession of delights: a carved lighthouse on the side of a Swiss bank; the bas-relief of two tube trains entering a tunnel above a doorway; an old fire-insurance plaque on the corner with London Wall; the fine stained-glass window of the City campus of the London Metropolitan University; and, where the street feeds into Finsbury Square, the strident art deco Triton Court with its secular spire topped by the statue of a man, standing astride a globe, with one arm raised to shield his eyes from the sun as he stares into the distance. Most central London streets conceal similar treats.

Top decks are also the best place to witness another London ritual: school going-home time. In a 2008 transport policy document, the Conservative Mayor Boris Johnson argued that 'Free travel for kids has brought a culture where adults are too often terrified of the swearing, staring in-your-face-ness of the younger generation.' But it's really not as bad as all that, and 'free' has nothing to do with it. For decades, schoolchildren have gone home by bus and in exactly the same manner – they swarm on, stampede upstairs, then spend the short duration of their journey shouting at each other about pop music and clothes, fighting and snogging, and occasionally waving wildly/gesticulatingly crudely to their peers, who are doing exactly the same thing on the top decks of neighbouring buses. Sure, it might get a bit noisy, but it's

only intimidating if you've never been a schoolchild on a London bus.

So, ignore Boris's nannying and catch any London bus at around 3pm (the 4 bus, between Waterloo and Archway, is particularly exciting) – you will, if nothing else, be able to impress your friends with some sensational new slang. You might even be pleasantly surprised: I was recently on a 68 when a gang of hoodies slouched on and stomped towards the back of the bus. Commuters nervously eyed each other – was this the dreaded 'in-your-face-ness' Boris had warned them about? However, a teenage gang war on the 8.47am to Euston seemed increasingly unlikely as the kids started an enthusiastic discussion about the best way to present a Thai green curry – they were catering students, threatening nothing but our taste buds.

Most tourists won't go anywhere near buses that serve the inner-London schools, though; they'll be too busy getting gushy over the (old) Routemaster. Yes, these still survive (just), rattling along one 'heritage' route, the 15 – between the Tower of London and Trafalgar Square. Tourists love them – and who can blame them? Boris Johnson has introduced a new-generation Routemaster to replace the articulated 'bendy buses'. The latter were a disappointment for many reasons, one of which was no top deck – meaning no chance to get above the London streets. Nobody would travel on a bendy bus for pleasure.

Which leads us to the big question: what buses should you catch for pleasure? One of the best for seeing the sights is the 11, which goes from Fulham Broadway to Liverpool Street, taking in everything from the boutiques of Sloane Square to the national monuments of Westminster and the City. The 360 is a good way of getting from the museums of South Kensington down to the brilliant Imperial War Museum, albeit by entertainingly circuitous means. The 73 is a London icon, being one of the capital's most regular services. The 24 is the most scenic way of getting from central London to Hampstead Heath. The 3 will take you all the way down south to London's magical Crystal Palace Park. And the 22 allows you to finish your journey in the charming surrounds of the Spencer pub on Putney Common, where the tables are big enough for you to get out your maps and contemplate your next voyage on London's best and cheapest form of transport.

259 *Learn Afro-Brazilian drumming*

Energetic carnival-style funkateers Tribo are a London-based Afro-Brazilian samba-reggae outfit, originally from Salvador, who run a weekly two-hour workshop for anyone interested in their indigenous percussive arts. It involves learning how to beat a huge samba drum to a set rhythm – not as easy as it sounds, but the emphasis here is very much on finding your groove at your own pace. The classes are casual and welcome all ages and abilities, ultimately working towards students being able to perform in *blocos* (street parades) in London (including Notting Hill Carnival) and in Brazil. Tribo beginners have even gone on to play with bands back in Salvador. The group is also a regular fixture at the capital's buzzing Latin American clubs, such as Guanabara (7242 8600, www.guanabara.co.uk).

Tribo *Maxilla Social Club, 2 Maxilla Walk, W10 6NQ (07772 470198, www.triboband.com). £10 per person.*

260

Go to a roller disco
All over the capital, roller
gals and guys are squeezing
into Lycra leggings and
donning fluoro leg warmers.
Check out www.skating
haven.com, www.ukroller
disco.moonfruit.com and
www.rollerdisco.com.

261

Spend Sunday with the French

For some guaranteed Gallic flair, pop along at 2pm on a Sunday to the Ciné Lumière's screenings of classy French flicks (tickets £6-£8). Launched by Catherine Deneuve in 1998, this plush cinema puts on a variety of excellent film seasons (including Turkish and Spanish movies) but its Sunday slot is always a French classic from the likes of François Truffaut, Jean Renoir and Jean-Luc Godard.
Ciné Lumière *Institut Français, 17 Queensberry Place, SW7 2DT (7871 3515, www.institut français. org.uk).*

262

Work out at a green gym

Are you keen to improve your fitness but not a fan of indoor exercise? Organised by the Conservation Volunteers (formerly the British Trust for Conservation Volunteers, 01302 388883, www.tcv.org.uk), Green Gym may be just what you're after. A fresh-air alternative to sweaty aerobics classes and soul-destroying treadmills, groups undertake a variety of tasks to enhance the local environment, such as clearing undergrowth, building an outdoor seat or reinstating a pathway. Research has shown that you can burn almost a third more calories in an hour doing some Green Gym activities than in a step aerobics class. If you fancy giving it a go, there are currently six groups in London (Camden, Hampstead, Harringay, Lewisham, Newham, Waltham Forest) – or you could start one yourself. The website has full details.

263

Sail from Tate to Tate

The inspired Tate to Tate boat service travels from Tate Britain to Bankside Pier (Tate Modern) every 40 minutes during the day, with a stop at Embankment en route. *www.thamesclippers.com.*

264-270

Be late

On the last Friday of every month, the V&A (www.vam.ac.uk) hosts evening events (6.30-10pm), with live performances, cutting-edge fashion, film, installations, debates, special guests, DJs, bars, food and late exhibition openings. Round the corner at the Science Museum (www.sciencemuseum.org.uk), Lates – last Wednesday of every month, 6.45-10pm – are for over-18s only; every month there's a different theme. Late at Tate Britain (www.tate.org.uk) occurs on the first Friday of certain months (6-10pm), with a range of music, workshops, special guests, performances and debates, while After Hours at the Natural History Museum (www.nhm.ac.uk) gives access to exhibitions, galleries and shops. The museum stays open until 10pm on the last Friday of every month (apart from December).

If that's not enough, the British Museum (www.britishmuseum.org) is open until 8.30pm every Friday night and offers a programme of events, open galleries, food and drink. Volunteers are available for free 20-minute spotlight tours. Also open every Friday night (until 9pm) is the National Gallery (www.nationalgallery.org.uk). There are free guided tours (7pm), and music in the Sainsbury Wing foyer. Visit the Museum of London website (www.museumoflondon.org.uk) to see details of their late nights. The events are free, but admission charges apply for some temporary exhibitions.

271

Observe 'A Rake's Progress'

William Hogarth was an archetypal Londoner but even he needed to escape the teeming streets of the city from which he drew so much inspiration – which is why he had a country retreat in Chiswick. Here, you can see his great series of satirical engravings including *A Rake's Progress* and *Marriage à-la-Mode*. Afterwards, make a pilgrimage to his tomb in the graveyard of nearby St Nicholas Church (Church Street, W4 2PJ).
Hogarth's House *Hogarth Lane, Great West Road, W4 2QN (8994 6757, www.hounslow.info). Free.*

272

Go up the creek in Deptford

Once an important industrial tributary of the Thames, for centuries Deptford Creek, with its huge, twice-daily seven-metre tidal surge – like an inhalation and exhalation – was an inherent part of Deptford's identity. Even the name Deptford means Deep Ford; a place where people could cross the creek's stony bottom at low tide. But as dockyards, slaughterhouses, tanneries, granaries and tidal mills moved elsewhere in the last century and the river's importance slowly diminished, the tributary sank into neglect and stagnation, gradually becoming a repository for shopping trolleys and other detritus.

That is until 2002, when the Creekside Centre charity decided to clean things up and bring the creek's fragile but unique ecosystem to people's attention. That's why we're now flailing around in an attempt to don thigh-high waders. It's a chilly Sunday morning in December and although it's perhaps not the most immediately enticing weekend activity, we're struggling to contain our excitement at the prospect of wading through the exposed mud of 'London's Grand Canyon'. Our infectiously enthusiastic guide is Nick Bertrand, local conservationist and Deptford Creek hero, and it's into a seemingly new dimension that he's about to lead us. Eventually, our group of around ten waddle off, armed with walking poles ('they're your third leg'), leaving behind the centre's wild grounds full of trolley sculptures and artworks assembled from assorted reclaimed creekside materials.

Down on the creek bed, the raucous world of the city, with its buildings hanging high above us, silhouetted darkly by the sun, does indeed seem almost threatening – or perhaps it's just that the river bed quickly becomes more of a comforting, if muddy, cocoon the further we tramp along its course.

Over our two-hour tour Nick shows us a stretch not more than about a mile in length, but even on this wintry day there's enough wildlife to see – from kingfishers and herons to chinese mitten crabs and other squiggly shrimp-like creatures, as well as delicate wild plants. In summer, the place is teeming with butterflies, dragonflies, flounder – the creek is an important breeding ground – prawns, crabs and around 120 species of wildflower, as well as a lot more birds, including cormorants and sometimes even the rare black redstart. You're so low down here that it's easy to get sucked (literally, in one case) into the opaque and mysterious world of viscous silt. We poke about like wannabe Swallows and Amazons, delighted not only by a caught mitten crab and the wriggling contents of our white 'pond dipping trays' but also by unidentifiable metal chunks that have perhaps fallen off one of the boats moored (and in some cases still inhabited) in the creek.

But it's worth looking up as well as down. There's a unique perspective to be had from the riverbed – just imagining what would happen to London if those towering flood-defence walls were breached makes you dizzy for starters. And those looming constructions even higher above you? Well, Nick's no fan of architects, but there's no denying the ingenuity of Joseph Bazalgette's pumping station; the simple, solid and pragmatic beauty of Mumford's Flour Mill; the graceful sweep of the DLR bridge or the shimmering chutzpah of Herzog and de Meuron's Laban dance centre with its pink, green and blue polycarbonate panels. But there's a problem here too: Deptford has been slated as one of London's key areas for residential housing development, and in the Deptford Creek area alone – about 25 hectares in all – a staggering 3,400 new homes are expected to be built in the next five years. All of which, of course, means that the creek and its inhabitants – human and animal – are under threat. Go and see it for yourself before the developers have their wicked way.

Creekside Centre *14 Creekside, SE8 4SA (8692 9922, www.creeksidecentre.org.uk). Low-tide walk £10.*

273-275

Search for bats in London's woods and wetlands

Once London's bats have crawled out of hibernation in late spring, you'll have a number of opportunities to observe these fascinating and endangered mammals close up in the city's wilder locations. Whichever sunset foray you choose (see www.londonbats.org.uk for a list of locations, further information on other walks and bat groups around London), you'll learn about the country's 17 species before heading out (armed with ultrasonic bat detectors) to look for the six that are found in London as they leave their roosts. The detectors translate the echo-location signals emitted by bats into sound audible

to the human ear. Once you've tuned in you're almost guaranteed a sighting of Britain's smallest bat, the pocket-sized pipistrelle, as it swoops in on its nightly dinner of around 3,000 midges. Popular bat walks in London take place at lovely Highgate Woods, which were granted to Londoners as an open space by the Lord Mayor in 1886. Here, you can bat-spot among the oaks and hornbeams of one of the city's most atmospheric parks. These events are free but very popular, so book ahead.

At the London Wetland Centre in Barnes (which has ten confirmed species), there are 30-minute introductory presentations before groups of around ten head out with guides and their bat detectors into the 100-odd acres of the award-winning Site of Special Scientific Interest. There's also a chance to spot Britain's biggest bat, the noctule, which can reach speeds of around 30mph. (Contrary to popular belief, they don't dive-bomb you.)

The London Wildlife Trust runs free bat-spotting evenings in various nature reserves – check the website for details of these events. In general, bat walks usually take place at twilight in the summer months and walk dates tend to be sporadic; ring ahead to check times and to book (sessions are often heavily oversubscribed). Even in summer, you may have to do a lot of standing around so dress warmly and take a torch. All start times vary with sunset.
Highgate Woods *Muswell Hill Road, N10 3JN (8444 6129, www.cityoflondon.gov.uk/openspaces). Bat watches June-Sept (at least once a month). Free.*
London Wildlife Trust *7261 0447, www.wildlondon. org.uk.*
WWT London Wetland Centre *Queen Elizabeth's Walk, SW13 9WT (8409 4400, www.wwt.org.uk). Big Batty Walks July-Sept (at least three a month). £10.*

276

Visit an Arts and Crafts gem

This Georgian house on the Thames conceals a splendid Arts and Crafts interior, with the decoration and furnishings preserved as they were in the lifetime of the owner, printer Emery Walker (1851-1933). There's a combination of Morris & Co textiles, wallpapers and furniture (Walker was a great friend of William Morris), 17th- and 18th-century furniture, and Middle Eastern and North African textiles and ceramics. The house – run by a small charitable trust – opens for small groups of visitors (eight at a time) from April to October.
Emery Walker House *7 Hammersmith Terrace, W6 9TS (www.emerywalker.org.uk).*

277

Catch blooms all year round

Kew Gardens may cost more than a tenner, but horticultural diehards on a budget can take solace from the fact that the Isabella Plantation, tucked away in the south-west corner of Richmond Park, is completely free. An enchanting ornamental woodland garden, dotted with clearings, ponds and streams, it was established in the 1950s and today there's always something in bloom – or at least colourful – among the collection of exotic plants and trees. It's also a good place to see birds: resident species include redpoll, bullfinch, woodpecker, sparrowhawk and tawny owl. *www.royalparks.org.uk.*

Isabella Plantation

Run London

*Ronnie Haydon **pulls on her trainers to pound the city's pavements and parks and trails.***

It's cheap. It makes you cheerful. It's a top calorie-burner. No gym fees or special kit. Fresh air. Camaraderie. The reasons runners give for their addiction sound insufferably smug, but they have a point. Throw in London's reputation as an A-plus running city (world-class marathon, the best green spaces, fantastic Olympic Park) and its rather B-minus public transport system (a cycling or running commute is often the swiftest option) and joining the ranks of the city's running nuts seems like a fine idea.

Off the treadmill

It's baffling how many people 'go for a run' in a noisy gym while within easy sweating distance of a beautiful London park. Exercising outdoors not only gifts your body more endorphins (feel-good hormones) and burns more calories (watching your step, swerving on to grass and climbing hills all require extra effort), but it's good for the soul and mental health too. A quick circuit of the nearest greensward before breakfast, during your lunch break or after work, in any weather, will make you feel happier, healthier

and glowier than any gym. Parks are free too. And if you really must get some reps in, many parks have outdoor gyms as well: log on to the Great Outdoor Gym Company (www.tgogc.com) to find the nearest.

On doctor's orders

If you've done little more than run for a bus since school PE lessons, pounding pavements every day is going to cause injury. So start out conservatively, interspersing running with walking, active days with rest days, weight-bearing exercise with kinder activities such as cycling or swimming. Follow the nine-week NHS Couch to 5K programme as a gentle start to your running career, before taking the next step.

With barcode downloaded

Parkrun (www.parkrun.org.uk) has turned thousands of aimless city joggers into 5,000-metre champs. There are about 50 'parkruns' in Greater London, taking place at 9am on a Saturday morning, in a park near you. It costs nothing. Before you show up, go online to

download your barcode, which is scanned on completion of every run. Each parkrun is staffed by a team of volunteers (sign up to do that too) and the camaraderie every Saturday morning is fantastic. Your time is emailed or texted to you a couple of hours later. The results table shows if you've managed a personal best (PB), how fit you are for your age group and how many points you've stacked up – and points mean prizes.

Parkrun started life as the Bushy Park Time Trial (BPTT), a five-kilometre race against the clock that only serious runners cared about. As it was timed, it proved an accurate way of gauging progress over the distance. The time trial became so popular that its founder, Paul Sinton-Hewitt, had the idea of staging other time trials in parks across the country. The rest, as he says, has made

running history: 'We started BPTT in 2004. At the time, we considered it too simple to reproduce to want to protect it. After we started Wimbledon Common Time Trial (WCTT), we realised we had something and so the growth began. The parkrun brand was conceived in late 2009. We then formed the not-for-profit company – parkrun UK – which allowed all the events at the time to be rebranded as parkruns. We welcome all walkers, joggers, runners and those who simply wish to volunteer. There are no time limits.'

With support from your club

Once you've enjoyed a few parkruns, and you can run for 30 minutes without stopping, you may want to progress further. Perhaps that running holy grail, the London Marathon, is your ultimate

aim. But to become a better runner, you'll need a coach. The best way to find one is to sign up with your local running club.

To some, the prospect of venturing on to a running track with all those sinewy Mo Farah lookalikes is daunting; they'd prefer to remain trotting around the park in their own private runner's world, earbuds in, enjoying the scenery. And that's all you need for baseline fitness. To improve, however, coaching is essential.

Club runners encourage each other and participate (for free) in club races – from muddy cross-country events to summer-evening park meetings, all marshalled and timed. Many clubs allow non-members to pay a track fee and run on club nights, especially if they're thinking of

joining at some later date. Clubs ask for a subscription fee (usually £25-£35 a year) and an optional annual UK Athletics affiliation fee (£12, which allows you to compete for your club and receive race fee discounts, plus reductions in sports shops). See below for a list of London's most popular running clubs.

All the way to the office

Run to work. Or from work. If your place of work is more than eight miles from your home (anything much more than a one-hour run is going to have you snoozing al desko), take the train or bus halfway and run the rest. Always have an Oystercard in your pocket in case of sudden prostration.

It requires a little organisation: a change of clothes under your desk, not to mention toiletries to stop your workmates complaining that you're still emanating a little too much 'runner's high'. Some people like to run to work with a special non-jiggly runners' rucksack (Deuter have a fine selection). For more inspiration about your running commute, visit www.runningtowork.co.uk.

Like a jolly good sport

If you've ever found yourself pounding the pavements and wondering 'what's it all for?', GoodGym (www.goodgym.org) has the answer. GoodGym matches a love of running with a community's need for good eggs. You sign up online, pick a group (currently in Camden, Hackney and Lambeth) and then join a group of runners and a qualified trainer on one of their 'missions'. It might be a Saturday-morning run to clean out a pond in Vauxhall or creating an allotment compost heap in Stepney. Other GoodGym runners get matched up with people in their community who are elderly or isolated and need someone to, ahem, run errands. There are weekly Tuesday workouts if you want to share your love of running with London's friendliest, and certainly most helpful, fitness club.

At an inspirational pace

If you're an experienced runner (and have a good watch), you could sign up to be an official race pacer. Pacers wear a light backpack with a hi-vis flag announcing the time they're contracted to finish the race in. Runners keep pacers in their sights if they want to complete a big race in a certain time. Many popular London races, such as the Royal Parks Half and, of course, the Virgin Money London Marathon, have pacers.

You have to be able to guarantee you can run the distance in a certain time, so most runners choose a mark about 20 minutes slower than their PB. You don't have to be a great runner: half-marathon pacers see runners through in a range of times, from 1hr 30mins to 2hrs 30mins. Every second counts in the fevered world of PB chasing, so pacers often gather a little posse of hopefuls around them during the race. What does the pacer get out of it? Free entry to expensive races, and a finisher's technical T-shirt and goody bag, as well as an enormous sense of well-being. Find out more from www.racepacing.com.

London's running clubs

Beckenham Running Club
www.beckenhamrunning.co.uk.
Training at Norman Park running track and surrounding areas.

Clapham Chasers
www.claphamchasers.co.uk.
Training at Trinity Fields, Wandsworth Common.

Dulwich Runners
www.dulwichrunners.org.uk.
Training at Dulwich College track (summer) and Crystal Palace Arena (winter).

Highgate Harriers
www.highgateharriers.org.uk.
Training at Parliament Hill athletics track.

Hillingdon Athletic Club
www.hillingdonac.co.uk.
Training at Hillingdon Athletics Stadium, Ruislip.

Kent Athletic Club
www.kentac.org.uk.
Training at Ladywell Track, Lewisham.

Serpentine Running Club
www.serpentine.org.uk.
Training at Seymour Leisure Centre, Marylebone, and Hyde Park.

Thames Valley Harriers
www.thamesvalleyharriers.com.
Training at Linford Christie Stadium, Wormwood Scrubs.

Victoria Park Harriers & Tower Hamlets Athletics Club
www.vphthac.org.uk.
Training in Victoria Park and Mile End Stadium.

Wimbledon Windmilers
www.windmilers.org.uk.
Training at Wimbledon Park track.

285-290
Pound along London's loveliest running routes

Royal parks, common green spaces and the sweet Thames – London has them all, and most Londoners aren't further than a short jog away. Avoid the South Bank, though; it's just too congested with tourists.

Green Lungs of Lewisham

A circular route starting at Ladywell Track and taking in Ladywell Fields, Hilly Fields Park, Brockley & Ladywell Cemetery and Blythe Hill Fields. About four miles.

Victoria Park & Limehouse Basin

Starting at Bethnal Green, taking in the V&A Museum of Childhood's gardens, followed by a circuit of Hackney's finest park, then tracking the Regent's Canal by Mile End Park, around Limehouse Basin and back on the other side of the canal. About 7.5 miles.

Time & Tide: Greenwich

Starting at the *Cutty Sark*, follow the river east as far as the Thames Barrier, then run inland towards Charlton, crossing the A206 Woolwich Road and taking in a steep climb over woodland across to Maryon Wilson Park. From there to Charlton Park, then west via Vanbrugh Park back to the top of Greenwich Park. This is a long 'un – about 8.5 miles.

Two Bridges West

Hammersmith and Barnes bridges. Start at either and run along the towpath to the other bridge; cross over and run along the other side of the river to end up back where you started. The south side of the river is a nice, leafy trail-type path, while the north side is a mix of paved roads and trails. About four miles – and there are any number of pleasant hostelries for rehydration purposes.

Northern Sights

A four-mile circuit of Hampstead Heath, starting at the railway station (not tube) along Parliament Hill to the Heath, past the ponds, then Kenwood House, heading for Highgate Ponds, past the cemetery into Waterlow Park, then back on to the Heath via Swain's Lane.

Royally crowd-pleasing

Bring a visitor to London with you on this seven-mile run following the Princess Diana Memorial Walk waymarkers (brass plates in the pavement), from the Kensington Gardens that she called home, through Hyde, Green and St James's parks – all the selfie opportunities a tourist could need.

291 Think positive in the West End

Rubbing shoulders with trendy hair salons and minimalist boutiques, Covent Garden-based meditation centre Inner Space offers the kind of spiritual free lunch we're told doesn't exist: you can take courses in raja yoga meditation or try workshops in effective stress resistance, heightened self-esteem techniques and progressive relaxation methods. Alternatively, drop in to its curious, mood-lit quiet room, listen to piped Zen-like music and sit among London's enlightened ones.

Inner Space *36 Shorts Gardens, WC2H 9AB (7836 6688, www.innerspace.org.uk). Free.*

292 Browse under Waterloo Bridge

Stroll along the South Bank and before long you'll find the second-hand book stalls beneath Waterloo Bridge, a venerable London institution and a great place to browse for literary classics, out-of-print books and old magazines and prints (many of which you'll get for less than a tenner).

293 Taste vintage wine at the Sampler

Wannabe wine buffs need look no further than the Sampler, an independent wine shop that offers 80 of its more than 900 wines for you to try, whether it's an inexpensive chardonnay from Australia or a fancy bottle of Château Latour from Bordeaux. The wines are rotated every two to three weeks, so there's always something new to savour, with prices starting at just 30p for a slug of fino sherry. Staff can provide expert help if needed.

Sampler *266 Upper Street, N1 2UQ (7226 9500); 35 Thurloe Place, SW7 2HP (7225 5091); www.thesampler.co.uk.*

294 *Remember lost luvvies at the Actors' Church*

St Paul's, Covent Garden is justly known as the Actors' Church. Thespians commemorated on its walls range from those lost in obscurity – step forward Percy Press, one-time Punch and Judy man – to those destined for immortality: that'll be Charlie Chaplin, then. Perhaps most charming are the numerous sublunary figures. William Henry Pratt, for example, better known as Boris Karloff, and universally famous as the real flesh behind unforgettable monsters – Frankenstein being one of them. Take a bow too, Hattie Jacques, archetypal matron in the interminable series of Carry On films. The Jacques memorial is so plain you may wonder if the inscriber felt that any embellishment would seem an impertinence in the face of such a big comic persona. And surely no more romantic tribute is paid anywhere in the city than that to Vivien Leigh. Her plaque is simply inscribed with words from Shakespeare's *Antony and Cleopatra*: 'Now boast thee, death, in thy possession lies a lass unparallel'd.' When we visit, however, our first homage is always paid to the memory of the mysterious 'Pantopuck the Puppetman', one AR Philpott, a master puppeteer whose work included films such as *The Dark Crystal*, *Labyrinth* and *Star Wars*. We choose to imagine his spirit wooing the excellently named Hollywood actress Edna Best, remembered not far away as 'The Constant Nymph'.

St Paul's Church *Bedford Street, WC2E 9ED (7836 5221, www.actorschurch.org). Free.*

295 *Go old-school...*

Ragged schools, providing tuition, food and clothing for destitute children, were an early experiment in public education, and this one was London's largest; Dr Barnardo taught here in Mile End. Today's kids love the mocked-up classroom, where formal lessons – complete with slate writing boards – are staged. There's also a Victorian kitchen, displays on local history and industry, and popular holiday activities. **Ragged School Museum** *46-50 Copperfield Road, E3 4RR (8980 6405, www.raggedschoolmuseum. org.uk). Free.*

296 *...or 'Suffer the little children' at the Foundling Museum*

England's first hospital for abandoned children was established by Thomas Coram in 1739 and was home to 27,000 children between then and its closure in 1953. The museum tells the story of these children (the exhibit of humble tokens left by the mothers who had to give up their babies is especially poignant) and the adults who campaigned for them, such as Thomas Gainsborough, William Hogarth and George Frederic Handel. Hogarth's support and gifts of paintings enabled the hospital to establish itself as Britain's first public art gallery, and a selection of Handel's manuscripts are also on display. **Foundling Museum** *40 Brunswick Square, WC1N 1AZ (7841 3600, www.foundlingmuseum.org.uk). £8.25.*

297 *Get a Wren's-eye view of St Paul's*

Over the 33 years that it took to transform an optimistic architectural plan into St Paul's Cathedral, Sir Christopher Wren resided across the river on Bankside at Cardinal Cap Alley (next to the Globe Theatre) in order to give him the best possible perspective on his work. It's a view you can take in yourself from the ceramic plaque that now marks the spot.

Foundling Museum

298-300

Find yourself a cure for... anything!

Focus your intelligence with the warmth of the *lin zhi* mushroom (ganoderma). Try *mo yao* resin (myrrh) to activate blood circulation. *Ju hua* (chrysanthemum) flowers dispel wind-heat, and are a common treatment for flu symptoms; and you can eliminate 'food stagnation and bloating' with the sweet, pungent seeds of the *lai fu* (radish) plant. Alternatively, ventilate your lungs with the roots and rhizomes of the aster plant or supplement your yang and give your kidneys a boost with the stripped bark of the hardy *du zhong* rubber tree (eucommia). London has hundreds of Traditional Chinese Medicine (TCM) practitioners: from those promising to 'Help You With Acne, Hair Loss, Gynecology!

Losing Weight In One Months!' to more authoritative-sounding places.

At the beautifully presented, traditional clinic Hong Yuen (22 Rupert Street, W1D 6DG, 7439 2408) in Soho, they are 'very low-key', according to its owner. 'No advertising. No propaganda.' What better recommendation than a centre that allows results to generate custom via word of mouth? The Institute of Chinese Medicine (44-46 Chandos Place, WC2N 4HS, 7836 5220, www.instituteofchinesemedicine.org) is one of several rival institutes that have attempted to form an affiliation of practitioners. It commands respect as a supplier of herbs to many of London's other practices, and runs its own highly rated treatment centres.

There's also the long-established AcuMedic Centre (101-105 Camden High Street, NW1 7JN, 7388 6704, www.acumedic.com), which has 18 treatment rooms offering Chinese herbal medicine, acupuncture and massage, plus a herbal health shop and a teahouse.

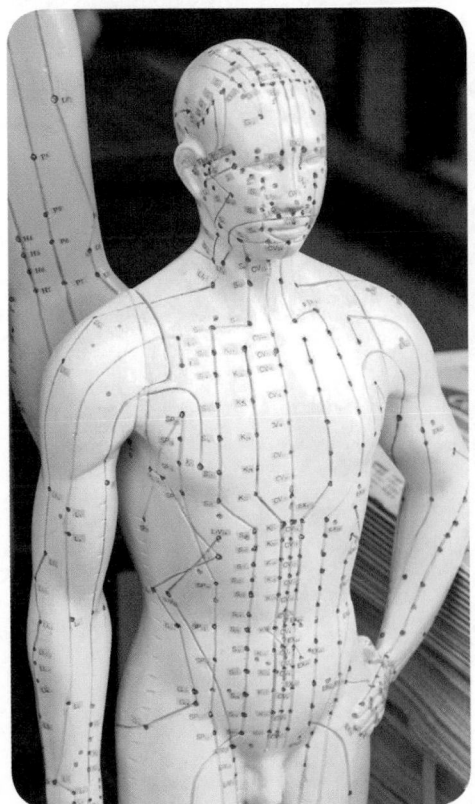

301
Muck out at Spitalfields City Farm

Given the smells and the sounds – it's all quack-quack, oink-oink, baa-baa round here – emanating from Spitalfields City Farm, you'd be surprised to learn that you're less than a mile from the Square Mile. Set up in 1978 on a disused railway goods depot just off Brick Lane, the farm has been a favourite with local Tower Hamlets families ever since. Kids and parents come down for workshops on healthy eating, sustainability and animal welfare, as well as to learn where milk and eggs come from. For children aged eight to 13, there's an after-school club on Thursdays and a Young Farmers Club on Saturdays, in addition to courses during the holidays (all are free; phone to book).

Unsurprisingly, though, the main attraction is meeting the animals – typical city farm beasts, friendly and made cocky from the vast amount of attention showered on them from visiting children. Favourites include donkeys (which can be ridden in spring and summer, at events), strokeable mice and rabbits, two pigs (Watson and Holmes) and Tilly, a cheeky – and chunky – shetland pony. There's also a shop and café, with rolls, simple snacks and cakes. Check the website for details of the volunteer programme if you fancy mucking in – or out.

Spitalfields City Farm *Buxton Street, E1 5AR (7247 8762, www.spitalfieldscityfarm.org).*

302-310

...then check out the others

Deen City Farm *Off Windsor Avenue, SW19 2RR (8543 5300, www.deencityfarm.co.uk).*
Freightliners City Farm *Paradise Park, Sheringham Road, N7 8PF (7609 0467, www.freightliners farm.org.uk).*
Hackney City Farm *1A Goldsmiths Row, E2 8QA (7729 6381, www.hackneycityfarm.co.uk).*
Kentish Town City Farm *1 Cressfield Close, off Grafton Road, NW5 4BN (7916 5421, www.ktcityfarm.org.uk).*
Mudchute City Farm *Pier Street, E14 3HP (7515 5901, www.mudchute.org).*
Newham City Farm *Stansfeld Road, E16 3RD (7474 4960, www.activenewham.org.uk/newham-city-farm).*
Stepney City Farm *Stepney Way, at Stepney High Street, E1 3DG (7790 8204, www.stepney cityfarm.org).*
Surrey Docks Farm *Rotherhithe Street, SE16 5ET (7231 1010, www.surreydocksfarm.org).*
Vauxhall City Farm *165 Tyers Street, SE11 5HS (7582 4204, www.vauxhallcityfarm.org).*

311-319 *Have cocktails*

It's hard to find exquisite cocktails when you're on a budget, so here are some top watering holes where your tipple will cost less than a tenner.

Bar Termini

Bar Termini does two things: coffee and cocktails. Coffee is overseen by Marco Arrigo, head of quality for Illy; cocktails are supervised by Tony Conigliaro, the alco-alchemist behind 69 Colebrooke Row and Zetter Town House, among others. Premises are tiny, but centrally located. The alcohol list has three negronis (£6.50) and a few other classics (bloody mary, bellini), none of them more than £10. A marsala martini contains

Beefeater gin, sweet marsala, dry vermouth and almond bitters served straight-up and is a model of simplicity and balance. Booking is essential after 5pm.
7 Old Compton Street, W1D 5JE (www.bar-termini.com).

Café Kick

As you might have guessed, football is the name of the game at this Clerkenwell hotspot. Table football is the main draw – you can reserve one of the three table-football tables – and soccer paraphernalia adorns the walls. The feel is retro meets Lisbon, and tapas, sandwiches and charcuterie can be washed down with great Kick cocktails – mojitos, caipirinhas, martinis and margaritas (£6.95, and only £4.85 between 4pm and 7pm). Sibling Bar Kick, in Shoreditch, has 11 football tables over two floors.
43 Exmouth Market, EC1R 4QL (7837 8077, www.cafekick.co.uk).

Callooh Callay

A funky, cosmopolitan, evening-only cocktail bar, where most cocktails are less than a tenner; the Rivington 65 (£9) contains Tanqueray gin with fresh pink grapefruit juice and own-made chamomile syrup topped with prosecco. The main bar room has low, purple seating and a long bar counter. Staff are savvy and DJs spin at weekends.
65 Rivington Street, EC2A 3AY (7739 4781, www.calloohcallaybar.com).

Christopher's Martini Bar

Christopher's has a super-sized list of martinis and cocktails. The choice includes a sloe gin martini and a classic martini (both priced from £9). The striking light fittings, glass-backed bar and high bar chairs add to the Big Apple art deco feel.
18 Wellington Street, WC2E 7DD (7240 4222, www.christophersgrill.com).

Happiness Forgets

This cosy cocktail cavern is small, subterranean and clearly slung together on a shoestring. But never mind all that, because it's really nice, with down-to-earth decor, extremely well-crafted cocktails, switched-on staff and good music. Simple, really. The 11-strong cocktail list changes every fortnight, and is devised by Alastair Burgess, formerly of Milk & Honey and New York's Pegu bar. Examples include the Perfect Storm (dark rum, plum brandy, ginger, honey and lemon) and the Louis Balfour (scotch, port, Picon bitters and honey (both are £7.50).
8-9 Hoxton Square, N1 6NU (7613 0325, www.happinessforgets.com).

Hawksmoor

The bar at the original Hawksmoor didn't used to be much to look at, but in 2012 it got all glammed up. Nevertheless, the drinks are still the most important factor, and the celebrated bar staff remain London's cocktail intellectuals. They know their stuff, and the menu makes for entertaining reading too. Silver Bullet (£8.50), with gin, kummel and lemon juice, a head-clearing concoction, is apparently Prince Philip's favourite cocktail, while under the heading 'disco drinks', you'll find Concealed Weapon, £9.50), containing absinthe shaken with Chambord, lemon and raspberries.
157 Commercial Street, E1 6BJ (7426 4850, www.thehawksmoor.com).

1 Lombard Street

Another converted bank in the heart of the City, this swanky fine-dining restaurant boasts a bright and suitably posh glass-domed circular bar, but a round of cocktails won't leave you in the red. Classic cocktails with a twist, such as espresso martini, cost £9.50, while a bellini (four variations) is £8.50.
1 Lombard Street, EC3V 9AA (7929 6611, www.1lombardstreet.com).

Shochu Lounge

Shochu Lounge is the chic basement bar of the Fitzrovia branch of Roka, the mini-chain of contemporary Japanese restaurants. It's named after a Japanese vodka-like spirit made from rice, barley and buckwheat, which forms the basis for its divine cocktails. These include the Noshino martini (shochu with cucumber, £8.60) and the Hei sour (jasmine shochu, lemon, almond syrup

Callooh Callay

and ylang ylang – fragrance in a glass). More recent additions include the Glass Maze (lychee shochu, lychee juice and ylang ylang) and the Ki-la Rose (shochu, rose petal vodka, lemon, cranberry and cucumber).
Basement, 37 Charlotte Street, W1T 1RR (7580 4850, www.shochulounge.com).

Worship Street Whistling Shop

This cellar room is darkly Dickensian, full of cosy corners and leather armchairs. In the back is a windowed laboratory crammed with equipment both modern and antiquated, used to create the wondrously described ingredients that constitute the cocktails (high-pressure hydrosol, chlorophyll bitters and so on). These are original and stimulating drinks; the house gin fizz costs £10. And staff are great – it would be easy to come across po-faced or pretentious with such a studied approach to drink-making, but they're staunchly friendly and helpful all night.
63 Worship Street, EC2A 2DU (7247 0015, www.whistlingshop.com).

320

Get paddling…
Thames Dragons (www. thamesdragons.com) trains crews to row in lung-bursting races, usually over 500 metres but occasionally longer distances – such as this 22-mile annual Great River Race marathon. The first training sessions are free, although there's a membership subscription if you then decide to join the club.

321-323

...or let others take the strain

Hang on a minute. Glass of Pimm's in hand? Balmy spring weather? Total absence of aching limbs? Maybe watching Oxbridge types grunt their way along the Thames is more your cup of tea? If so, join 250,000 fellow revellers along the riverbank for the next installment of the 150-year-old Boat Race (www.theboatrace.org, late March or early April). See the two 'eights' power past from viewpoints at the start (Putney Bridge, Putney Embankment and Bishops Park), by the bridges at Hammersmith or Barnes, or at the finish (Dukes Meadows or Chiswick Bridge), perhaps taking advantage of big screens (usually in Bishops Park and Furnival Gardens) to watch the rest of the race.

If watching two crews of burly ringers isn't to your taste, try the Doggett Coat & Badge Race (www.watermenshall.org): much more sparsely supported, but far more historic. Contested since 1715 by young watermen (once a Thames-borne equivalent of the modern-day cabby), the race is rowed each July in traditional 'gigs' over four miles and five furlongs (nearly five miles) from London Bridge to Chelsea.

Or you could try the Great River Race (8398 8141, www.greatriverrace.co.uk). Every September, 300 traditional rowed boats from all over the world – and a variety of historical epochs – race a lung-bursting 22 miles from Millwall Riverside to Richmond's Ham House. Hungerford Bridge, the Millennium Bridge and Tower Bridge are all good viewpoints. It's a great spectacle.

324

See a performance at the Scoop

The Scoop at More London (www.morelondon.com/scoop.html), to use its full name, is a sunken, open-air amphitheatre seating 800 people on the South Bank (in front of City Hall) that runs a programme of free films, concerts, plays and other events from May to October each year. One evening each Christmas, it's also a magical setting for carols and storytelling.

325

See a bit of New England in old England

The Grosvenor Chapel on South Audley Street is widely known as the American Church in Mayfair. Virtually unaltered since its construction in 1731, with its Tuscan portico, square tower and steeple, it now looks as though it could have been airlifted in from New England: that's how popular the look subsequently became in the States. The secluded gardens between the chapel and the Roman Catholic Church of the Immaculate Conception on Farm Street is full of benches dedicated to Americans, and became a favourite dead-letter drop during the Cold War.

Grosvenor Chapel *24 South Audley Street, W1K 2PA (7499 1684, www.grosvenor chapel.org.uk).*

326

Go to the Proms

True to its original democratic principles, you can still attend Promenade concerts for around a fiver. Of the 70-odd performances held at the Royal Albert Hall during the Proms season (www.bbc.co.uk/proms, mid July to early September), most offer same-day cheap tickets – up to 1,400 standing tickets are released 30 minutes before each performance. You have a choice of standing (or sitting on the floor) in the Arena pit in the middle or standing in the gallery running round the top of the hall.

Queues form early and snake around the block for the popular shows; but for many of the concerts you will rarely have to wait more than half an hour to see world-class classical-music performances. Forget the slightly frightening bombast of the Last Night (you're unlikely to get tickets under a tenner for this anyway) – there's so much more worth queuing for.

327

Check out Maltby Street

On the streets around the railway arches in SE1, a clutch of food and drink specialists holds court at the weekend (9am-4pm Sat; 11am-4pm Sun). Well-known names include Monmouth Coffee in arch 3 on Maltby Street (www.maltbystreet.com), and St John Bakery in arch 72 on Druid Street, but there are plenty of smaller-scale suppliers here too. We love Topolski (selling produce from Poland, including sausages and pickles), which shares an arch (104 Druid Street) with a couple of cheese importers, among others. Further food and drink purveyors can be found along nearby Ropewalk and at Spa Terminus (www.spa-terminus.co.uk).

Maltby Street

328

Get lost in the maze

Hampton Court Palace has one of the UK's oldest surviving hedge mazes. Tickets, for the maze only, cost £4.40 per adult and £2.75 per child.
Hampton Court Palace *East Molesey, Surrey, KT8 9AU (0844 482 7777, www.hrp.org.uk).*

329-330

Experience alfresco Dalston

Dalston Eastern Curve Garden (3 Dalston Lane, E8 3DF, http://dalstongarden.org) is an appealing 'micropark' created along a disused railway line. There's a café, plus drop-in gardening sessions and folk nights (http://woodburnermusic.co.uk; £4).

Two minutes' walk away, Dalston Roof Park is located atop the Print House (www.bootstrapcompany.co.uk). It's open from May to September, and there are activities – poetry nights, clothes swaps, yoga, film screenings, bands – organised for most evenings. Summer-long membership costs £5.

331

Give something back

Volunteering charity TimeBank (http://timebank.org.uk) runs projects in London, recruiting and training people to act as mentors in a range of situations: with young adults leaving care, for example; helping ex-military personnel who have mental-health problems; or directly supporting carers themselves. The TimeBank website also links to the enormous Do-it UK national database of volunteering opportunities (https://do-it.org). The range of roles available in and around London is astonishing: hospitals need 'meal buddies' for patients who have problems with eating and drinking; regional parks want monitors to look out for wild mink; cash-strapped arts groups are looking for help with their accounts. The upside? You help, meet and interact with people, and gain experience – and it costs you nothing but time.

332 Encounter butterflies

Every year, from April to mid September, the Natural History Museum's east lawn is home to Sensational Butterflies, a special display in a temperature- and humidity-controlled enclosure where you can get up close and personal with actual, living butterflies. Each spring, tropical chrysalises are shipped to the museum, where an expert lepidopterist nurtures them in an appropriate environment. If you're lucky, when you visit you might even see one emerge, extend its wings, then take flight.

Natural History Museum *Cromwell Road, SW7 5BD (7942 5000, www.nhm.ac.uk). £5.90.*

333 Find the word on the street in Notting Hill

Paved with gold? Pah! How coarse! West London's streets are paved with something infinitely more profound (and probably more useful in these bleak economic times) – poetry. Thanks to local artist and lifelong resident Maria Vlotides, Notting Hill now boasts seven specially designed manhole covers. Each is engraved with a lyrical ditty from other local writers, including Margaret Drabble (who describes the Coronet Cinema as a place of 'diamonds, dreams and tears'), PD James, Sebastian Faulks and John Heath-Stubbs. All are based near Notting Hill Gate; start at Daunt Books (112-114 Holland Park Avenue, W11 4UA) and stroll around to see if you can find the rest.

334 Enjoy an island

Just south of the Olympic Park, this island on the River Lea takes its name from the three mills that ground flour and gunpowder here. The House Mill, built in 1776, is the oldest and largest tidal mill in Britain and is occasionally opened to the public (www.housemill.org.uk, £3, £1.50 reductions, free under-16s). Even when that's closed, the island provides pleasant walks that can feel surprisingly rural – and the new Wild Kingdom children's playground is a joy.

Three Mills Island *Three Mill Lane, E3 3DU (08456 770600, www.visitleevalley.org.uk).*

335 Watch hockey for free

Unlike the premier division games of most other team sports, professional hockey is usually free to watch – though you might be quietly nudged into buying a programme for £1. Games are played at weekends: check out the likes of the Hampstead & Westminster, Old Loughtonians and Surbiton. For details of who to see and where to see them, check the website.
www.englandhockey.co.uk.

336-345 Search for beautiful trees

London still has hundreds of magnificent trees despite disease and redevelopment. Here are our top ten: for detailed information on how to get to them, see www.treesforcities.org.

Ash (*Fraxinus excelsior*) in Old St Pancras Churchyard, King's Cross, NW1.

Fig (*Ficus carica*) in Amwell Street, EC1. Free food.

Holm oak (*Quercus ilex*) in Fulham Palace Gardens, SW6. A 500-year-old evergreen oak.

Huntingdon elm (*Ulmus x hollandica*) on Marylebone High Street, W1. The last elm surviving in Westminster.

Hybrid strawberry tree (*Arbutus x andrachnoides*) in Battersea Park, SW11.

Indian bean tree (*Catalpa bignonioides*) in the yard outside St James's Church, Piccadilly, SW1.

London plane (*Platanus x hispanica*) in Berkeley Square, W1. The quintessential street tree.

Queen Elizabeth's oak (*Quercus robur*) in Greenwich Park, SE10. The remains of this ancient oak, where Henry VIII wooed Anne Boleyn and young Bess played, are fenced off and marked by a plaque. A new sapling has been planted in its place.

Royal oak (*Quercus robur*) in Richmond Park, TW10. This tree is 700-800 years old.

Yew (*Taxus baccata*) in the yard of St Andrew's Church, Totteridge, N20. Over 500 years old.

Hybrid Strawberry Tree

Going underground

*Hankering for the glamorous – and grimy – world of latter-day espionage, Time Out's agent **Robin Saikia** goes undercover.*

If you stand outside Tate Britain on Millbank and look across the Thames, you can't miss Vauxhall Cross, the striking headquarters of MI6, the British secret service. But for all the moody green cladding and bullet-proof glass, and despite its guest appearances in a couple of recent Bond films, this is a resolutely practical and functional building. As such, it may be something of a disappointment for the espionage fan in search of mystery, deception, eccentricity, romance and sleaze.

However, these attributes are all to be found in greater or lesser degrees in former secret-service headquarters: 54 Broadway, SW1, with its brass plaque proclaiming 'Minimax Fire Extinguisher Company'; 21 Queen Anne's Gate, SW1, lair of Captain Sir Mansfield Smith-Cumming – the first 'C' – with his swordstick, wooden leg, false moustaches and phoney German accent; Bush House, WC2, HQ of Claude Dansey – 'Uncle Claude' or 'Colonel Z' to his few friends and many enemies – originator of 'Z Organisation', an alternative MI6 of his own devising; Curzon

Street House, W1, the quarters (it was rumoured) of hundreds of specially trained carrier pigeons – and home to the 'Registry', an ever-expanding filing system including the details of over two million people, hidden behind windows so encrusted with grime that they could doubtless have resisted a massive explosion.

Those were the days – and if Vauxhall Cross has any glamour at all, it is surely a corporate, ostentatious glamour, not remotely redolent of the covert blackmail, silk stockings and cyanide of yesteryear. For mementos of those, one has to go north of the Thames: Dolphin Square in Pimlico, SW1, an eminently respectable development of some 1,250 flats built in the mid 1930s, delivers a good measure of intrigue, sleaze and secret-service history. There are 13 blocks in the square, each named after a naval hero – Drake House, Collingwood House, Hood House and so on. There is an agreeable bar, a good restaurant and pleasant gardens.

Former residents include Princess Anne, Harold Wilson, William Hague and Peter

Finch, as well as a steady stream of judges, politicians, writers and journalists. But there were dark horses too.

Call girl Christine Keeler (a subtenant of Dolphin Square) caused a national scandal when it was revealed in 1961 that she had had affairs with both the Conservative politician John Profumo, Secretary of State for War, and Yevgeny Ivanov, a Soviet naval officer.

But despite the nation's outrage, these were trifling indiscretions in comparison with the antics of John Vassall, resident of Hood House in the late 1950s. Vassall, a naval attaché in the British Embassy in Moscow, was lured to a homosexual party organised by the KGB and photographed in what he later conceded was 'a complicated array of sexual activities with a number of different men'. The KGB blackmailed him into working for them, though many claimed that Vassall, poorly paid and yearning for the high life, needed little coercion. He subsequently sold secret documents to the Russians, smuggling them out of the Admiralty in a copy of *The Times*, squandering the proceeds on expensive suits from Savile Row, rare antiques and exotic holidays.

The Square's respectable spy – an important figure in the history of British espionage – was Maxwell Knight, who, from 1925, ran Section B5(b) of MI5 from his flat in Hood House. The purpose of B5(b) – 'Knight's Black Agents' to those in the know – was to infiltrate subversive groups, which under Knight's leadership it did with some success. (Knight also pursued a successful career as 'Uncle Max', broadcasting nature programmes for children for the BBC.)

A well-run hotel is the perfect spot to strike a Faustian bargain, and hotels will probably always be popular meeting places for secret agents. Brown's Hotel (Albemarle Street, W1S 4BP) was an occasional and very elegant secret-service rendezvous, notably for the interrogation by Peter Wright of the scientist Alastair Watson, suspected in the 1960s of passing technical information to the Soviets.

As Roy Berkeley observes in his excellent book *A Spy's London* '…the Soviets took their people to the basement of the Lubyanka, while the British took their people to Brown's'.

Wladislaw Sikorski, the Polish prime minister and commander-in-chief of Polish forces in World War II, set up his headquarters at the Rubens Hotel (39 Buckingham Palace Road,

SW1W 0PS) in 1940. From here the Polish Resistance operated an extensive spy network until Sikorski's death in 1943.

The Mount Royal Hotel (now the Thistle Marble Arch, Bryanston Street, W1H 7EH) was a meeting place for Russian double agent Oleg Penkovsky and agents from MI6 and the CIA. Penkovsky passed on invaluable secrets to his new colleagues in British and US intelligence, detailing the extent of the Soviet nuclear arsenal. In 1962, as a result of a tip-off from the British agent George Blake, he was arrested by the KGB. It is said that he was tied to a board with piano wire before being fed feet first into the oven of Moscow Crematorium.

The former Ebury Court Hotel (now Tophams Hotel, 28 Ebury Street, SW1W 0LU) was a known meeting place for the secret service and the Special Operations Executive (SOE) during World War II, and it is still an agreeable place to meet for a quiet drink. Its unassuming wartime manageress, Yvonne Rudellat, was recruited into SOE and subsequently became a heroine of the French Resistance, successfully running a network in France. She was eventually captured by the Germans and died in a concentration camp.

St Ermin's Hotel (2 Caxton Street, SW1H 0QW) was another wartime outpost. Here, potential recruits were routinely interviewed in the subdued glamour of the restaurant, successful candidates (among them Noël Coward) being spirited up to the fifth and sixth floors, which in those days had been completely requisitioned by MI6. It was here that Kim Philby was interviewed and recruited into the secret service by Guy Burgess – a deal they sealed with a weekend of heavy drinking prior to an early start in Section D (for 'Destruction' – stirring up active resistance to the enemy) in the summer of 1940.

MI9, the World War II escape and 'exfiltration' department, set up shop on the second floor of the old Great Central Hotel (now the Landmark Hotel, 222 Marylebone Road, NW1 6JQ), having outgrown its former ad hoc HQ in room 424 of the Metropole Hotel (no longer in existence) on Northumberland Avenue. An underrated and too little known wing of the secret service, MI9's principal task was to help Allied servicemen stranded or imprisoned in enemy territory to escape or find their way back home. Footsoldiers such as Airey Neave masterminded the repatriation of troops and agents after disasters such as Operation Market Garden at Arnhem, while resourceful agents such as the theatrical conjuror Jasper Maskelyne and former pilot Christopher Clayton Hutton developed a series of useful gadgets and devices – tools concealed in cricket bats, maps in gramophone records, compasses in buttons, and so forth.

These survival innovations are not to be confused with the rather more sinister devices developed at 35 Portland Place, W1, by SOE: exploding rats, exploding pencils, exploding animal droppings, collapsible crossbows, suicide pills, a .22 calibre cigarette gun, garrottes and a tear-gas fountain pen. (Gadgets of this sort are the stock in trade of spies of all allegiances. Later, during the Cold War, the KGB developed the 'Kiss of Death', a lipstick tube containing a 4.5mm single-shot pistol that was used by both female agents and by the notorious KGB 'ravens', gay men on entrapment missions.)

Throughout World War II, SOE progressively requisitioned whole blocks in Baker Street, to the extent that members would refer to themselves and the section simply as 'Baker Street'. No.64 became the operational HQ in October 1940. No.83, Norgeby House, had a plaque proclaiming it as the 'Inter-Services Research Bureau', but in reality the whole of 'F Section' ('F' for France) was run here by Colonel Maurice Buckmaster. F Section was split into cells, some large, some consisting of a single agent or a small team. Their codenames and personnel are resonant to this day: 'Wrestler', run by Pearl Witherington, the 'best shot in the service'; 'Salesman', with Violette Szabo, nicknamed 'la p'tite Anglaise'; 'Physician', a larger team that included Yvonne Rudellat, formerly of the Ebury Court Hotel, and the beautiful Indian agent Noor Inayat Khan, the first female radio operator sent to France by SOE.

Agents needed a wide range of skills to survive in the field – everything from lockpicking to noiseless assassination – and these were taught at Michael House, 82 Baker Street. The second-floor flat in Orchard Court, Portman Square, with its famous black onyx and marble bathroom, was a briefing and debriefing station for SOE recruits. Officers would check that agents looked and behaved in a suitably Gallic fashion before despatching them on a tour of duty with the French Resistance. Chiltern Court was HQ to the Scandinavian section of SOE, while 221 Baker Street housed the clothing and disguise section, where tailors would work round the clock making 'authentic' continental clothing for agents.

Buckingham Palace may seem an odd landmark to include – but it was there, after all, that art historian Anthony Blunt continued to fulfil his duties as Surveyor of the King's (and subsequently the Queen's) Pictures, long after he had confessed in 1964 to Arthur Martin of

> 'The KGB developed a 'Kiss of Death' lipstick containing a 4.5mm single shot pistol that was used by agents on entrapment missions.'

MI5 that he was a Soviet agent. Blunt was a member of the Cambridge Spy Ring – a group working for the Russians that had met at Cambridge University and included fellow KGB agents Guy Burgess, Donald Maclean and Kim Philby. Blunt was spared exposure and imprisonment in exchange for a full confession. Until his retirement as its director in 1974, Blunt also had the run of the Courtauld Institute of Art, then housed at 20 Portman Square. It was only in 1979, after the publication of Andrew Boyle's book *Climate of Treason*, that he was finally publicly disgraced (though he was never prosecuted). Named as a traitor by Margaret Thatcher in 1979, Blunt was stripped of his knighthood and, memorably, booed out of a cinema in Notting Hill Gate. Ever the cosmopolitan scholar and boulevardier, and seemingly unfazed by these very English setbacks, he quietly set about completing a definitive book on the Italian painter Pietro da Cortona without so much as a twang of piano wire to trouble him.

362
Get into korfball

Korfball, a mix between netball and basketball, was invented in 1901 in Holland. Which is perhaps surprising, given the '90s-fad-sounding name and the impressively progressive basic premise: fat, thin, tall, short, male or female, the only thing that matters is your ability to cooperate with your teammates. Twelve teams – each comprising four men and four women – compete in London's regional league, and they all welcome beginners; see the website for more information.
www.londonkorfball.com.

363
Be careful you don't get nicked in Trafalgar Square

The smallest police station in London is to be found hidden away in a lamp pillar in the south-east corner of Trafalgar Square. If you didn't know, you might take it for an ice-cream kiosk; but, no, it's really a one-man, auxiliary police station.

364
Watch nature amid brutalist concrete

Ducks? Check. Reeds? Check. You're at the London Wetland Centre, right? Wrong, wrong, wrong. The Barbican Centre (Silk Street, EC2Y 8DS, 7638 8891, www.barbican.org.uk) is dismissed by those who loathe it as a concrete monstrosity, but city-lovers know to linger by its lake and ponds, the water and waterfowl all the more delightful for the unlikely setting. Take a coffee to one of the outdoor tables and gaze out over the main lake, taking in the fountains, the waterfall (at the eastern end), St Giles's church (Milton's last resting place, directly opposite the café) and, yes, nature: waterlilies in summer; mallards, moorhens and their offspring in spring; even the occasional heron. You can pop out here during the interval – it's just as lovely at night – and there are more landscaped water gardens if you arrive at the Barbican on the Highwalk from Barbican station. Even more transporting is the steamy Conservatory (open 11am-5pm Sunday, unless there's a private event), a lush jungle of tropical plants and carp ponds. You won't believe you're still in the centre of town.

Barbican Centre

365-371 *Check out the city's best streets for window-shopping*

As long as you're happy looking rather than buying, there's fun to be had on London's shopping streets.

In the last few years, concept stores, independents and pop-ups have reinvigorated the London shopping scene. Nowhere is this more apparent than in Redchurch Street, E2, still grimy in parts but often hailed as London's trendiest street. Here, you'll find established but niche brands such as Aesop (no.5A),the botanical beauty shop from the Aussie skincare brand, and pared-back homewares store Labour & Wait (no.85). A world away in atmosphere, but equally fashion conscious, is posh Mount Street, W1, home to master butcher Allens of Mayfair (no.117) and cigar supplier Sautter (no.106) but also increasingly the likes of Marc Jacobs (nos. 24-25), perfumer Annick Goutal (no.109) and Christian Louboutin (no.17). Ledbury Road, W11, also makes for upmarket gawping: here, fashion boutiques such as Matches (nos.60-64) and Aimé (no.32) are joined by lifestyle boutique Wolf & Badger (no.46).

More villagely in feel is Lamb's Conduit Street, WC1. This partially pedestrianised stretch holds a nicely diverse bunch of shops, from the People's Supermarket (nos.72-76) at one end to the French House (no.50) homewares store at the other. In between are individual fashion outlets such as Folk (nos.49 & 53), not to mention delightful Persephone Books (no.59).

Equally charming is Camden Passage, N1. Once the haunt of antiques dealers, it's now more mixed, with upmarket knitting shop Loop (no.15) rubbing shoulders with womenswear designer Susy Harper (no.35) and Paul A Young Fine Chocolates (no.33). We're also very fond of Smug (no.13), which sells a covetable range of homewares.

Broadway Market, E8, has the added attraction of a swathe of stalls. Saturday is when the market is in full swing, but shops such as deli L'Eau à la Bouche (nos.35-37), accessories trove Black Truffle (no.4) and Broadway Books (no.6) are open all week.

Finally, Pitfield Street, N1, is short but interesting – stubbornly grotty for years, without a decent shop or café to its name, it now features some fantastic shops, including designer tattoo parlour Nine Nails Tattoos (no.25) and a smart interiors store with a café, Pitfield London (nos.31-35) – with more to follow, no doubt.

A few of my favourite things

372-378

Paul Sinton-Hewitt,
Founder, parkrun UK

Standing on Waterloo Bridge, no matter what the weather, looking east and west along the Thames, you get a sense of the power, grandeur and splendour of the city I love so much. I'm also a fan of Tower Bridge, which epitomises London and is a constant reminder of the marathon – my favourite running event.

From Waterloo Bridge, it's just a little jog along the South Bank to the mighty Tate Modern (Bankside, SE1 9TG, 7887 8888, www.tate.org.uk) – a modern platform, indeed – and a good place for all of us to brush shoulders with the most creative members of our society. Much as I love the Tate, however, it's the Victoria & Albert Museum (Cromwell Road, SW7 2RL, 7942 2000, www.vam.ac.uk) I most enjoy spending time in. It holds some stunning, inspiring and intricate pieces that I go back to repeatedly, and the café is excellent too. As you might imagine, I prefer to be outdoors. Hampstead Heath has the vastness of a wild park (by UK standards, anyway) in the middle of a metropolis. It takes you away from the city but also joins you with the city. **Another delight for me is Highgate Cemetery (Swain's Lane, N6 6PJ, 8340 1834,** www.highgatecemetery.org). At first I found it, not surprisingly, eerie, but I've grown to love its quite singular atmosphere. The tours are very unusual and informative. Serene Bushy Park – the first ever parkrun venue – a stone's throw from where I live, is also vast by city standards and, more importantly, a place where I meet many of my friends. Not far away is Richmond Park: wilder than Bushy and with more contours (for both, see www.royalparks.org.uk). I think of it as a park with many personalities. I particularly like the stretch of river between Richmond Park and Hampton Court – it's a perfect place to walk, and has much of interest, not just the stately Thames but all those stately homes. **I'm so fortunate to have Kew Gardens (8332 5655, www.kew.org) – an amazing, expansive, exotic botanical garden – on my doorstep. It is the best place to stroll and think. If I want to stroll and shop, however, I eschew the West End for a more local hub: Teddington. It's quaint, boutique and friendly, a real gem – so please don't tell anyone else!** I must include the Virgin Money London Marathon (www.virginmoneylondonmarathon.com) in this list. It's my favourite running event through my favourite city organised by some of my favourite people. If you're looking for a more frequent running challenge, however, I recommend the weekly Mile End parkrun (www.parkrun.org.uk) – a joyful and welcoming experience in what is a deprived part of town. The people who make it happen epitomise what it is to give back to the community.

379 *Take the long view in Richmond Park*

You can put this 'thing to do' on the back burner, if you like – the view is not likely to change any time soon because it is protected by law. That means nothing can be built that obstructs the ten-mile sightline from the top of King Henry's Mound in Richmond Park (the Tudor monarch used to hunt in these parts) all the way to St Paul's Cathedral in the City to the east. After you've taken in the vista, make your way to the lovely Isabella Plantation (*see p97*).
Richmond Park, TW10 (0300 061 2000, www.royalparks.gov.uk).

Richmond Park

380 *Read history in stained glass at St Margaret's*

The parish church of the House of Commons since 1614, St Margaret's is well worth a visit for its stained-glass windows alone. As old in foundation as Westminster Abbey, the building standing today dates largely from the 16th century. Highlights include the east window, which is 15th-century Flemish and was paid for by Catherine of Aragon. It depicts the Crucifixion scene, flanked by St George and St Catherine of Alexandria. Underneath is the sickly Prince Arthur, elder brother of Henry VIII (and Catherine of Aragon's first betrothed). The west window is by the eminent Victorian Arts and Crafts window-makers Clayton and Bell, and shows Sir Walter Raleigh (in the middle) – who was executed only a few yards away, in Old Palace Yard. The south aisle windows are by John Piper and were added in 1966.

St Margaret's Church *20 Dean's Yard, SW1P 3PA (7222 5152, www.westminster-abbey.org).*

381-384

Go for a walk in a wood

Epping Forest

The big one. Nearly 6,000 acres of woodland, interspersed with heaths, lakes and trails. The wood formed after the last Ice Age and consists mainly of oak, beech and hornbeam. Look out for the massive branches of previously pollarded trees, left to grow since the passing of the Epping Forest Act in 1878. A good starting point for walks is the area around Queen Elizabeth's Hunting Lodge, which is now a museum.

Queen Elizabeth's Hunting Lodge, Ranger's Road, E4 7QH.

Highgate Wood/Queen's Wood

Highgate and, on the other side of Muswell Hill Road, Queen's Wood are remnants of the ancient forest of Middlesex, which once covered most of north London and the county of Middlesex. The smaller Queen's Wood has the more diverse ecology, with its predominant oak and hornbeam canopy and strangely named 'wild service tree' – a marker for the age of the woodland. Highgate Wood also has a café, a playground and playing fields.

Muswell Hill Road, N10.

Holland Park

Although Holland Park is one of London's grand formal parks, there is a surprisingly extensive wood in its northern half. Set off down one of the shaded paths and within a minute the sounds of the city will become muffled and then all but disappear.

Abbotsbury Road, W11.

Shooters Hill Woodlands

Oxleas, Jack and Shepherdleas woods – remnants of the post-glaciation wildwood that once stretched over the whole country – cover Shooters Hill with a mixture of oak, sweet chestnut and hazel, plus the telltale maple-like leaves of the wild service tree. The rare palmate newt lives in ponds in the woods.

Shooters Hill, SE9.

385

See the future, now

In mid September each year, design junkies descend on the London Design Festival (www.londondesignfestival.com), which showcases the best of the capital's creative designers, artists and fashion makers. Held at various locations across town, the fun usually centres on Brick Lane's Truman Brewery, and the programme features a couple of hundred commercial and cultural events.

386

Get into the Tower for free – but don't be late

The ticket price puts a normal visit to the Tower of London beyond the scope of this book, but – if you're organised – you can see something the hordes of paying tourists won't be able to see… and without paying a penny. Dating back seven centuries, the Ceremony of the Keys happens at exactly 9.53pm each evening, when the Yeoman Warders begin the process of locking the Tower's entrances. They have failed to do so on the dot only once since the ceremony began, when shockwaves from nearby Blitz bombs tumbled the party to the ground, causing a delay of several minutes. (The Yeoman Warders were sufficiently ashamed of this failure that they wrote an apology to King George VI.)

The ticketed public assembles at the West Gate at 9pm, through which they enter the outer wall and follow the ceremony around each gate. When it's all over, at about 10pm, the Last Post sounds. This little piece of repeated history is understandably popular, of course, so you'll need to apply for tickets (offering two possible dates) at least two months (probably much longer) in advance. For full details, see www.hrp.org.uk/toweroflondon/whatson/theceremonyofthekeys.

Tower Hamlets residents are, however, unusually blessed: they can get into the Tower of London for just £1, without applying in advance for anything. And they get to see the Crown Jewels and inside all the various towers. Just take proof of residence and a library card with you when you go to the ticket office.

387-394

Savour the capital's finest kebabs...

London may be beset with dodgy doner houses, but it's also blessed with some of the best kebabs this side of Istanbul. Here are our favourites.

19 Numara Bos Cirrik I

It's appropriate that the dominating feature of this ocakbaşı in Dalston is the embossed copper extractor hood at one end of the counter: the place is all about that smoking charcoal grill. The main event is the meat: shish, adana and chicken kebabs, spare ribs, beyti and köfte – perfectly charred without being burnt, and all saltily, juicily magnificent. The extras are done right too – expect a great feed for pleasingly little cash.
34 Stoke Newington Road, N16 7XJ (7249 0400, www.cirrik1.co.uk).

Abu Zaad

This restaurant in Shepherd's Bush has reasonably priced Damascene food ranging from meat-heavy kebabs to vegetarian-friendly meze and, being Syrian, the odd spicy kebab and lots of oven-baking in yoghurt. Try the kebab bil tahina – a traditional dish of spicy lamb topped with yoghurt and rich tahini.
29 Uxbridge Road, W12 8LH (8749 5107, www.abuzaad.co.uk).

E Mono

The food here is a cut above: the lamb shish is excellent, the salad fillings are varied and tasty, and the portions are enormous. Chips are merely satisfactory, though. Warning: chilli sauce is applied with abandon – if you don't love the burn, ask for less of it. There is ample seating space if you don't fancy taking your kebab for a walk down Kentish Town Road.
287 Kentish Town Road, NW5 2JS (7485 9779).

Kebab Kid

Forget greasy doners of fatty minced lamb – this little takeaway in Parsons Green serves proper shawarmas (chicken or lamb) of prime cuts of meat (from Smithfield Market), or shish kebabs cooked on skewers to order. We also like the crunchy shredded salad and the (optional) smear of own-made taramasalata. A medium shawarma costs £5.90.
90 New King's Road, SW6 4LU (7731 0427).

Mangal 1

Come to the original branch of Turkish Mangal in Dalston for heaps of prime meat at low prices – and its BYO policy. There's no printed menu; you choose skewers of meat from the glass display counter and they're grilled in front of you. Shish (marinated lamb chunks), beyti (spicy minced lamb) and pirzola (lamb chops) are all exemplary and served in generous portions with a huge mound of salad and warm leavened bread (from £9.50 to eat in).
10 Arcola Street, E8 2DJ (7275 8981, www.mangal1.com).

Patogh

This tightly-packed Iranian café off the Edgware Road offers wonderful flatbreads with minced lamb or chicken wrapped around skewers, then chargrilled (from £6). Most mains are served on grim metal plates, but somehow it all adds to the authentic experience. The salads include whole fronds of fresh mint and tarragon, which really make the flavours sing.
8 Crawford Place, W1H 5NE (7262 4015).

Ranoush Juice

The original branch of this Lebanese café chain is a great pit stop for either an easy lunch or post-partying sustenance. The meze of houmous, chicken livers, sujuk sausages and so forth are all excellent, but the pièces de résistance are the two formidable shawarmas

(chicken and lamb) rotating at the front of the shop. Juicy slices are deftly shorn off by the staff and scooped into bread.
43 Edgware Road, W2 2JR (7723 5929, www.maroush.com).

Tayyabs

This Pakistani canteen in Whitechapel is consistently popular: there's almost always a queue. Among the starters are chicken or mutton tikkas, lamb chops, seekh kebabs and shami kebabs – all of which are seriously low-priced (starting at £1) and beautifully cooked.
83-89 Fieldgate Street, E1 1JU (7247 9543, www.tayyabs.co.uk).

395 *...or make your own*

Many butchers sell meat ready prepared to kebab; try M Moen & Sons in Clapham (24 The Pavement, SW4 0JA, 7622 1624, www.moen.co.uk) or Macken Brothers in Chiswick (44 Turnham Green Terrace, W4 1QP, 8994 2646, www.mackenbros.co.uk).

Ranoush Juice

396

Enjoy a free concert in the Union Chapel

Regularly voted London's best music venue, Islington's Union Chapel (Compton Terrace, N1 2UN, www.unionchapel.org.uk) is a glorious place in which to spend a few hours. Tickets to its usual programme of gigs will almost always cost more than a tenner, but you can catch interesting musical acts for free most Saturday lunchtimes, thanks to Daylight Music (www.facebook.com/daylightmusiclondon). The long list of artists who played in 2015 includes Darren Hayman, Laetitia Sadier, Martin Carr and a group of teenage Texan handbell ringers. Expect to see some memorable performances, and make sure to bring a little cash for some home-made cake from the charity-run café.

397 Remember the watergate scandal

Between the bottom of Buckingham Street and Embankment Gardens stands a weathered stone gate – once the watergate belonging to the great 17th-century York House, which stood between here and the Strand. It isn't now immediately recognisable as a watergate that once led from a grand garden down to the Thames – primarily because it's fully 150 yards from the river, thanks to Joseph Bazalgette's 1864 construction of the Embankment.

Today, clues to York House's ownership still lie in the surrounding streets. George Street, Villiers Street, Duke Street (now gone) and the absurdly named Of Alley (now York Place, formerly Of Alley), in the immediate vicinity of Buckingham Street, together serve to remind us of George Villiers, Duke of Buckingham. Sexy George swanned into London in 1614, and quickly became the court favourite of King James I, who referred to him as 'sweet child and wife': rumour and intrigue followed him for the rest of his life, but if nothing else it was a canny short-cut to having a whole corner of London named after oneself.

398 Visit a music market

Since launching in 2011, the buzzy, free Independent Label Market (www.independentlabelmarket.com) has become so popular that it now appears several times a year (usually in summer and at Easter – check the website for dates). It takes place in the vast Old Spitalfields Market building, which bulges with small stalls hosted by the hippest independent record labels, such as Moshi Moshi, Ninja Tune and Hyperdub, selling vinyl, CDs and even cassettes – remember them?

399 Revel in digital nostalgia

Ever wonder what happened to all those arcade machines you spent your youth chugging 50-pence pieces into? Chances are, some of them ended up at the Four Quarters – a bar dedicated to all things '90s on Peckham's Rye Lane. The good news is that classic games such as Point Blank and Daytona USA are just as much fun as they ever were – the even better news is that here they cost just a quarter a go (you can buy the US 25¢ pieces from at the bar for 25p). Free-to-play consoles (N64s, Megadrives), prize-laden tournaments and regular food promos (grilled cheese, hot dogs) add to the thrifty time-warp vibe.
Four Quarters *187 Rye Lane, SE15 4TP (www. facebook.com/fourquartersbar).*

400 Make the most of your youth at Matilda

The witty, energetic and completely joy-packed musical that is *Matilda* could help anyone feel youthful, but it's only those aged between 16 and 25 who can buy a whole evening of West End entertainment for less than the cost of a cinema ticket. Just 16 seats per performance are available to young adults at the bargain price of £5; they can be bought from the theatre at 10am on the day of the show (one ticket per person, ID required). You can treat yourself to an ice-cream at the interval with the money you saved. See http://uk.matildathemusical.com/tickets/special-rates-discounts. for more details.

401 *Learn Brazilian dance at Guanabara*

Salsa is a bit 1990s and tango is a little too technical – if you want to learn to dance Latin style, go Brazilian. One of the capital's best Brazilian bars, Guanabara (Parker Street, W2CB 5PW, 7242 8600, www.guanabara.co.uk), runs free dance classes on Sundays; try samba, forró and even Brazilian ballroom dancing, gafieira. Classes take place before the place fills up with regulars, which means that when the lesson ends you can practise your moves on the dancefloor with those who really know their stuff. Alternatively, hit the bar for a caipirinha.

402

Check out the street furniture in SE15

In Peckham's Bellenden Road, street bollards are designed by Antony Gormley; pavements and bus stops are by Zandra Rhodes; and local artist Tom Phillips created the curlicue lamp posts and wall mosaics. Restored Georgian and Victorian terraces, upmarket bistros, and boutique fashion and book stores all add to the burgeoning café culture.

403

Drink sherry

The choice includes everything from the light, tangy Puerto Fino through to intense fruity PX sherries such as the 1975 Don Pedro Ximenez Gran Reserva. Perch at the bar at Moro (34-36 Exmouth Market, EC1R 4QE, 7833 8336, www.moro.co.uk) and sip an old favourite such as manzanilla (£3.50 a glass) and snack on the excellent tapas dishes, or visit offshoot tapas bar Morito (32 Exmouth Market, EC1R 4QE, 7278 7007). Another small, no-bookings tapas bar is José (104 Bermondsey Street, SE1 3UB, 7403 4902, www.josepizarro. com), where the list of sherries is longer than the tapas menu. Tiny Bar Pepito (3 Varnishers Yard, N1 9DF, 7841 7331, www.camino.uk.com) is dedicated to sherry – to sample the breadth of flavours, try a flight of sherries (starting at £7.90). The bright, stylish surroundings at mini-chain Barrafina (www.barrafina.co.uk) are also fine options – sherries start at £4.50 a glass.

404-405

Examine the new blue plaques

Famous London residents newly celebrated include comedian Tony Hancock at 20 Queen's Gate Place, SW7 5NY (opposite the Science Museum in South Kensington); and film makers Michael Powell and Emeric Pressburger at Dorset House, Gloucester Place, NW1 5AG (just round the corner from Baker Street tube).

406

Watch out for Appearing Rooms

Danish artist Jeppe Hein's water sculpture *Appearing Rooms* has proved so popular (especially with children) that it returns to the South Bank every summer. The rows of fountains, in grid formation, are liable to squirt unpredictably – trapping you in one of the square 'rooms', unless, of course, you're up for a soaking. Find it in front of the Royal Festival Hall, SE1.

407

Get the most out of your Mac

If you've splashed out on a Mac, it makes sense to take advantage of the free in-store aftercare and learn more about getting the most out of your investment. Check the website for details of the frequent workshop sessions.
Apple Store *235 Regent Street, W1B 2EL (7153 9000, www.apple.com/uk/retail/regentstreet).*

408

Board Hammerton's ferry

This tiny boat, taking just 12 foot-passengers (and the odd bicycle), operates daily from Marble Hill House to Ham House (and vice versa) from March to the end of October, and weekends only in winter. It's the sole survivor of the numerous ferries that plied this stretch of the river for hundreds of years. Times have changed: the boat has an electric motor these days, and the fare – a penny when it was started in 1908 by one Walter Hammerton – is now £1 for adults, 50p for children (plus 50p for adult bikes). *www.hammertonsferry.com.*

409

Don't touch anything in the Islington Museum

In the Islington Museum, you'll find a bust of communist leader Lenin (who published his radical newspaper *Iskra* at nearby 37A Clerkenwell Green). Originally gracing the Russian Embassy, it was moved to Finsbury Town Hall, but, following repeated vandalism, it's found a safer, and perhaps more appreciative, audience here. Once you've finished doffing your cap to Lenin, check out the museum's curiously ironic relic: the books from Islington's libraries that were famously defaced by playwright Joe Orton and his lover Kenneth Halliwell. What a difference a few decades make: back in 1962, the pair were jailed for six months for their doodling.
Islington Museum *245 St John Street, EC1V 4NB (7527 2837, www.islington.gov.uk/islington/history-heritage/heritage_museum). Free.*

410

Experience the heavy hand of the law

Members of the public can watch British justice in action at the Central Criminal Court (open 10am-1pm, 2-5pm Mon-Fri), so long as they leave any bags, cameras, dictaphones, mobile phones or food at home (there are no storage facilities provided at the court). The front door details forthcoming trials.

Central Criminal Court *Old Bailey, EC4M 7EH (7248 3277, www.cityoflondon.gov.uk). Free.*

411-415

Take a whistle-stop tour of Roman London

In 1985, Museum of London archaeologists discovered a 2,000-year-old Roman amphitheatre, now opened to the public, underneath the Guildhall Yard. Admission into the savage realm of slaves, gladiators and wild animals is via the Guildhall Gallery (Guildhall Yard, EC2V 5AE, 7332 3700, www. guildhallartgallery.cityoflondon.gov.uk, free). It's an amazing chance to step back into the city's bloody past, which even trumps the previous chart-topping subterranean Roman thrill –

admiring the pavement and villa remains in the undercroft of St Bride's Church (Fleet Street, EC4Y 8AU, 7427 0133, guided tours £6), hidden treasures that had been lost before bombs struck during the Blitz.

The fortifications of London Wall were constructed and continually developed between AD 200 and 410, when the Romans upped and left for home. Its six gates are still easy to find in the *A-to-Z*, with the best surviving stretches at Tower Hill (along with a statue of Emperor Trajan) and on the Barbican Estate, where one of the regular lookout towers, or bastions, survives next to the church of St Giles-without-Cripplegate.

Nearby, the grounds of the Museum of London (150 London Wall, EC2Y 5HN, 7001 9844, www. museumoflondon.org.uk) boast a 13th-century tower built on top of London Wall and a Roman fort gate beneath pavement level (unfortunately, only rarely open for public viewing). Inside, the museum houses 47,000 Roman objects uncovered by building work over the centuries, including the wonderful marble sculptures of gods from the Temple of Mithras (Minerva, Venus combing her hair, the Egyptian god Serapis, and, of course, the bullfighting Mithras himself) as well as ceramics, coins, metalwork, mosaics – and leather bikinis. Discovered in 1954, the foundations of the Temple of Mithras – the soldier's temple, later rededicated to the wine god, Bacchus – are, at the time of writing, temporarily in storage.

Central Criminal Court

DEFEND THE CHILDREN OF THE POOR & PVNISH THE WRONGDOER

416 *Make the world more beautiful...*

In late 2004, gardening radical and Elephant & Castle resident Richard Reynolds set up his own underground movement, inviting others to join him 'to fight the filth in public spaces with forks and flowers'. The idea is to overhaul neglected areas of greenery; a particular favourite is roundabouts – often unattractive spaces, yet seen by hundreds of people every day. You can check out which digs are planned – and suggest your own – on the website, www.guerrillagardening.org, which also has news of similar popular gardening initiatives, talks and communities overseas.

417 *...or take a short cut and visit a garden that is already beautiful*

During Open Garden Squares weekend (held in June, www.opensquares.org), wrought-iron gates are swung back and city oases, usually hidden behind high laurel hedges, are opened to the public. There are around 200 gardens and squares to choose from, and they come in all shapes, colours and sizes. The impressively grand set pieces include Belgrave Square, SW1, an enormous four-acre garden with an enviable collection of statuary and a tennis court.

Hill Garden & Pergola, Hampstead

Waterlow Park Kitchen Garden

Take it to the
bridges

Wealth, death and a lot of bad language – Charlie Godfrey-Faussett talks us through traversing the Thames.

It was thanks to Hadrian that Londinium, with its timber bridge over the river, was able to consolidate its prestige a century after being sacked and burned by Boudicca. And without London's bridges, it's quite possible that we'd still be waiting for a waterman to ferry us across to the other side of the river in his boat – though we probably wouldn't have to wait very long. In Elizabethan times, when there was still only one bridge in London, there were some 40,000 watermen working the river (to put that in perspective, there are around 20,000 licensed black cabs in the city today). A famously feisty and foul-mouthed bunch (a law was once passed attempting to moderate their backchat), when more bridges were proposed in the 17th century, it was the watermen (along with the City of London) who successfully opposed the idea. Let's give thanks, then, that you can now walk across the Thames free of charge, keeping your feet dry and your thoughts clean, on no fewer than nine different bridges in the two miles or so between the Tower of London and the Houses of Parliament.

A pleasant stroll through Tower Gardens leads round the medieval walls of the Tower of London and up some steps on to Tower Bridge Approach. And what an approach it is: this preposterous neo-Gothic construction, the first bridge ever built downstream of London Bridge, has become even more iconic than the fortress it was supposed to complement. And what's more, it actually works. With its lifting 'bascules' and pedestrian skywalks, it looks more like the entrance to an elfin wonderland than a bridge. But perhaps the real reason it's so popular is that it has buildings on it – harking back to Old London Bridge, which was packed with houses – and you can hire the Bridge Master's Dining Room in the south abutment for a day (or evening) of private dining.

Thanks to one of those feats of continuity that the City of London does so well, the Bridge House Estates, founded in 1097 by King William Rufus for levying taxes for the repair of London's only bridge, are still paying for the upkeep of the five City bridges today. The Estates grew

considerably in importance during the Middle Ages, after the new stone bridge became the City's lifeline, and were given a Royal Charter in 1282. They now manage some £700 million worth of assets and, as the City Bridge Trust, also give £15 million to charitable causes in London each year. They also paid for Tower Bridge, which opened with much pomp and ceremony in 1894.

At the south end of the bridge, head down the steps and turn right on to the riverside Queen's Walk. It passes the glass kidney of City Hall, the gleaming office blocks of MoreLondon and HMS *Belfast* – which is moored at the end of Battle Bridge Lane, apparently named after the supposed site of Boudicca's final rout by the Romans. Further along, a plaque on the embankment wall marks the site of Old London Bridge, its first stone laid in 1176. It was replaced in 1831 by a new one designed by the indefatigable Scottish engineer John Rennie (who also built the first Waterloo and Southwark bridges). His London Bridge was famously sold to McCulloch Oil in 1968 and rebuilt in Lake Havasu City, Arizona. The new London Bridge, finished in

1973, with its three arches, is hardly a beauty but it's still well worth crossing for the view of Tower Bridge downstream – and for the beeline it makes into the City, towards the imposing offices of the Guardian Royal Exchange Assurance Group (1921). On the left, Cannon Street station's brick towers, and its iron railway bridge, were constructed in 1865 and are early works of John Wolfe Barry, who later saw Tower Bridge through to completion (he was the son of Sir Charles Barry, who designed the Houses of Parliament).

At the north end of London Bridge, by the Egyptian art deco Adelaide House, take the steps down to the riverside on the right. Carrying on

'There were some 40,000 watermen working the river – to put that in perspective, there are around 20,000 licensed black cabs in the city today.'

upstream from here, great views of Southwark Cathedral open up across the river from Watermen's Walk (a name loaded with cruel irony, given that they would surely have preferred you to take a ride in their boats). On the north side of the river, Watermark Place, with its swish wooden gantries and euro-chic dining options, recently opened in the place of Mondial House, the stylish 1970s bomb-proof telephone exchange that once stood here. On the other side of the water, you can see Pickford's Wharf, Winchester Wharf, the old Thameside Inn, and the replica of Sir Francis Drake's world-circling little *Golden Hinde* in its dock.

Just before you pass under Cannon Street station, note the plaque unveiled in 2005 'to celebrate 60 years of peace between the peoples of Britain and Germany, and to commemorate

600 years during which some 400 Hanseatic merchants inhabited peacefully in the City of London from the 13th to 19th centuries, in the German self-governing enclave on this site known as the Steelyard'. Steelyard Passage, running under the bridge and lit by dinky blue lights dotted on the ground, leads to a refreshing stopover in the shape of the Banker pub on Cousin Lane. Its funny little outdoor deck, right on the river, looks across to the more famous (and busy) Anchor inn on Bankside, but this one gets all the sun in the afternoon. Fortify yourself before continuing along Walbrook Wharf past Cory Environmental's Transfer Station, where the City of London's garbage is containerised before being floated out of town on big barges to the Mucking Marshes (thankfully a remarkably odourless operation these days).

The approach to Southwark Bridge is up Fruiterers Passage (check out the Fruiterers' crest on the wall showing Adam and Eve in the garden, proving what a serious matter fruit and veg can be). Southwark Bridge, built between 1913 and 1921, and designed by Sir Ernest George, mentor to Edwin Lutyens, has a beautiful old gold, eau-de-Nil and cream colour scheme and lovely lamps which are especially atmospheric when there's a mist hanging over the river at night. Crossing south over the bridge – apparently aligned with the older Blackfriars Bridge upstream to minimise tidal turbulence – you'll be confronted by the spinnaker façade of Riverside House, home of media regulator Ofcom. Head right along Bankside at the end of the bridge, and you'll pass the reconstructed Globe Theatre, its thatched roof now authentically mossy.

However, St Paul's Cathedral and Tate Modern are the big events here – and the Millennium Bridge connects the two. Also in the care of the Bridge House Estates, the first new pedestrian bridge over the river for a century is a shining wonder to walk across. Famously wobbly on first opening, the cunning design of its flattened-out suspension cables means that there are great views to the left and right, and it's a memorable approach straight across towards the great dome of St Paul's.

Don't get distracted by the cathedral, though: you've got more bridges to cross. From the north end of the Millennium Bridge, drop hard left on to riverside Paul's Walk. Outside the entrance to the City of London School is a polar sundial, the time indicated by the shadow of its oxhead gnomon (a gnomon is a sundial's 'needle'; in this case, positioned in the centre of the sundial and vaguely resembling an oxhead). Paul's Walk continues along the river past flower-filled tubs, wooden pergolas and benches backed up against the brick wall of the Blackfriars Bridge Underpass. Pass beneath Blackfriars Railway Bridge (another of John Wolfe Barry's works, with Henri Brunel, son of Isambard, opened in 1886), which stands next to the shadow of its former self – the massive supports of the London, Dover & Chatham railway bridge of 1862 jutting purposelessly out of the water.

The original Blackfriars Bridge was put up in 1769 (then only the third bridge in London) and the watermen were duly compensated. Its replacement was opened exactly 100 years later by Queen Victoria, at the time so unpopular she was hissed at by the crowd at the opening ceremony (a statue of her stands at the northern end of the bridge, notwithstanding). Dickens described the bridge as 'one of the handsomest in London... the general outline is bold and the ensemble rich, if perhaps a trifle gaudy, especially when the gilding, of which there is an unusual proportion, has been freshly renewed.' In honour of this being the river's tidal turning point – the point at which fresh and saline water meet – you'll notice that the bridge's piers are decorated with stone seagulls and seabirds on the downstream (seaward) side, and kingfishers, herons and other freshwater birds on the upstream side. It also has a surprisingly low Venetian-Gothic balustrade: could it be coincidence that it was from this bridge that the Italian banker Roberto Calvi, known as the Pope's banker, was found hanging in 1982?

At the south end of the bridge, ugly Sea Containers House has been handsomely refurbished and now houses a fancy hotel, with bars and restaurants lining the riverside walkway. Turn the corner past the successful OXO Tower Wharf redevelopment into the attractive, tree-lined and laid-back approach to Waterloo Bridge. Before long, however, the great blocks of the National Theatre announce a different, concrete world – sterner and more practical, perhaps, but certainly, in the case of the bridge at least, more beautiful. Not only are the views from the bridge itself inspiring – wedged as it is on a sharp bend in the river – but with it, the architect, Sir Giles Gilbert Scott, surely produced his finest work. Bearing its name proudly on its side, like a ship, its five leaping spans, supported

by massive concrete box girders, manage to appear wonderfully light. It was completed during World War II, in 1942, and much of the construction work was carried out by women. It is the people's bridge.

> '*Waterloo Bridge, bearing its name proudly on its side like a ship, was completed during World War II.*'

After a break at the terrace café in Somerset House on the northern side, Victoria Embankment Gardens are well worth strolling through on the way to your penultimate bridge. The Golden Jubilee footbridges on either side of Hungerford (railway) Bridge were opened in 2003, making them the newest bridges on the river. Take the left-hand footbridge to see the City; take the right-hand one to see Westminster.

Now you're in the busiest and most popular bit of the South Bank, home to the London Eye and County Hall, but you can avoid the crowds (nearly) by going through the tunnel beneath the Coade stone South Bank lion, then taking the southern pavement of Westminster Bridge towards the Houses of Parliament. The first bridge on this site was constructed in 1750, after overcoming the usual long-held objections from the watermen and the City. Wordsworth immortalised it with his reflections from it on the city at dawn, but the current structure replaced Wordsworth's in 1862. It was designed by Thomas Page with input from Sir Charles Barry, architect of the Houses of Parliament, and possibly the reason why it complements them so neatly. Follow the bridge to its west end on the north bank and you'll find a striking statue of Boudicca. If she – or the watermen – had had their way, there might never have been any London bridges at all.

427-430

Listen to church choirs

There are many glorious church choirs in London and all of them can be heard for little more than the cost of a bus fare or whatever donation you feel inclined to leave in the plate. The choirs of Westminster Abbey (www.westminster-abbey.org), St Paul's Cathedral (www.stpauls.co.uk), Westminster Cathedral (www.westminster cathedral.org.uk) and the Brompton Oratory (www.bromptonoratory.com) are all well known (visit their websites for details), but there are also several less prominent churches that offer a great opportunity for musical uplift.

One such is the Parish Church of St George (Hanover Square, W1S 1FX, 7629 0874, www.stgeorgeshanoversquare.org), an elegant Queen Anne church. There is animated carving on the reredos from the workshop of Grinling Gibbons, and the 16th-century Flemish glass in the east window has a uniquely smoky beauty. Famous for high society weddings, St George's was the venue of choice for Eliza's upwardly mobile dustman father, Alfred Doolittle, in *My Fair Lady*. The choir sings every Sunday morning at the Parish Eucharist.

At the end of one of north London's most lovely residential streets, you'll find a grand church and graveyard, dating back to 986. The Parish Church of St John-at-Hampstead (Church Row, NW3 6UU, 7794 5808, www.hampsteadparishchurch.org.uk) has a strong musical heritage originally created by its great organist and choirmaster, the late Martindale Sidwell, and generously supported by the urbane and enthusiastic Hampstead congregation. There is a sung Parish Eucharist and Choral Evensong every Sunday (4.30pm in winter, 6pm in summer; check website for details).

St Mary's Church (Bourne Street, SW1W 8JJ, 7730 2423, www.stmarysbournest.com) is an offbeat haven in the heart of Belgravia. The church is Anglo-Catholic, and you are therefore just as likely to hear a polyphonic *Salve Regina* by Juan de Aranda as you are Anglican music by the likes of Stanford and Parry sung by the 'invisible' choir on high in the west end gallery.

The Parish Church of St Mary the Virgin (Elsworthy Road, NW3 3DJ, 7722 3238, www.smvph.org.uk), near Swiss Cottage, offers a sung Eucharist every Sunday morning and Evensong

once a month. St Mary's figures prominently in the Anglican choral tradition; its vicar in Edwardian times, Percy Dearmer, collaborated with Ralph Vaughan Williams on the *New English Hymnal*. Dearmer was as much renowned for his sense of sartorial style as he was for his interest in music, favouring a cassock, gown and velvet cap during day-to-day parish rounds. 'To hell with the Pope!' shouted a rude little boy on seeing Dearmer in this outfit. 'Are you aware,' replied Dearmer, 'that this is the precise costume in which Latimer went to the stake?'

431

Hide away at Greenwich Peninsula Ecology Park

At the Greenwich Peninsula Ecology Park, you can delight in being in a way-out wet place bouncing with life and beauty – just a stone's throw from the O2 centre. If it's astonishing enough that a park like this should exist, given the area's industrial history, it's even more amazing that the creatures living here are not put off by the encroaching city. But then the park was always intended as an urban project, providing a new wetland habitat and enabling scientists to find out more about urban ecology. Abundant wildlife – frogs, toads, newts, beetles, brightly coloured dragonflies and damselflies, butterflies and wild flowers – throngs the inner and outer lakes. You can go on evening bat walks (*see p96*) and there are also specially designed hides from which to survey the various resident and visiting bird species. Check the website for details of the different monthly and seasonal events.

Greenwich Peninsula Ecology Park *Ecology Park Gatehouse, Thames Path, John Harrison Way, SE10 0QZ (8293 1904, www.tcv.org.uk/urbanecology/urban-ecology-sites/greenwich-peninsula-ecology-park, www.greenwichecologypark.com).*

432

Spend a Sunday morning on Columbia Road

One of London's most visually appealing markets, Columbia Road overflows with bucketfuls of flowers on a Sunday morning – and rings with the patter of chirpy Essex barrowboys. The market opens at 8am – early birds can get breakfast when they arrive.

Start at the Ezra Street end of the market, next to the Royal Oak gastropub (73 Columbia Road, 7729 2220, www.royaloaklondon.com). A mooch around the Courtyard, also on Ezra Street, will provide drooling opportunities with the restored furniture of B Southgate (4 The Courtyard, 07905 960792, www.bsouthgate.co.uk) and the art in Columbia Road Gallery (7 The Courtyard, 07812 196257, www.columbiaroadgallery.com).

Back on Columbia Road itself, check out the shops that run either side of the flower traders. This end is best for gawping at art, with Elphick's (no.160, 7033 7891, www.elphicksshop.com),

Nelly Duff (no.156, 7033 9683, www.nellyduff.com) and Start Space (no.150, 7729 0049, www.startspace.co.uk). Fun shops include friendly accessories boutique L'Orangerie (no.162, 8983 7873) – chunky bead necklaces, straw sun-visors and fat glass rings are among the cheaper items – as well as old-fashioned sweetshop Suck & Chew (no.130, 8983 3504, www.suckandchew.co.uk); A Portuguese Love Affair (no.142, 7613 1482, www.aportugueseloveaffair.co.uk), which stocks gifts from Portugal, including beautifully packaged soaps and sardines; and gorgeous stationery specialist Choosing Keeping (no.128, 7613 3842, http://choosingkeeping.com). Columbia Road institution Milagros (no.61, 7613 0876, www.milagros.co.uk) offers Mexican curiosities and trinkets, including single tiles for 70p. Ready for lunch? Try Brawn at no.49 (7729 5692, www.brawn.co).

433-442 *Splash out on chocolate*

Forget those cheap bars at supermarket checkout counters: instead, spend £10 on chocolate from the capital's finest chocolatiers.

Artisan du Chocolat

Artisan du Chocolat, London's most experimental chocolate shop, is a good bet for spectacular ganaches, truffles, mints and candied fruits. Irish-born proprietor Gerard Coleman makes all of his trademark tobacco 'couture chocolate' (smoky, silky and intense) by hand. He has also created many other delicious innovations, among them the best-selling liquid salt caramels.
89 Lower Sloane Street, SW1W 8DA (7824 8365, www.artisanduchocolat.com).

La Maison du Chocolat

Robert Linxe's Parisian choc palace is a browser's paradise: spacious and slick, with giant windows, the store sells seasonal individual cakes – perhaps a chocolate, mango and ginger Maiko in summer, or a Rigoletto caramel mousse-filled cake for winter.
45-46 Piccadilly, W1J 0DS (7287 8500, www.lamaisonduchocolat.com).

Mast Brothers

The bearded American siblings (Michael and Rick) that are the Mast Brothers look just the part for hipster-heavy Redchurch Street. Their clean-lined flagship store/factory is where to pick up some of their beautifully packaged single-estate and single-origin chocolate bars – perhaps maple, almond, goat milk or sea salt.
19-29 Redchurch Street, E2 7DJ (7739 1236, www.mastbrothers.co.uk).

Melt

Watch the chocolates being made in the pristine white open kitchen at the rear of this pretty Notting Hill boutique. Melt's bars are all made by hand and come in inspired flavours such as milk chocolate with raspberry and black pepper, or sesame. Love bars (silky milk chocolate with a creamy filling) have a secret pocket in the pack for your own private message. The takeaway hot chocolate is dark and delicious.
54 Ledbury Road, W11 2AA (7727 5030, www.meltchocolates.com).

Montezuma's

In contrast to the precious attitude of some of their competitors, Montezuma's has a light-hearted attitude towards chocolate, and their variety of giant chocolate buttons, animal shapes and dipped fruits makes for quirky, colourful presents. Much of the range is organic and fair trade. They also offer a service where you can create your own one-kilo bar.
51 Brushfield Street, E1 6AA (7539 9208, www.montezumas.co.uk).

Paul A Young

A gorgeous boutique with almost everything – chocolates, cakes, ice-cream – made in the downstairs kitchen and finished in front of customers. Young is a pâtissier as well as a chocolatier and has an astute chef's palate for combining flavours. In summer, try Pimm's cocktail truffles featuring cucumber, strawberry and mint flavours, and white chocolate blondies made with raspberries and blueberries.
33 Camden Passage, N1 8EA (7424 5750, www.payoung.net).

Philip Neal

Phil Neal hand-makes the chocolates spread over the counter and adjacent dresser of this cosy Chiswick shop. There are large truffles, fruit-flavoured whips in chocolate cups and good marzipan options, but our favourites are the cocoa-dusted chocolate 'sticks', rich enough to serve as dessert in themselves. Look for the discreetly boxed chocolates featuring *Kama Sutra* positions.
43 Turnham Green Terrace, W4 1RG (8987 3183, www.philipnealchocolates.co.uk).

Prestat

Another British business that has long since proved itself next to the chocolate masters of Brussels, Prestat's 'Appointment to the Queen' status is echoed in glorious packaging

William Curley

– pretty boxes in regal purples and ruby reds, embellished with gold crowns and elegant script. The store's strongest product is its plump, round, velvety truffles.
14 Princes Arcade, SW1Y 6DS (7492 3372, www.prestat.co.uk).

Rococo
Rococo's Chantal Cody has a fondness for unusual flavours (cardamom, chilli pepper or orange and geranium bwars, say), but combines this with some nostalgic ones: English rose and violet creams, plus fresh cream truffles, for example. Rococo has also been a pioneer in the UK when it comes to ethical practices. Try the Grenada 71% bar, made on the same estate on which the cocoa is grown.
321 King's Road, SW3 5EP (7352 5857, www.rococochocolates.com).

William Curley
This charming pâtisserie is the brainchild of husband and wife duo William and Suzue Curley. The couple opened their first shop in Richmond in 2004, to rave reviews. It sells an exquisite range of cakes and chocolates, including a tropical entremet, orange and praline cake and sea-salt caramel chocolate.
10 Paved Court, Richmond TW9 1LZ (8332 3002, www.williamcurley.co.uk).

443 Relive the jet set days at Croydon Airport's museum

If the words 'terminal building' invariably summon 'terminal boredom' to mind, you'll find an antidote in the free visitors' centre at Croydon Airport. Defunct as an airport since 1959, this vestige of Empire relives the early days of aviation: a time when getting airborne and staying there was no mean feat, when air traffic control was a thing of the future, and when the expression 'jet set' was invented to imply impossibly glamorous luxury. The beautifully crafted art deco terminal building was constructed on two World War I airfields, and this was the main commercial airport for London until Heathrow opened in 1953. In its heyday, the great aviators all came here – Charles Lindbergh touched down in 1927 shortly after his solo transatlantic flight, and Amy Johnson flew from Croydon to Australia – and, incredibly, back again. All the surprising romance of Croydon's lost past is celebrated at the visitors' centre in the old control tower, where the world's first air traffic control system (1921) has been recreated with original equipment. You can see Amy Johnson's flight bag and even dress up as a passenger from the 1930s. There's a De Havilland Tiger Moth in the preserved booking hall and a Heron outside the door. All it lacks is Hercule Poirot, en route to solve a high-class murder in Paris. Never let it be said that romance is dead in Croydon.

Croydon Airport Visitors' Centre *Airport House, Purley Way, Croydon CRO OXZ (8669 1196, www. croydonairport.org.uk).*

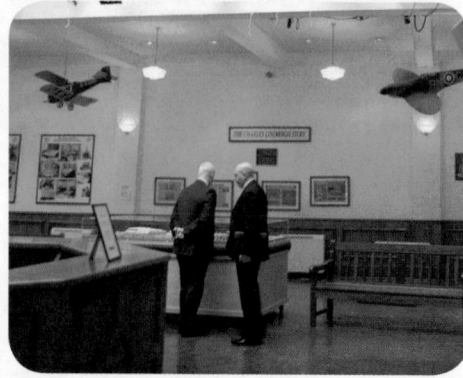

444-448 *Pedal...*

The odd argument with drivers aside, the capital can be a great place to cycle through – and it's free! We especially like the following routes.

...through the City at night

This five-mile jaunt is best left for the weekends, when the hordes of suited workers have gone home and the place is shrouded by an eerie calm. It's the ideal time to drink in the stagily magnificent architecture – from Richard Rogers' ultra-modern Lloyd's building to the Acropolis-like Royal Exchange – especially at night, when it's all aglow and the lack of traffic allows you to pause in front of buildings without dismounting. Start at Bishopsgate, continue on to Leadenhall Street, St Mary Axe, Cornhill, Threadneedle Street, Poultry and Cheapside, before ending at St Paul's.

...to the shops

Head to Holborn, Farringdon and Islington for a spot of window shopping and bargain browsing. Start at Bayley Street and go along Russell Square and Guilford Street, before heading up Calthorpe Street into Farringdon, Rosebery Avenue, Upper Street and Camden Passage. Highlights, in order of appearance, include the lovely Russell Square Gardens, Lambs Conduit Street – with its idiosyncratic independent outlets, including Persephone Books and the People's Supermarket – and Exmouth Market with its array of eateries. After zipping past Sadler's Wells, you'll reach Camden Passage near Angel, a cobbled lane with everything from high-end jewellers to heavily laden vintage shops.

...around the south-east

This is a workout for serious cyclists that meanders through 13 miles of gorgeous river views and renovated docks. The route takes in two quirky river crossings as well as great maritime institutions, dockside industries and plenty of parkland. Begin at Greenwich and head to village-like Charlton and Woolwich, where you'll cross the river by ferry. Then it's on to car-free Canary Wharf and Island Gardens, where you can get the lift down to the Greenwich foot tunnel (you have to dismount here) and head back south under the river to the station and where you started. Unless, of course, you're tempted to do the whole thing again.

...by Battersea

This pleasant 12-mile waft along the Thames to Kew starts at Westminster Pier (you can return by ferry). Take the road behind the Houses of Parliament and continue along to Millbank, past Tate Britain and Vauxhall Bridge; soon, Battersea Power Station pops up on the other side. Further on, just before Battersea Bridge, there's a little colony of houseboats on the river. (The path is privately owned for some stretches here, so you may have to dismount.) The ferry back to Westminster leaves from Kew Pier and takes about an hour and a half (7930 2062, www.wpsa. co.uk). If it's busy, you might not be able to take your bike, but you can always catch the train from Kew Bridge station to Waterloo.

...from east to west

This nine-mile schlep starts with the trendy grit of London Fields in Hackney, before heading north-west towards Islington, where at Canonbury Park you may be shocked to discover that some Londoners have gardens the size of your street. Next, it's over Upper Street through leafy Barnsbury and down to Camden, pristine Regent's Park and on to the grand streets surrounding St John's Wood. After Lord's cricket ground, head downhill to Maida Vale before scooting round swish Sutherland Avenue and along the foliage-shaded canal to Portobello Road. Where it's time for a sit-down and a cup of tea.

449 Get into the Inns of Court

Meandering in a broad zig-zag from Holborn down through Chancery Lane to Blackfriars and the Embankment, the Inns of Court are the four self-contained precincts where barristers traditionally train and practise – an oasis of academic calm in the middle of the city. Like hushed and venerable Oxbridge campuses with their Grade I-listed medieval chapels, Tudor-style libraries, quads and lawns dominated by majestic plane trees, it's no wonder so few Londoners realise that they are open to the public.

The Inns – Lincoln's Inn, Gray's Inn, Inner Temple, Middle Temple – trace their history back to the 14th century, when the old manor house belonging to Sir Reginald de Grey, Chief Justice of Chester, was converted into a 'hostelry' for law students fleeing the disarray of King Edward's court (hence Inns). They then spread to incorporate land owned by the medieval Christian military order of the Knights Templar (hence Temples). While the Inns no longer accommodate students, judges are still entitled to stay overnight in advantageously apportioned apartments, though they rarely do in practice (it's 'a security nightmare', according to those in the know).

In true Dickensian style, the first thing you'll notice when you visit are the off-putting signs announcing the removal of anyone 'constituting a nuisance'. (The best of these is at the entrance to Staple Inn, just by Chancery Lane tube station, which expressly forbids the presence of 'old clothesmen' and 'rude children'.) Anyone bold enough to venture further, however, will find paved courtyards dominated by tinkling fountains and impressive swards such as Gray's Inn Gardens or the rolling fields of Lincoln's Inn.

As well as being well and truly pickled in history, the Inns of Court are, unsurprisingly, no strangers to celluloid either: the huge Tudor Hall dominating Lincoln's Inn (a 19th-century facsimile of the 15th-century original) was one of the settings for *Bleak House*, just one period drama (after *Wilde*, *Pride & Prejudice* and, of course, *Harry Potter and the Order of the Phoenix*) to use the Inns as a backdrop for Ye Olde London. In fact, the place is so popular with location finders that the road around Lincoln's Inn Fields can often be blocked up with camera crews. When it isn't, however, we urge you to stop on one of the generously sized benches and watch the gas lamps being lit as dusk falls (*see p41*). Squint just enough to blur out the modern appurtenances – the Audis in the parking slots, the synthetic colours of the cyclists' Lycra – and you can imagine yourself in a precursor of the modern, frenetic city that lies outside the gates; a London that's more tranquil, more civilised and, somehow, more mysterious.

If you want to visit the redoubtable Halls, with their august stained glass and old-buffer wood panelling (and, in the case of Middle Temple Hall, genuine minstrels' gallery), you'll need to be organised (or riding on a barrister's coat-tails). You must group-book ahead, and even then you're strictly forbidden to disturb the Inns' most sacred ritual: dining.

But the Inns also have their own places of worship – and these are generally open to the public (11am to noon and 1pm to 4pm, outside of special services). The Inner Temple Church is built on the site of a 12th-century Knights Templar church and graveyard. Here, you'll come across effigies of crusty old knights, as well as Nicola Hicks' sculpture of a pair of knights on a scrawny horse that sits on a plinth in the adjacent square. If you turn up on Fridays, you can catch the current 'Master' of the church, Robin Griffith-Jones, lecturing weekly to tourists on the inadequacies of Dan Brown's 'research' for *The Da Vinci Code*.

Conspiracy theories and Dickensian locations aside, however, there's plenty to keep you occupied here. The Inns have a singular ambience; and a simple stroll along the cobbled lanes – through archways and into secret gardens – is reward enough for most, especially on a crisp sunny day.

450 *Start skateboarding*

Although skateboarding in some parts of the city may incur a fine if you get caught, it's fair to say that the capital's skateboarders have never had it so good as far as legitimate or semi-legitimate skate spots are concerned. Up north, there are the streety bowls in the southern corner of Finsbury Park, N4, and Cantelowes skatepark (www.camden.gov.uk), halfway up Camden Road, NW1. There's a new concrete skatepark in Clissold Park, Stoke Newington, N16. In west London, you'll find the oddly named skatepark siblings Meanwhile One (a series of interconnecting concrete bowls next to the Regent's Canal at Westbourne Park tube) and Meanwhile Two (a small, smooth, covered concrete street course with a 1970s freestyle ramp under the Westway at Royal Oak tube). There's also the large, covered Bay66 skatepark near Ladbroke Grove (Bay 66, Acklam Road, W10 5YU, 8969 4669, www.baysixty6.com).

Just behind Brixton Academy in south London is the expansive and recently resurfaced Stockwell skatepark (Stockwell Park Road, SW9),

while out east there's the tight concrete Mudchute skatepark, near Mudchute DLR (the corner of Westbury Road and Spindrift Avenue), and Mile End skatepark (in Mile End Park), which is free and really popular. More central is the imaginatively designed White's Grounds concrete skatepark underneath the railway arches off Tooley Street, SE5, next to Tower Bridge. More centrally, Shoreditch's skaters have two grindblocks in Shoreditch Park, N1.

But no discussion of skateboarding in the city would be complete without mention of the hallowed blocks, banks and steps of the South Bank, SE1 (in the undercroft below the Royal Festival Hall), which, after a campaign to preserve its status as UK skating's spiritual home, is as busy as ever.

For the latest places to skate, the Slam City Skates shop (16 Neal's Yard, WC2H 9DP, 7240 0928, www.slamcity.com) has a tourist-friendly map of London skateparks. Ask nicely and they'll also give you the lowdown on up-and-coming spots.

Stockwell skatepark

451-460

Go in search of heroes and kings

Tick off some of London's quirkiest and most fascinating statues, starting at Trinity Church Square in SE1. Here stands a weather-worn full-length statue, probably dating from the 14th century, usually identified as King Alfred. The only statue of the great English hero in London, it was moved here from medieval Westminster Hall in 1824.

The oldest outdoor sculpture in London must surely be the 3,600-year-old carving of Egyptian warrior goddess Sekhmet, which has guarded the door of Sotheby's Art Auctioneers (34-35 New Bond Street, W1) since the firm's move here in 1917. The black basalt bust was the subject of 'Sotheboy', Bruce Chatwin's first published piece of work, in 1966.

In Victoria Embankment Gardens, WC2, you'll find a memorial to composer Arthur Sullivan (the tuneful half of Gilbert and Sullivan). This bust was carved by the Welsh sculptor William Goscombe John and depicts a scantily draped embodiment of Music fainting on Sullivan's pedestal, having apparently just let slip the score of *The Yeomen of the Guard* from her hand.

Hyde Park is home to a huge bronze statue of Greek hero Achilles wielding his short sword and buckler behind the Duke of Wellington's former home, Apsley House (149 Piccadilly, W1J 7NT, 7499 5676, www.english-heritage.org.uk). Made from captured French cannons and paid for by 'the women of England' in gratitude to the Duke, it was erected in 1822 – the first nude public statue in Britain. The fig leaf added later to protect the Greek hero's modesty has been removed twice – most recently in 1961.

Best viewed from the top deck of a bus, John Bunyan looks down from a niche above the door of Baptist House, Covent Garden (6 Southampton Row, WC1). The full-length statue of the great nonconformist preacher is underscored by the first lines from his most famous work, *Pilgrim's Progress*: 'As I walked through the wilderness of this world, I lighted upon a certain place, where was a den, and I laid me down in that

place to sleep, and as I slept I dreamed a dream.' It's hard to imagine that happening on Southampton Row today.

A bust of Virginia Woolf, apparently a copy of the only one ever taken from life, was erected in Tavistock Square. It was unveiled in 2004 by 'the last member of the Bloomsbury Group', Anne Olivier Popham Bell, wife of Quentin Bell, Virginia's nephew. Anne was a member of the Monuments, Fine Arts and Archives section (MFAA) during World War II. The 'Monuments Men', as they were known, a group of 345 people from 13 different countries, are credited with locating and eventually returning some five million artworks looted by the Nazis. The gardens also contain a cherry tree planted in 1967 to commemorate the victims of Hiroshima – and a beautifully contemplative statue of Mahatma Gandhi.

Mary, Queen of Scots surveys Fleet Street from the first floor of a building now called Mary Queen of Scots House (143-144 Fleet Street, EC4). The statue was erected in the 1880s by the MP for Caithness, Sir John George Tollemache Sinclair. Sir John released various recordings on Columbia, Gramophone and Odeon in 1906, including his recitation of 'Adieu of Mary, Queen of Scots', an English translation of the French poem by the revolutionary Napoleonic poet Béranger.

Shakespeare can be found leaning out of the first-floor window of a corner pub on Carnaby Street, W1, casting a quizzical (if poorly modelled) eye on the swinging street scene below. Ashen-faced, looking like a clown, and wearing blue-striped pyjamas and a ruff, he appears to be staying in the Shakespeare's Head pub behind Liberty, which was once owned by the Shakespeare brothers, supposedly distant relatives of the playwright. The figure has been in place since just before World War I and lost a hand to a bomb in World War II.

Sir Winston Churchill and Franklin D Roosevelt are relaxing in conversation on a park bench on New Bond Street, W1. The bronze, entitled *Allies*, was modelled by Lawrence Holofcener and unveiled by Princess Margaret in 1995, to commemorate a half century of peace. The sculpture shows little evidence of Roosevelt's famous distrust, bordering on dislike, of Churchill, though he did once concede to the drunken PM that 'it is fun being in the same decade as you.'

461 Ponder the mystery of Pages Walk tank...

Take a left off the Old Kent Road in south London on to Mandela Way, just after the Tower Bridge Road roundabout, and you are quickly confronted with an enormous 32-ton Russian T-34 tank that someone has seen fit to park in a garden at the end of Pages Walk. Rumour has it that a doting father bought this Soviet relic for his seven-year-old son's birthday. The years may have passed but the gift never palled and it's still there for all to see (one year it was painted pink, now it's back to black and white camouflage). Apparently, the council once tried to have it removed but failed because the overgrown land it sits on also belongs to the tank's owner. He may not have forgiven them: according to local legend, its gun points towards Southwark Council's offices.

462 ...or head along to the Imperial War Museum

Housed in the old lunatic asylum known as Bedlam (the Bethlehem Royal Hospital), just down the road from Pages Walk in Lambeth, is a more impressive collection of military hardware. Focusing on the history of conflict from World War I to the present day, the newly revamped Imperial War Museum has a vast tank, antique guns, aircraft and artillery parked in its main atrium – and a gratifying wealth of information about them too.

Imperial War Museum *Lambeth Road, SE1 6HZ (7416 5320, www.iwm.org.uk). Free.*

463 Play giant Snake with Granary Squirt

The expanse of unpredictable play fountains in Granary Square, King's Cross, N1, is fun to watch, dash through or splash about in at any time of the day, but it becomes truly magical in the evening. Download the Granary Squirt app and between 8pm and 10pm you'll be able to control the water jets using your smartphone, steering a line of them around the grid as if you were playing Snake on your old Nokia 3210. Up to eight people can play at once, so you can embark on a very modern kind of water fight.
www.kingscross.co.uk/granarysquirt.

464

Marvel at the Sky Garden

The Walkie-Talkie, a 525-foot-tall skyscraper (20 Fenchurch Street, EC3M 3BY), has its share of haters, but there's no denying that the garden that occupies its top three floors offers a spectacular panorama. The tiered planting was designed especially for the space, and you can admire miles of London rooftops in every direction from observation decks and an open-air terrace. It's free to visit providing you book your slot in advance, though be warned that evening and weekend times are rarely available. If it's a sought-after sunset view you want, you'll have to reserve a space in one of the bars instead and treat yourself to a sundowner. Details on http://skygarden.london

465

Head for Belgravia

With its grand white houses, secluded gardens and elegant squares, Belgravia is another world – and a fantastically rich one at that. You'd need a small fortune to own even a kitchenette in these rarified surroundings, but going for a walk is free – though it may cost you your soul in envy. Start outside the Thomas Cubitt pub (44 Elizabeth Street, SW1W 9PA, 7730 6060, www.thethomas cubitt.co.uk), dedicated to the memory of the master builder who constructed most of this district in the 1820s. Cubitt was supposedly the first to introduce tea breaks for labourers, so celebrate his humanity with a pint, before heading north-west along Elizabeth Street to Eaton Square, one of London's most expensive addresses. Notable residents have included Neville Chamberlain at no.37, Sean Connery at no.6 and Vivien Leigh at no.54. But to really get a sense of how the other half lives, head for no.100, London residence of Gerald Grosvenor, sixth Duke of Westminster and owner of the freehold on most of the square and surrounding district. The area is named after him too – given that he's Viscount Belgrave, as well as a duke.

From this elegant abode, it's a short stumble up Belgrave Place to fabulous Belgrave Square, one of London's grandest Victorian squares. As well as a sprinkling of swish embassies (the German, Turkish, Portuguese and Norwegian among them), there are statues of great explorers (Christopher Columbus, Prince Henry the Navigator), the Liberator of South America (Simón Bolívar) and the first Marquess of Westminster, who was the grandfather of the first Duke of Westminster and another key figure in the development of this area.

Make your final salute to the follies of the rich in the south corner of the square. This mansion – known in the early 20th century as Downshire House – was the London home of Lord James Pirrie. It was here that, one evening in July 1907, the managing director of the White Star Line came to dinner and planned the production of three new ships, the largest in the world. One of them was, of course, the *Titanic*.

466-470
Have dinner at a night market

Make Market
Most often found in Kingston, this occasional food and crafts market is well worth seeking out for its fun, friendly atmosphere. Carefully chosen food vendors provide the dinner options and the live music almost always leads to dancing. *www.makemarkets.co.uk.*

Model Market
The south London outpost of Street Feast's delicious empire is packed with character. A disused 1950s indoor and outdoor market has been turned into a fun-filled maze of food stalls and themed bars. An old hair salon serves slushies and DJs play vinyl while you eat. *www.streetfeastlondon.com/where/model-market.*

Pop Brixton
Although not strictly a market, Brixton's new event and retail space made of shipping containers is a fine place in which to grab some food and spend an evening. There are 20 food and drink vendors to choose from; look out for street-food stars such as Baba G and his Indian spiced burgers, and Miss P's Barbecue, whose pulled pork is the real deal. *www.popbrixton.org.*

Street Feast Dalston Yard
Arguably the first London night market to make eating street food a date for the diary, Street Feast's Dalston outpost is vast, lively and packed with temptation. Get there early to avoid the £3 entry fee (and the queues). Do some food research before you go, so that you can make a beeline for what your belly will think is unmissable. *www.streetfeastlondon.com/where/dalston-yard.*

Urban Food Fest
What this Shoreditch car park-based market lacks in foodie credentials, it makes up for in enthusiasm: entry is free and there's a fancy dress theme most weeks, with free drinks for those who put in the effort. Around a dozen traders offer food from all over the world and there's everything from shots to champers at the bar. *www.urbanfoodfest.com.*

Pop Brixton

471-478

De- (and re-)clutter your house at a car boot sale

There's no question that car boot sales are more fun than the depersonalised world of eBay – yes, you lose the thrill of swooping in with a last-second winning bid, but you gain ridiculous sales patter, the opportunity to offload your unwanted junk, bargains aplenty and the chance to just potter around laughing at the tat. Here are our suggestions for the best places to find cut-price loot. Note that the entry fee listed is for buyers; the cost for sellers varies, but expect to pay between £10 and £15 for a pitch.

Battersea

The Battersea Tech College transforms itself into a lively trading hub each Sunday. It attracts a mix of house-clearance vultures as well as well-heeled local residents having a de-junk.
Battersea Park School, 401 Battersea Park Road (entrance in Dagnall Street), SW11 5AP (07941 383588, www.batterseaboot.com). Open 1.30-5pm Sun. Entry 50p.

Cuffley

Well over a hundred pitches sell a varied selection of second-hand and antique items every Sunday in this north London suburb.
Just north of Potters Bar, at the junction of Cattlegate Road and Northaw Road, Cuffley, Herts EN6 4 QZ (01707 873360, www.jumbocarbootsales. co.uk). Open Apr-Oct from 7am Sun, bank holiday Mon. Entry 50p.

Epsom

This site outside Epsom, half an hour from Waterloo by train to Ewell West station, is the daddy of bank holiday car boot sales. Expect a great mix of new and second-hand gear from its 700 pitches.
Hook Road Arena, at the junction of Hook Road and Chessington Road, Epsom, Surrey KT19 8QG (07788 132977). Open from 7.30am Sun, bank holiday Mon. Entry 50p (£1 before 7.30am); children free.

Hatfield

There are loads of bargains to be found at this impressive sale. It's strictly second-hand.
Birchwood Leisure Centre, Longmead, Hatfield, Herts AL10 0AN (01992 468619, www.countryside promotions.co.uk). Open Apr-Oct from noon Sun. Entry free.

Holloway

This small sale on the Holloway Road is worth a rummage. It attracts a mix of sellers – from regulars peddling DVDs, electrical goods and fake perfume to local homeowners looking to profit from a one-off clearout.
Opposite Odeon Cinema, Holloway Road, N7 6LJ (01992 717198). Open from 8am Sat; from 10am Sun. Entry free.

Kilburn

Kilburn's big car boot sale has a wide variety of new and second-hand stock from sellers from across north and west London.
St Augustine's Church of England Primary School, Kilburn Park Road, NW6 5SN (8440 0170, www. thelondoncarbootco.co.uk). Open from 11am Sat. Entry 50p (£3 before 11am)

Orpington

The stock at this well-established sale is high in both quantity and quality thanks in part to the affluent location. You'll find mainly second-hand goods at the 75 pitches. There are around 14 sales a year, mostly from January to April and October to December. There's also a well-stocked farm shop on site.
Hewitts Farm, Court Road, Orpington, Kent BR6 7QL (01959 532003, www. hewittsfarm.co.uk). Open from 9am Sun. Entry free.

Wimbledon Stadium

This is a big, spread-out boot sale with a commendable mix of sellers peddling all manner of unexpected second-hand goods. It's especially good for bargains on furniture and crockery. You need to act fast to get your hands on the real treasures.
Wimbledon Stadium, Plough Lane, SW17 0BL (07785 706506). Open from 6.30am Sat; froom 7am Sun. Entry £1 (£5 before 8.30am; £2 before 10am).

Have a laugh

*Ben Williams, **Time Out Comedy Editor**, tells you how to split your sides without breaking the bank.*

A room, a microphone and an audience: that's basically all that's needed to host a comedy night. London is widely regarded as the best city in the world in which to see live comedy. Each week, hundreds of comedians take over pub rooms, small theatres, trendy restaurants, churches, boats, barber shops – you name it – and there are heaps of shows that cost less than a tenner.

In the West End, weekdays are best for cheapo laughs. Every Monday, long-running comedians' favourite Old Rope takes place at the Phoenix (37 Cavendish Square, W1G 0PP, www.facebook. com/oldropecomedy), just off Oxford Circus. Hosted by panel-show regular Tiff Stevenson, it's where TV-name comics and circuit pros – incuding Rich Hall, Frankie Boyle and Milton Jones – come to test new material. A noose hangs over the stage, and if a comic's freshly thought-up jokes aren't going so well, they can grab the rope and tell some tried-and-tested gags. It's always fun, and entry is just £8 (£6 in advance).

Covent Garden's no-frills Top Secret Comedy Club (170 Drury Lane, WC2B 5PD, 07826 099023, www.thetopsecretcomedyclub.co.uk) hosts shows every night of the week. On Tuesdays, improv troupe Shoot From the Hip make up scenes and play silly games for zero entry fee. Tickets for other nights never top a tenner; Sundays and Mondays will cost you just one shiny pound, and sometimes, before the main show, a comic will roadtest their new solo offering for free. The line-ups are a mix of reliable stand-up stalwarts and hand-picked rising stars, and the relaxed, no-nonsense vibe has made it a favourite drop-in gig for big-name comedians. Eddie Izzard, Russell Howard, Simon Amstell, Jack Whitehall and John Bishop have all stopped by unannounced in recent years. Who knows, you could just catch an arena-filler in a basement under an Italian restaurant…

At weekends, the Piccadilly Comedy Club (The Comedy Pub, 7 Oxendon Street, SW1Y 4EE 07568 352828, www.piccadillycomedy.co.uk) is the best option for low-priced laughter. While it might lack the glamour of the famous Comedy Store just up the road, the line-ups are much more varied and exciting than other weekend clubs, with some of the best up-and-comers performing alongside panel-show favourites. It runs every Friday, Saturday and Sunday, with tickets costing between £7.50 and £10.

Up towards King's Cross, the Schadenfreude Cabaret (The Harrison, 28 Harrison Street, WC1H 8JF, www.facebook.com/the.schadenfreude. cabaret) runs twice a month, on Saturday nights. Guaranteed entry costs a fiver in advance; or take a chance and turn up on the night and it's pay-what-you-want. Smart, angry, beardy comic Garrett Millerick is the regular compère, and he introduces consistently excellent bills mixing stand-ups with character acts, sketch troupes and musical comics. Previous acts include *Never Mind the Buzzcocks* favourite Tony Law, Foster's Edinburgh Comedy Award-winner Adam Riches and XFM DJ John Robins.

Just the other side of Pentonville Road is permanent comedy venue the Invisible Dot (2 Northdown Street, N1 9BG, 7424 8918, www. theinvisibledot.com). It's the trendiest comedy club in town: a 100-capacity room with plain white walls where craft beers are sipped by men

with craft beards. It offers line-ups at the more leftfield, experimental end of the spectrum, and the shows are pretty spectacular. On Saturday nights, the inventively titled Saturday Night Show features three offbeat acts (regulars include the quizzically minded James Acaster, TV regular Sara Pascoe and thinker-comedian Liam Williams) for just a tenner. Plus the venue often hosts big-name comics – such as Simon Amstell, Adam Buxton and Tim Key – workshopping new material for next to nothing.

Walk a little further, over the Regent's Canal, and you'll find the Star of Kings pub, which hosts ace pay-what-you-want club the Comedy Grotto (126 York Way, N1 0AX) in its dark, sticky basement. It usually runs twice a month, on a Monday or Tuesday, with donations going towards the Fringe Free branch of the Edinburgh Festival. The bills are always superb: multimedia character comic Joseph Morpurgo and loony stand-up Lou Sanders often pop along to test new jokes. Kevin Eldon – who's been in *Big Train*, *Nighty Night*, *Brass Eye* and practically every other British comedy series that's any good – has been known to drop in on occasion.

Head further north and you'll find an abundance of bank-balance-friendly comedy gigs. Cheapest of all is Angel Comedy (Camden Head, 2 Camden Walk, N1 8DY, www.angel comedy.co.uk). This hugely popular club hosts shows seven nights a week, for free. Well, we say 'free' – there's a collection bucket at the end of the show and punters are strongly encouraged to donate, but if you can't afford to, don't worry, the acts won't be upset. On Fridays and Saturdays, you can catch hand-picked rising stars alongside professional comics performing their funniest sets, and weekdays feature either new material spots, improv troupes or solo shows. Get there early, though – at weekends, long queues form

outside the venue and the promoters usually have to turn people away. You have been warned.

From N1 to NW1: the Camden Comedy Club (upstairs at the other Camden Head, 100 Camden High Street, NW1 0LU, 7485 4019, www.camden comedyclub.com) plays host to a whole variety of shows, most for under ten quid and a lot for nothing at all. Different promoters and comedians take over the L-shaped room on different nights, so the programme's nicely varied. Each Saturday, it's home to the confusingly titled Hampstead Comedy Club (www.hampsteadcomedy.co.uk). Veteran comedian/promoter Ivor Dembina (who moved the club to Camden from a venue in Hampstead – he's not being deliberately abstruse) hosts enjoyable line-ups for £10 a pop.

Prefer comedy that's a bit more chaotic? Shambles (Aces & Eights, NW5 2HP, www. clubshambles.co.uk) lives up to its title. This tiny basement venue in Tufnell Park is perfect

Angel Comedy

for stand-up: dark, cosy and just a little bit grimy. The club is run by comedian/promoter/professional failure Harry Deansway, who knows just about every alt-comic in the business. His line-ups are stupidly good value at £6 a ticket, with regulars including Foster's Award-winning absurdist John Kearns, *Mighty Boosh* star Rich Fulcher, drunken poet Tim Key and bombastic BBC Three star Nick Helm. Deansway is in charge of the other cheap comedy gigs at the Aces & Eights, including the Comedians' Cinema Club – where comics recreate box-office hits live, fuelled by booze – and the venue is a favourite of Harry Hill, who often pops along to workshop new ideas.

Or if fresher, newer comedy's your thing, Kentish Town's Freedom Fridge Comedy Night (Rose & Crown, 71-73 Torriano Avenue, NW5 2SG, http://thefreedomfridge.weebly.com) is one of the best open mic nights in the capital.

Each Thursday, a large group of newbie comics (often 14 or 15 of them) perform short sets. It can be hit and miss – many acts have only been performing for a few months, after all – but it's relaxed and friendly, and you could spot the next household name.

On the other side of London, in studenty New Cross, Happy Mondays (Amersham Arms, 388 New Cross Road, SE14 6TY, www.happy mondayscomedy.com) is one of the finest clubs south of the river. The fact that it's also super-cheap (just £6, or a fiver in advance) is a bonus. It takes place every fortnight at the Tardis-esque Amersham Arms. What looks like a small, cosy pub from the street also looks that way inside. But it's all a front for a huge club and music venue out the back, with a capacity of 300. Some of the best names in the business – Stewart Lee, Reginald D Hunter, Milton Jones, David Cross – have played here to lively crowds.

Just down the road in Greenwich is much-loved, long-running club Up the Creek (302 Creek Road, SE10 9SW, 8858 4581, www.up-the-creek.com). It was originally set up by the late, great, alt-comedy legend Malcolm Hardee, and was renowned for being an absolute bear pit. It's less rowdy these days, but still a heckler's favourite. On Sundays, they drop the ticket price to seven quid for Sunday Special (www.sundayspecial. co.uk). It's much more relaxed than the Friday and Saturday gigs, and features far better line-ups. Russells Brand and Howard have both popped along over the years, as have Stephen Merchant, Jon Richardson and Rich Hall.

The Always Be Comedy team (www.always becomedy.com) run a bunch of ace comedy nights in south London, including Brixton (Prince of Wales, 467-469 Brixton Road, SW9 8HH), Balham (Exhibit, 12 Balham Station Road, SW12 9SG) and their flagship Kennington gig (Tommyfield, 185 Kennington Lane, SE11 4EZ). It's a comedians' favourite – Katherine Ryan and Nick Helm both claim it's the best club in the capital. Prices hover around the £8 mark, with an impressive line-up guaranteed. ABC has even branched out to west London, opening up shop at the Putney Arts Theatre (Ravenna Road, SW15 6AW).

Speaking of west London, Knock2Bag (Bar FM, 184 Uxbridge Road, W12 7JP, http:// knock2bag.co.uk) in Shepherd's Bush is always incredibly good value. The bills at this monthly club (£10 on the door, £8 in advance) are packed to the rafters, with often seven or more top-quality acts in one night. There's always a mix of inventive sketch troupes, weirdo character acts and slick stand-ups, from household names to the finest new comics.

But, wherever you are in the city, Laugh Out London (www.laughoutlondoncomedyclub. co.uk), one of the best little clubs in the capital, has pretty much got you covered. The team runs shows in locations across town, and they're always superb. Choose from Islington (Old Queens Head, 44 Essex Road, N1 8LN), Camden (Camden Head, 100 Camden High Street, NW1 0LU), Stoke Newington (Lion, 132 Stoke Newington Church Street, N16 0JX), Victoria Park (People's Park Tavern, 360 Victoria Park Road, E9 7BT) and Brixton (Dogstar, 389 Coldharbour Lane, SW9 8LQ). Tickets are a bargain, usually costing no more than £7, while the line-ups are worth three times that price. They showcase a mix of TV big 'uns (such as Harry Hill and Stewart Lee), multi-award winners (Bridget Christie and John Kearns) and the very best alt-circuit acts out there. LOL provides a friendly environment for comics to experiment in, and it works a treat. We particularly recommend the chaotic conceptual nights in Camden – they're totally stupid and so much fun. It just goes to show: in London, you really don't need much money to find the funny.

Piccadilly Comedy Club

494

Go down to the docks for the river view on London history

Nowhere in the capital gives you a better sense of the importance of the Thames to the evolution of London than this museum. Set in a 200-year-old warehouse (itself a Grade I-listed survivor of the city's extensive trading history), this isn't a place that ducks the big subjects: witness the thought-provoking 'London, Sugar and Slavery', examining the city's involvement in the transatlantic slave trade, and the hard-hitting 'Docklands at War' section. Models, videos, artefacts and reconstructions tell the story of the river from Roman times through to the commercial redevelopment of the docks in the 1980s and '90s. The impressive exhibits include a full-scale, walk-through mock-up of a working quay and of a 'Sailortown' back alley.
Museum of London Docklands *No.1 Warehouse, West India Quay, Hertsmere Road, E14 4AL (0870 444 3851, www.museumoflondon.org.uk/docklands).*

495

Hound Holmes and Watson through the streets of London

It's got to be one of London's most agreeable cheap thrills, emerging from the Baker Street tube only to bump into a certain long-striding, meerschaum-sucking, deerstalker-sporting figure drumming up business for his detective agency… his gentleman's lodgings… OK, the eponymous museum at 'The World's Most Famous Address' (221B Baker Street, NW1 6XE, 7935 8866, www.sherlock-holmes.co.uk, admission £15). The whole point about Sir Arthur Conan Doyle's appropriation of 221B Baker Street was that the address didn't exist at that time, but never mind, the study here is now a loving re-creation and a splendid photo-op for fans of Victoriana; the bedrooms are scattered with appropriate personal effects, make-believe papers and other paraphernalia, while waxwork tableaux depict scenes from the stories.

Near Baker Street, 2 Devonshire Place (the site of Conan Doyle's medical practice) and 9 Queen Anne Street (where Dr Watson roomed) are essential destinations for fans, and, if you can find a Hansom cab and a foggy night, it's still possible to recreate the route of Holmes – and the murderous Moriarty – from *The Memoirs of Sherlock Holmes*: 'As I passed the corner which leads from Bentinck Street on to the Welbeck Street crossing, a two-horse van furiously driven whizzed round and was on me like a flash. I sprang for the footpath and saved myself by the fraction of a second… I kept to the pavement after that, Watson, but as I walked down Vere Street a brick came down from the roof of one of the houses and was shattered to fragments at my feet…'

Further south, a walk along the Strand can take in 12 Burleigh Street, once the offices of the *Strand Magazine* and where many of the stories were first published. Then there's the site of the original Scotland Yard and the Sherlock Holmes pub (10-11 Northumberland Street, WC2N 5DA, 7930 2644, www.sherlockholmes-stjames.co.uk) – formerly the Northumberland Hotel, which appears in *The Hound of the Baskervilles*. Upstairs, a waxwork Holmes awaits, but the main attraction is another replica of Holmes and Watson's sitting room and study.

496

Visit Chatsworth Road market

Clapton's Chatsworth Road in east London has a long history. In the 1930s it had up to 200 stalls peddling their wares up to five days a week. After the war, the market dwindled and finally petered out in 1990, leaving Chatsworth Road slightly bereft. In November 2010, a band of locals and traders aimed to bring back the bustle and campaigned to get the market back on its feet. After a couple of successful test runs, the market returned regularly (11am-4pm Sunday, www.chatsworthroade5.co.uk), with more than 40 stalls selling gourmet foods, vintage bric-a-brac, crafts, cakes and preserves, clothing and jewellery – and more than its fair share of hipsters. (A handful of the traders also have stalls at Broadway Market.)

497

Spot the fake houses

Strolling past the grand stuccoed terraces in Bayswater's Leinster Gardens, you might notice the windows of nos.23 and 24 look a little strange. That's because they're trompe l'oeil works of plaster and paint. Walk round the back, to Porchester Terrace, and you can see the great iron struts that support the film-set façade of these fake houses – and you might catch a District line tube train thundering through the 'garden' below.

498

Brush up on anarcho-syndicalism

Hidden down Angel Alley, just off Whitechapel High Street by the Whitechape Art Gallery, you'll find the headquarters of Freedom Press & Bookshop, England's oldest anarchist publishers. Pass the mural of prominent anarcho rabble-rousers and head up the stairs into a cosy den of books and pamphlets that cover history without government, sex without rules and struggle without end. They also sell cool posters and T-shirts.
Freedom Press & Bookshop *Angel Alley, 84B Whitechapel High Street, E1 7QX (7247 9249, www.freedompress.org.uk).*

499

Follow the South London Art Map

SLAM is a handy online guide to all the contemporary art galleries, both mainstream and underground, on the south side of the river. Covering Bankside, Bermondsey, Deptford, Peckham and – the newest area – Greenwich, it's a great way of getting acquainted with an ever-growing community of artists, galleries and interesting locals. You can download a map for each area from the website, or get the phone app. On SLAM Fridays (the last Friday of the month), galleries open their doors for evening viewings,

Chatsworth Road

talks, performances and refreshments. SLAM also arranges walking tours led by a local artist or curator. These give you exclusive access to and knowledge about the spaces you'll be visiting, and usually focus on just one area of the map. Tours are ticketed – and cost exactly a tenner if you book online. *www.southlondonartmap.com.*

500
See the birthplace of a very special relationship

Scientist, diplomat, philosopher, inventor and a Founding Father of the United States, Benjamin Franklin lived behind the doors of this grand, Grade I-listed Craven Street house between 1757 and 1775. Because much of his time here was spent brokering peace between Britain and America on the eve of the American Revolution, it is considered to be the site of London's first de facto US embassy; the birthplace, then, of our enduring transatlantic love-in. It is also Franklin's only home to have survived. The 45-minute tour gives a strong sense of the scale of the man's myriad achievements, as well as the times in which he lived.
Benjamin Franklin House *36 Craven Street, WC2N 5NF (7839 2006, www.benjaminfranklin house.org). £7.*

501
Make chess mates in Holland Park

Most days in Holland Park, chess enthusiasts gather for friendly competition. All ages and abilities are welcome; just turn up at the park's open-air café – with or without your own chess set – and ask to join in. Play usually takes place between 2pm and 9pm in summer, and 2pm and 5pm in winter (when it gets really cold, players move inside the café). Children will also love the park's giant chess set, which is free to use every day.
www.hollandparkchess.com.

502
Join the Carnival of Chariots

Spiritual bliss is the promise of the spectacular annual Carnival of Chariots (www.rathayatra. co.uk), a day-long parade in June organised by the capital's supernal street noiseniks, the International Society for Krishna Consciousness. In celebration of the Hindu god Krishna's return to his home, three brightly decorated wooden chariots bearing waving, toga-clad Hindu deities ('who come out of the temple to freely distribute their loving glances to anyone and everyone') are pulled by hand (quite a feat in itself) by the chanting faithful from Hyde Park to Trafalgar Square. Here, among the street performers and stalls selling crafts and books, a free vegetarian feast (prasadam) is available to all.

503
Get naked – and rich

If you're an exhibitionist, the tendency will pay off at the Bare Facts workshop, designed for aspiring life models. You won't make Jordan-scale money (the fee is £12.50 an hour), but there are worse things you could do with your time… You'll be assessed for basic aptitude and blush factor, and – if you are deemed to be up to scratch (most are) – you can join as a life model, then watch the cash roll in. You get to test your inhibitions on Wednesday evenings at the life drawing classes held at the Islington Arts Factory (2 Parkhurst Road, N7 0SF, 7607 0561, www.islingtonartsfactory.org); should you wish to draw rather than doff your pants, classes cost £10 a session.

504
Take in the views from Severndroog

Hidden away high in Oxleas Wood in Eltham is the 18th-century folly, Severndroog Castle (www. severndroogcastle.org.uk). It's usually closed to the public, but you can sometimes visit during Open House weekend (*see p21*). From the top, on a clear day, there are views out over seven counties.

505-513
Eat more for less

We spill the beans on our super-cheap favourites.

Baozi Inn

The decor – Beijing, circa 1952 – favours kitsch over culture, but the street snacks served at this Chinatown eaterie are the real deal. The eponymous baozi (steamed bread filled with pork or vegetables) are typical of northern China and can be accompanied by a bowl of slightly sweet millet porridge to make up an inexpensive meal.

Otherwise, try the spicy dan dan noodles, which are handmade on the premises daily.
26 Newport Court, WC2H 7JS (7287 6877).

Battersea Pie

This bargain-priced pie and mash house with its bright white tiles and polished marble tables is something of an anomaly among the tourist traps

of Covent Garden Market. Fillings include steak and mushroom with stout, chicken and mushroom, salmon, cod and prawns, and a vegetarian option (butternut squash and goat's cheese, perhaps), with creamy mash or roast potatoes on the side.
28 The Market, WC2E 8RA (7240 9566, www.batterseapiestation.co.uk).

Benito's Hat

London's Tex-Mex eateries are ten a peso, but this mini-chain, its bright lime walls overlooking sturdy wooden tables, serves some of the best burritos in town (£6.90 with guacamole, £6.10 without). A hearty meal in themselves, the soft, floury tortillas come loaded with slow-cooked pork (or chicken, beef or grilled veg), fiery salsa brava, refried or black beans and avocado.
56 Goodge Street, W1T 4NB (7637 3732, www.benitos-hat.com).

Bi Bim Bap Soho

Bright Bi Bim Bap is just the place to try the delicious, filling and cheap Korean national dish of bibimbap – rice and assorted veg, plus meat, seafood or tofu, served in a sizzling stone bowl and often topped with a raw egg. Ten versions are available, from mixed seafood to spicy pork (most cost around £7). There's a branch in Charlotte Street and a takeaway in Leadenhall Market.
11 Greek Street, W1D 4DJ (7287 3434, http://bibimbapsoho.co.uk).

Comptoir Libanais

This chain of Lebanese cafés, serving fresh dishes with zingy citrus and herb flavours, is remarkably affordable. The small meze platter (£8.75) allows you to try several of the warm and cold dips and salads; there are also tagines (most under a tenner).
65 Wigmore Street, W1U 1PZ (7935 1110, www.comptoirlibanais.com).

Hummus Bros

The formula at this canteen-style café/takeaway is to serve creamy, flavoursome houmous as a base for a selection of toppings, which you scoop up with warm, fluffy pitta bread (£4-£9). Options include zingy guacamole with falafel, slow-cooked beef and aubergine, and tabbouleh. Round it all off with a chocolate brownie, baklava or malabi (a milk-based dessert with date honey).
88 Wardour Street, W1F 0TH (7734 1311, www.hbros.co.uk).

Rasa Express

This Keralan curry house is legendary among local office workers. A chicken biryani, for example – comes with chapati, a chickpea curry, a mild mung bean curry, a dry lentil side and a sweet rice pudding – for just £3.50 or £4.
327 Euston Road, NW1 3AD (7387 8974, www.rasarestaurants.com).

Regency Café

This classic caff in Westminster with its black-tiled art deco exterior, brown plastic chairs and Formica-topped tables has been in business since 1946. Choose from lasagne, omelettes, salads, baked potatoes, every conceivable cooked breakfast (the chunky bangers are especially fetching) and own-made specials such as steak pie, served in huge portions, with mugs of tannin-rich tea on the side.
17-19 Regency Street, SW1P 4BY (7821 6596).

Yalla Yalla

Bijou, charming and with walls decorated with photos of old Beirut, this is an informal spot. Near-faultless meze dishes include dense, garlicky houmous, crisp fattoush salad and spicy little sujuk sausages, served in a tomato-based, herby sauce. Grills augment the meze menu.
Green's Court, W1F 0HA (7287 7663, www.yalla-yalla.co.uk).

Yalla Yalla

514-518

Play games in the pub...

The Shipwrights Arms (88 Tooley Street, SE1 2TF, 7378 1486, www.shipwrightsarms.co.uk) really pushes the boat out with its free Wednesday board games night, from about 6pm to 11.30pm, run by the Swiggers Games Club. As well as the usual Monopoly-type offerings, you'll have the opportunity to play the likes of Civilization, Diplomacy, Escape from Colditz, Family Business, History of the World, Settlers of Catan, Antike, Louis XIV, Power Grid, Puerto Rico, Shadows over Camelot and Zepter Von Zavandor.

If you'd rather stick to the classics, though, there are loads of pubs that can oblige. We particularly like the Three Kings of Clerkenwell (7 Clerkenwell Close, EC1R 0DY, 7253 0483), the Big Chill House (257-259 Pentonville Road, N1 9NL, 7427 2540, http://wearebigchill.com) and the Flower Pot (128 Wood Street, E17 3HX, 8520 3600), which all have chess, draughts and dominoes. The Westbourne (101 Westbourne Villas, W2 5ED, 7221 1332, www.thewestbourne.com) ups the ante with backgammon, Cluedo and Monopoly.

519

...or in London's first games café

Based in the heart of Hackney, in a railway arch near Haggerston Overground station, Draughts is London's first board game café. There are over 500 games to choose from, ranging from every family's favourite, Monopoly, to games you're not quite sure should exist, such as Nuns on the Run. Gaming sessions costs £5 per person, and there are also tournaments, themed evenings and workshops. Craft beers and other drinks and snacks are available to maintain energy levels.
Draughts *337 Acton Mews, E8 4EA (www.draughtslondon.com).*

520 Attend the Royal Opera House

Go to the opera – or ballet – for a tenner? Certainly. First off, you can attend the Royal Opera House's excellent weekly series of free lunchtime concerts. Starting at 1pm and always held on the premises (in the splendidly baroque Crush Room, the Linbury Studio Threatre or the Paul Hamlyn Hall), the music ranges from Debussy to Wagner. You must collect your tickets from the box office by 12.40pm, but a limited number can be reserved online a few days in advance. Check the website for the current programme.

Also gratis is the annual Deloitte Ignite festival (www.roh.org.uk/deloitteignite), which brings an inventive and madcap array of street performers, dance events, concerts and workshops, spread throughout the opera house building and the Covent Garden Piazza outside. It's held over three weekend days across September; book a festival day pass online.

You will have to pay for the traditional tea dances, held on monthly Friday afternoons in the airy Paul Hamlyn Hall, but your ticket buys you the opportunity to waltz and cha-cha-cha to the exemplary Royal Opera House Dance Band. No tuition is given (unless one of the friendly dancers takes pity on you), but you do get free tea and biscuits. Wannabe songbirds might want to turn up for the informal group singing – from showtunes to opera in English – on Big Sing Fridays, also in the Paul Hamlyn Hall. Be sure to book ahead for both these events; for forthcoming dates, see the website.

And, perhaps most surprising of all, you can get into a proper, 24-carat opera for less than £10. Honest. Restricted-view seats start from £4, and while you might be perched rather uncomfortably up in the gods, you can console yourself with the thought that some fellow auditors will have paid as much as £195 to see the same glorious show. Tee hee.
Royal Opera House *Bow Street, WC2E 9DD (7304 4000, www.roh.org.uk).*

521 Watch the Great Gorilla Run

This annual charity fundraising event in September gets runners dressed up as gorillas to pound the pavements in an effort to raise awareness and money for the endangered gorillas of Rwanda. The five-mile circular route begins and ends (amusingly) at Mincing Lane, passing Tate Modern and Tower Bridge, and the 'run' is all about having fun, not who's fastest. Participants are encouraged to customise their outfits, so you'll see anything from power-pramming mums with their little monkeys dressed in furry suits to hirsute blondes in bikinis – even the route marshals are in fancy dress. If you want to take part, the registration fee is £58 (including a complimentary gorilla suit and fundraising support), but you can always watch for free and donate a voluntary £10 to the cause. For more details, see www.greatgorillarun.org.

522 *Get bowled over*

Bowling was once synonymous with suburbia: alleys were situated in bland retail parks, the decor comprised blaring arcade machines and sticky floors, and sustenance peaked at the level of chicken nuggets and fluorescent blue 'raspberry' slushies that surely came from no earthly fruit. Even then, the bowling always seemed to take a back seat to birthday parties and boy-girl groups of randy teenagers. No longer.

'Boutique bowling alleys' – darker, less sticky, with bars serving cocktails, and no kids – are flourishing in the US. And now, in the wake of Britain's current cultural obsession with retro Americana, Londoners can score strikes in properly cool venues: Bloomsbury Bowling Lanes (basement of Tavistock Hotel, Bedford Way, WC1H 9EH, 7183 1979, www.bloomsbury bowling.com) and the burgeoning All Star Lanes mini-chain (www.allstarlanes.co.uk), with locations in Bloomsbury (Victoria House, Bloomsbury Place, WC1B 4DA, 7025 2676), Bayswater (6 Porchester Gardens, W2 4DB, 7313 8363), Brick Lane (95 Brick Lane, E1 6QL, 7426 9200) and Stratford (2nd floor, Westfield Stratford City, E20 1ET, 3167 2434). All Star charges per person (£8.95 a game at peak times), while Bloomsbury Bowling Lanes charges per lane (£39 per hour during peak time). Both operations come with a swanky diner and cocktail bar.

Bloomsbury Bowling Lanes

523-539

See the City's architecture on a Sunday stroll...

Sundays, when the traffic is much reduced, are perfect for architectural rambles in the City. Construction has gone into overdrive in recent years and there are interesting buildings popping up all over the place. Here's a jaunt round some of the less obvious new buildings (and a few of the older ones), all of them only a short distance from St Paul's Cathedral.

Start at one of the City's most striking new structures: the very pointed City of London Information Centre beside St Paul's (2007, Make Architects), then head down towards the Millennium Bridge approach. At 101 Queen Victoria Street, you'll find Sheppard Robson's elegant, light-filled Salvation Army HQ (2005), with its 'floating' ground floor supported by splayed, white-painted legs. Next, go east up Queen Victoria Street and cross over to the dark brick Renaissance-style palazzo of Bracken House (1959, Albert Richardson), sitting on its red sandstone plinth at nos.110-112. Turn left beside it to see the Michael Hopkins 1992 revamp that gutted the building. Outrageous vandalism or fabulous update? You decide, but while you are here, take a look at the old Cannon Street frontage with its wonderful zodiac clock.

Cross Cannon Street and look back at the flirty concrete arcades of no.30 (1973-77, Whinney, Son & Austen Hall) – very 1970s, but also suddenly looking very now. Turn north up narrow Bow Lane and then right along Watling Street to the corner of Queen Street. You're now at Peter Foggo's HSBC Building (1999), with its bluish-green chemically created patina and external window grilles. From here, go north up Queen Street, turn left on to Cheapside, right on to Wood Street and stop at Gresham Street. Kohn, Pedersen, Fox's 20 Gresham Street (2008) is on your right, and Norman Foster's 10 Gresham Street (2003) is on your left. Walk further left to see the cantilevered 'handstitched' frontage of Nicholas Grimshaw's 25 Gresham Street (2002), which extends over the trees of a churchyard.

Heading west on Gresham Street, turn right up Noble Street. Take another right on to Oat Lane and straight through the light-grabbing scoop of Norman Foster's 100 Wood Street (2000) to one of the City's most fascinating assemblages of architectural heavy-hitters. In the middle of the road is the surviving tower of Wren's St Alban's church – one of two bombed-out Wren churches in the City that are now private residences – and on the east side of Wood Street is McMorran & Whitby's police station (1966), a compelling pale-stone riff on a Renaissance palazzo (compare with Bracken House). Beside Foster's building is Richard Rogers' 88 Wood Street (2000), while across the road is the back of Eric Parry's coolly elegant 5 Aldermanbury Square (2007), with its silvery external steel frame and classical entasis tapering towards the roof. The street ends with the very 1980s, postmodern bombast of Terry Farrell's Alban Gate (1992) at 125 London Wall.

Cut through Parry's building to see its Aldermanbury Square frontage, then return by continuing along the side of 88 Wood Street, allowing you to see the full extent of Rogers' airy masterpiece, sheathed in glittering Saint-Gobain glass. Now, you get a splendid view of yet another Foster building: curvy, deco-ish 1 London Wall (2003). Turn left down Noble Street again and along Foster Lane, ending at Michael Aukett's 150 Cheapside (2008) and Jean Nouvel's huge One New Change (2010).

540

...then see the Lloyd's building lit up at night

Time your day tour of the City's buildings carefully so that you're heading east along Cornhill to 1 Lime Street just as the streetlights are coming on. The Lloyd's of London building is still the City's best-known example of high-tech architecture, its commercial and industrial aesthetics combined by Richard Rogers to create what is arguably one of the most significant British buildings constructed since World War II. Mocked on completion, the 'inside out' building still manages to outclass much of its more recent, much-vaunted competition. You can usually see the inside of the building during Open House weekend (see p21), though you'll have to arrive early and expect to queue.

Lloyd's of London *1 Lime Street, EC3M 7HA (7327 6586, www.lloyds.com).*

541

Automate
Automate
**Operate the
nutty slot machines
of Novelty
Automation
(1A Princeton
Street, WC1R 4AX,
http://novelty-
automation.com),**
*most of which have been lovingly crafted by Tim
Hunkin. Admission free; tokens £1 each.*

542

Experience peace and reconciliation at St Ethelburga's

A place for people of all faiths and none, St Ethelburga's Centre for Reconciliation and Peace is a tiny spiritual oasis in the heart of the City. Step through an unassuming medieval door on Bishopsgate and you'll find yourself in an interfaith prayer tent, before the entrance to the building proper. A church dedicated to St Ethelburga stood here for nearly 800 years before it was destroyed by an IRA bomb in 1993. Rebuilt as a centre for reconciliation and peace – it is no longer a parish church – it hosts lectures and discussion evenings on conflict and faith, as well as concerts ranging from flamenco to Afro-Caribbean music, and nights of African storytelling. Past sessions have brought together dissidents and secret police from South Africa; another looked at violence and the sacred in film. And if it's old-fashioned spirituality you're after (or simply a break from urban life), there are several free weekly meditation sessions, including one every Tuesday lunchtime.
St Ethelburga's Centre for Reconciliation and Peace *78 Bishopsgate, EC2N 4AG (7496 1610, www.stethelburgas.org).*

543 *Don't get Court!*

Marlborough Street Magistrates Court, opposite the northern end of Carnaby Street, was once infamous for cases involving unfortunate notables such as Oscar Wilde, Christine Keeler and the *International Times* obscenity defendants. It was drugs offences that saw the Rolling Stones, Johnny Rotten and Lionel Bart kept here under lock and key, while John Lennon was pulled up for exhibiting a little too much of Yoko Ono in his sketches on show at the London Art Gallery. Now, at the Courthouse Hotel, you can enjoy Indian fusion food in Number One Court, or a drink in the cells – complete with hard bunk, 'ice-bucket' lav and warden's peephole in the lead door.
Courthouse Doubletree Hotel *19-21 Great Marlborough Street, W1F 7HL (7297 5555, www.courthouse-hotel.com).*

544

Hear classics in the City's halls

The City of London Festival (7796 4949, www.colf.org) is a well-established favourite, both for music fans and those intrigued by the Square Mile's many historic buildings. A huge range of concerts takes place from late June to early July each year, in some of the finest churches and halls in the Square Mile. While concerts in the grander venues (among them St Paul's Cathedral) are likely to be ticketed, many of those held in the City's atmospheric churches and livery halls are absolutely free. The programme is mostly traditional classical music, but there are also more unusual offerings from the worlds of jazz, dance, visual art, literature and theatre.

545

Visit the address Richard Rogers must wish he could have

One Hyde Park – the name of Rogers Stirk Harbour & Partners' super-prime, exquisitely located block of duplex flats – is pretty impressive, but how much do you think the architect would have paid to get his hands on No.1 London instead? You and those Russian oligarch flat owners have equal rights to visit the latter: stump up £8.30 and step in. Right on Hyde Park Corner, Apsley House was called No.1 London back when Kensington was still a village, since it was the first building you reached on the way into the city. For more than three decades, it was the Duke of Wellington's residence (a Goya portrait of the Iron Duke is among the treasures on display), and parts of the building – strictly out of bounds to the public – are occupied by his descendants to this day.
Apsley House *149 Piccadilly, W1J 7NT (7499 5676, www.english-heritage.org.uk).*

546
Get slammed, the literary way

You think you know all about book readings? The silences, the shuffling feet and smothered coughs, the pitiful bribe of precisely two wineboxes – one lukewarm white and one ice-cold red. Well, you've clearly never been to Book Slam (www.bookslam. com). This is a monthly musical-literary club night for which you're best advised to book tickets well in advance. Still organised by co-founder Patrick Neate – now with Elliot Jack and Bernie Critchley – it rotates between the Tabernacle (35 Powis Square, W11 2AY, 7221 9700) and Clapham Grand (21-25 St John's Hill, SW11 1TT, 7223 6523). Tickets are £6-£8 in advance (more on the door), for which meagre sum you might get lucky and see authors such as Zadie Smith, Will Self or Dave Eggers, supported by musicians such as Moss Project or Plan B.

547
Get near to the Neolithic

Ask most East Enders if it is possible to walk the ramparts of an Iron Age hill fort in their manor, and they'd most likely suggest you were having a proper larf. Head out to Epping Forest on the further reaches of the Central line, though, and you'll find two of them – the huge wooded circles of Ambresbury Banks and Loughton Camp. A natural spring rises in the former, and both can be cut off by their broad moats in rainy weather. An awesome discovery, half an hour from Oxford Street. Visit www.eppingforestdc.gov.uk for details of how to get to them.

548
Add a string to your bow at the Royal Academy of Music

Here, you can inspect hundreds of different musical instruments, including over 200 violins and a number of pianos dating from the early 19th century, and see temporary exhibitions.
Royal Academy of Music *Marylebone Road, NW1 5HT (7873 7373, www.ram.ac.uk/museum). Free.*

549

Experience dance

Dance Umbrella is a leading international dance festival, featuring a range of events (many of them free) in unusual spaces. **Dance Umbrella** *7407 1200, www.dance umbrella.co.uk.*

550

Look up at Gresham's grasshopper

Spend less time staring at the pavement – look up! You'll be endlessly rewarded. We're particularly fond of the stone relief grasshopper at the top corner of the Royal Exchange, EC3. It's the family symbol of Thomas Gresham, pioneering Tudor financier, sometime arms smuggler and founder of the original version of this building. Another (golden) grasshopper makes the Exchange's weathervane, and a third hangs from a wall on nearby Lombard Street.

551

Drink vodka in a Polish bar

More often than not, bars in the West End merely nod towards a theme. But Bar Polski (1 Little Turnstile Street, WC1V 7DX, 7831 9679) is the real deal. Polish sausages, bigos, pierogis and Polish sweetmeats are available all day, but by the evening all anyone's seriously interested in are the vodkas. Divided into 'dry and interesting', 'clean and clear', 'kosher' and 'nice and sweet' (try the Lancut rose petal) – they're here by the vatload. Most cost around £3 a shot.

552 *Visit Dulwich Picture Gallery*

Sir John Soane's neoclassical, purpose-built art gallery (the first of its kind) has been described as the most beautiful art gallery in the world, but its contents are worth a look too: you'll find work by Rubens, Van Dyck, Rembrandt, Gainsborough, Hogarth, Raphael, Canaletto and Reynolds, among others. It's a fiver's worth of admission very well spent.

Dulwich Picture Gallery *Gallery Road, SE21 7AD (8693 5254, www.dulwichpicturegallery.org.uk).*

553 *Admire an original Crapper*

You can see the Methodist founder John Wesley's nightcap, preaching gown and personal experimental electric-shock machine in his austere home, but if you head downstairs (to the right), you'll see some of the finest public toilets in London, built in 1899 by Sir Thomas Crapper. Some parts are now replicas, but the cisterns are original.

John Wesley's House & Museum of Methodism *Wesley's Chapel, 49 City Road, EC1Y 1AU (7253 2262, www.wesleyschapel.org.uk).*

Dulwich Picture Gallery

A few of my favourite things

554-562

Des Yankson, Actor

I'm not a very good swimmer, but in order to progress you have to put in time at the pool. And there is nowhere finer than the London Aquatics Centre in the Queen Elizabeth Olympic Park (E20 2ZQ, 8536 3150, http://londonaquaticscentre.org). The facilities are amazing and it costs only £4.50 for a swim.

For an actor and film buff, the Mediatheque at the BFI Southbank (Belvedere Road, SE1 8XT, 7255 1444, www.bfi.org.uk) is a brilliant resource. It is a trove of the best of British, from TV (such as *Ab Fab* and *EastEnders*) to factual (1926's *After the Blizzard*) to cinematic classics (*The Long Good Friday*).

Postman's Park is a small park in the City, off a street called Little Britain (which the TV show was named after), which contains the Victorian Memorial to Heroic Self Sacrifice – a wall of ceramic tablets dedicated to ordinary people who died saving the lives of others. As with most thing these days, there's now an app, The Everyday Heroes of Postman's Park, detailing the lives of those commemorated. It's also a lovely spot for lunch.

When I was younger, we used to drive across town regularly and my mum would always take a very scenic route. I was often gazing out the window, making up stories in my head, and I would always glimpse the ruined church and garden of St Dunstan in the East (St Dunstan's Hill, EC3R 5DD) as we drove down Lower Thames Street. When I finally got there in person, it was definitely better than all the the the stories I'd concocted. A friend called Ellen once took me and Annabel (Williamson, a theatre producer and lawyer) around the Houses of Parliament (SW1A 0AA, 7219 4114, www.parliament.uk/visiting), as neither of us had been. It was brilliant: the grandeur, the ridiculous artworks, the different areas depicted by differing colour schemes – green for the Commons, red for the Lords, blue for royalty.

Leicester Square is still where most of the UK's film premières happen. It's also the place to go if you want to experience ice-cream heaven – at the Häagen-Dazs café (14 Leicester Square, WC2H 7NG, 7287 9577, https://haagen-dazs.co.uk). I only ever go with my friend Mandy from York; we always decide what we want beforehand, so that there's more time to enjoy the goodness and less time standing in front of their extensive menu in shocked awe.

By day, the fifth-floor balcony at the Royal Festival Hall (Belvedere Road, SE1 8XX, www.southbankcentre.co.uk) is heaven for anyone with a laptop to sit, read, type, talk, learn, chat and generally put the world to rights. By night, it's a great escape from the busy South Bank – and the view is excellent. You can get drinks and take them out on the balcony and pretend that all you survey is actually your domain.

Borough Market has some of the best food producers and vendors in London, including the Bread Ahead bakery (3 Cathedral Street, SE1 9DE, 7407 7853, www.bread ahead.com). Their deliciously moreish doughnuts often sell out within an hour of being put out fresh from the oven. My faves are the brilliant vanilla cream or the insane crème caramel with a piece of honeycomb sticking out of it.

I went on a date to the Worship Street Whistling Shop (63 Worship Street, EC2A 2DU, 7247 0015, www.whistlingshop.com) in Shoreditch. It was raining and it was a back-up as the first place we tried was busy. She was unimpressed by the small doorway, steep stairs (she was in heels) and dark interior. But the olde-worlde Victorian charm (waistcoated bar staff, a private room based around a bathtub) and inventive drinks were a cracking start to the night. I'm not sure if it was the kookiness of the place or the tastiness of the cocktails, but we're still together, so it's all good in my book!

Walk the Ring

Alex Dudok de Wit **discovers the joys of London's long-distance orbital footpath.**

Halfway between the Circle Line and the M25, the Capital Ring traces its course through the leafiest suburbs of London. Over 78 miles, this orbital walking trail takes in parks, forests, cemeteries, docklands and residential streets, occasionally running into an obstacle, such as a canal or City Airport. The route was dreamed up by ramblers in 1990; today, it's fully signposted and supported by Transport for London. Walking its length brings home both the sheer scale of the capital and the abundance of greenery nestled among its roads and buildings.

I don't yet know any of this when I happen upon one of the Ring's trademark lime-green signposts in Highgate. Curious, I follow it, and find myself on the Parkland Walk: once a railway line, now a footpath popular with dog owners. One of the most appealing features of the Capital Ring is the way it moves between stretches of bucolic tranquillity and busy, populated areas. Before long, I'm in Clissold Park where I'm greeted with a Richard Curtis vision of London:

mums pushing prams and eating ciabattas in the sunshine. As I stroll into Stoke Newington, the mums give way first to Hasidic Jews, then to latte-toting hipsters, who will be my company until Stratford. The terrain levels out into Hackney Marsh and the route joins the River Lea. Jostling with cyclists on the towpath, I look ahead to the Olympic Park, which rudely imposed itself on the Ring a decade ago. Now the trail diverts awkwardly around the site before finding its groove again on an elevated walkway near Plaistow. I spot the byzantine turrets of Joseph Bazalgette's Abbey Mills Pumping Station, a relic of an era when sewage was dignified with sublime architecture. In one day, I've seen more of London than I would in an average year.

Keen to discover more, the following week I resume my walk from Plaistow tube. The flatlands between here and the Thames make for the weirdest stretch of the Ring. Signposts lead me through post-industrial districts as bland as they are fancifully named ('Cyprus'? Not quite), but they can't cope with the complex network of docks that surrounds City Airport, and I'm forced to use the map I've downloaded on my phone to find the entrance to the ominously lit Woolwich Foot Tunnel, which takes me beneath the river.

Starting off again from Woolwich, I'm now beyond the reaches of the tube and therefore off the average Londoner's mental map. It's their loss: this south-eastern leg features some wonderfully wild landscapes, especially among the dense copses and wide meadows of the ancient Oxleas Wood. Soon, the trees yield to manicured gardens, and rows of grand mock-Tudor houses prepare me for the real deal: Eltham Palace, childhood home of Henry VIII, though only the Great Hall remains of the building that Henry knew.

I tackle the next couple of legs over a stormy autumn weekend. For two dozen miles, I wend my way through quiet neighbourhoods and familiar Sunday afternoon destinations: Crystal Palace, Wimbledon Common, Richmond Park. Inclement weather has turned the grasslands into bogs; by the time I reach Richmond Bridge, I'm muddy up to my knees. Even the sumptuous scenery along the riverbank at Isleworth isn't enough to lift my spirits. Around Brentford, the heavens open. I've been under the weather for a while, but now I find myself harassed by it, as driving rain turns me into a sodden mass. Cue a bleak stretch along the Grand Union Canal and up to the River Brent. Intrepid walkers and homesick Brummies can pursue the canal all the way to Birmingham; I continue north towards Greenford.

The final section of the Ring, which runs through the hilly suburbia of north-west London, is pretty sparse and short on landmarks. But it has its moments: St Mary's church in Harrow, where Byron used to lounge around composing verse; and Brunel's mighty Wharncliffe Viaduct, the view from which Queen Victoria was said to admire (for once, I agree with her). It is, in a way, the most memorable leg of my journey, summing up what the Capital Ring is about: seeing the most beautiful parts of London you'd never otherwise visit. As I hobble up to Highgate station, cursing the calluses on my toes, I feel that bit better acquainted with my city.

Seven stages of the Capital Ring

The terrain is mostly flat and accessible, though walking boots are advised. The trail is officially divided into 15 legs, but you can walk it in seven (distances are approximate).

For maps, see www.tfl.gov.uk/modes/walking/capital-ring.

North-east London
Start: East Finchley tube
Finish: Hackney Wick Overground
Distance: 11 miles

East London
Start: Hackney Wick Overground
Finish: Woolwich Arsenal DLR
Distance: 9 miles

South-east London
Start: Woolwich Arsenal DLR
Finish: Grove Park rail
Distance: 11 miles

South London
Start: Grove Park rail
Finish: Streatham Common rail
Distance: 12.5 miles

South-west London
Start: Streatham Common rail
Finish: Richmond tube/Overground/rail
Distance: 12.5 miles

West London
Start: Richmond tube/Overground/rail
Finish: Sudbury Hill tube
Distance: 12.5 miles

North-west London
Start: Sudbury Hill tube
Finish: East Finchley tube
Distance: 13.5 miles

Woolwich Foot Tunnel

564

Search for the original Chinatown

Stepping off the DLR at Westferry, where once hundreds of ships' masts towered over fortified docks, there's nothing left on Limehouse Causeway to suggest the maze of alleyways, Chinese cafés and grocers that clustered here from the 1880s to the 1930s. Nothing to suggest the exotic hubbub of real docklands, the whiff of opium smoked openly, the excitement of the *puck-apu* numbers racket or the gambling den at Ah Tack's Lodging House – all conjured up by the fiction of Conan-Doyle and Sax 'Fu Manchu' Rohmer. Even Dorian Gray dropped by E14 for his opium.

Well – almost nothing. A tin dragon sculpture at the end of Mandarin Street hints at what used to be, as does Ming Street, now lined with 1960s blocks instead of the Confucian temple and local Tong HQ – all of which were part of the slums that were razed in 1934.

Among the ships chandlers and mastmakers, the Merchant Navy Officers' Club and Dock Constables' houses – traces of real docklands, all recycled as flats – Amoy Place was once the epicentre of those 'kind of Limehouse Chinese Laundry Blues.' The old wharves (and new 'gated communities') of riverside Narrow Street were once Fu Manchu's lair – 'the river was his highway, his line of communication along which he moved his mysterious forces.' Now, the street houses a Gordon Ramsay pub, the Narrow.

The decline in the docks, from the 1930s onwards, meant the dwindling of the Chinese population of the area. At Commercial Road is the striking British & Foreign Sailors' Hostel (or 'Sailor's Palace'), one window ablaze with the telltale pictograms of the Chinese Association of Tower Hamlets. Opposite, the Star of the East pub (805A Commercial Road), with its original gaslights outside, is a hulking Victorian Gothic take on a Chinese temple. At the end of Canton Street lies the Chinese Sunday School & Chun Yee Society, with an old people's drop-in centre in the basement. At last, somewhere where you might find people with actual memories of London's original Chinatown.

There's lots more information on the website http://limehousechinatown.org.

565 *Pitch and putt near Richmond Park*

Just adjacent to the one-time regal hunting grounds of Richmond Park lie the more modern delights of Palewell Common Pitch & Putt Golf Course. A gentler and cheaper alternative to the capital's 18-hole options, it's more about honing your skills and enjoying a quick round than thrashing 3-woods and clomping off down the fairway. It boasts pretty surrounds too – the nine holes are spread either side of babbling Beverley Brook – and the greens are well maintained. Coaching sessions are also offered; ask at the golf kiosk, which is staffed daily in summer. In short, it's the kind of place you can have a swing without worrying about disdainful eyes. If golf doesn't appeal, Palewell Common also has a pétanque pitch (free to use), four tennis courts (£8 per hour) and plenty of green open space in which to kick a football around or throw a frisbee.

Palewell Common Pitch & Putt Golf Course
Palewell Common, SW14 8RE (8876 7005).
£5 for 9 holes.

566 *Test Albert Bridge*

'All troops must break step when marching over this bridge', says the sign on the end of Albert Bridge, but you could always plan a meet up with a battalion of friends and see what happens if you don't.

567
Get digging

Annie Dare digs for victory with some of the capital's community gardening projects.

This meeting of the Transition Town's (TT, www.transitionnetwork.org) Belsize Park branch has something of the Women's Institute about it. Twenty-two of us sit in a circle in a dimly lit room in a local library; there's a marked preponderance of ladies in cardies and practical heels, and we're knitting a (somewhat symbolic) scarf together. And then there's the baking: side tables groan with home-made fare. Yet the ambition here is somewhat loftier than the staging of a village fête.

TT's goal is to inspire local communities to prepare for the end of the 'Oil Age', and at its heart is 'local resilience' – in other words, community cohesion and sustainable environmental practice, particularly with

regard to food and energy use (hence tonight's hand-fired hurricane lamps, to spare the National Grid a few gigawatts). It may sound like a radical fringe, but there are now hundreds of Transition Towns worldwide, with lots in London, including Brixton, Kingston and Belsize Park.

Although there is some hand wringing about the urgent need to change Londoners' shopping habits and convince us all to eat and waste less – at which point those who lived through rationing 'tsk' approvingly – by and large, the group seems optimistic and avoids being overly earnest. There's home-grown hooch to wash down the home-made cakes and jams, and a local gent waxes wonderfully lyrical about the history of fruit trees. Nor is it all 'knit-one, purl-one' in the Transition movement: the Brixton branch's festive shindig was at a bar.

Tonight's main aim is to establish a local food-growing strategy, so we're scoping out possible plots that we can take over within the borough: housing association plots, school yards, derelict gardens and even cemeteries are the prime contenders – and World War II survivors suggest we arm-twist the Corporation of London into allowing us to turn Hampstead Heath back into vegetable plots, as happened during the 1940s Dig for Victory campaign.

Over the past few years, growing your own reached a tipping point, and actually became cool. Cool – and cheap. It looks likely that the food-growing phenomenon will continue to expand at grassroots level too. Lucie Stephens, head of co-production at the left-wing thinktank the New Economics Foundation (NEF), sees the Transition Town movement and community food-cultivation schemes across London as symptoms of a larger trend: that of local communities making positive, non-financial-based interventions to prevent social breakdown. She cites Rushey Green in Catford, where a local doctor's surgery began prescribing voluntary work and community involvement to patients suffering from poor mental health largely caused by isolation.

Whatever their reasons for getting involved, it seems that Londoners are queuing up to get dirt under their fingernails. Dozens turn up for bimonthly conservation digs set up by the Conservation Volunteers (www.tcv.org.uk), Britain's largest practical conservation charity. TCV also runs the Green Gyms in London (*see p92*), which rebranded gardening as a sport every bit as legitimate as pilates or ab crunching. There's no membership fee, and you can't help feeling that brandishing shears in a park, with dog walkers and joggers beaming at you as you work, certainly beats a session on the running machine.

568

Join a flash mob

Have you ever stumbled across a mass pillowfight outside Tate Modern or a rabble dancing like maniacs in the middle of a railway station? Welcome to the surreal world of the flash mob. First staged in 2003 in New York, when 100 people gathered, for no apparent reason, around an expensive rug at Macy's department store, flash mobs are bizarre spectacles that involve a crowd of strangers assembling briefly in a public space and performing some strange ritual (the second-ever flash mob consisted of 200 people suddenly bursting into applause for 15 seconds in the lobby of the Hyatt hotel).

They may seem like a relic of the early noughties, but London's mobs continue, coming up with new and intriguing spins on the format. Public pillowfights became particularly popular for a while and then waterfights were all the rage. To find out about the next weird happening, visit the website.
www.flashmob.co.uk.

569

See a new piece of architecture every year at the Serpentine Pavilion

With its consistently acclaimed and thought-provoking exhibitions, the Serpentine Gallery has long been a great pit stop on a leisurely stroll around Hyde Park. But since 2000, there's been even more to entice you here each summer. Designed by a host of high-profile architects, the gallery's temporary summer pavilion is now one of the most anticipated annual events in the architectural calendar. Past designers have included Frank Gehry, Rem Koolhas, Zaha Hadid and Oscar Niemeyer.

Serpentine Gallery *Kensington Gardens, near Albert Memorial, W2 3XA (7402 6075, www.serpentinegallery.org).*

570-579 Investigate ten of London's lesser-known squares

Bonnington Square, SW8

Incorporating a 'Pleasure Garden' designed by local residents, this bohemian pocket of Vauxhall is a community hub, complete with a vegetarian restaurant (*see p15*) operating a chef-rotation system and hosting weekly vegan nights. An inexplicable wooden rowing boat suspended above the entrance welcomes visitors into what is an overgrown jungle of a square.

Cabot Square, E14

Although Canada Square, with Ron Arad's impressive *Big Blue* sculpture as its centrepiece, has its advocates, we're more taken with neighbouring Cabot Square. Located to the west of Canary Wharf tower, it has a broad, calm fountain, as well as views over the docks on either side. Wander south to see the beautifully manicured Japanese-style garden by the Jubilee line exit from Canary Wharf station.

Cleaver Square, SE11

Just off Kennington Park Road, this quiet residential square was beautifully restored using Lottery money. It's a peaceful place for a game of pétanque or to sup a beer.

Cloudesley Square, N1

Holy Trinity Church, which sits in the middle of this square, was built by Charles Barry in 1828 and is said to be an imitation of King's College Chapel in Cambridge. The diminutive square (built in 1826) was the earliest of the Barnsbury squares, all of which boast late Georgian and early Victorian architecture.

Edwardes Square, W8

Built by Louis Changeur in the early 19th century, this superb garden square in Kensington features a Greek Revival-style gardener's lodge, a rose pergola and a croquet lawn. It's normally closed to the public, so visit on the annual Open Garden Squares Weekend (*see p134*).

Fitzroy Square, W1

Designed by Robert Adam in 1793, Fitzroy Square was built in two stages: the first, from 1793 to 1798,

saw the construction of the east side (a unified Portland stone palazzo of individual houses); the second produced the stucco-fronted north and west sides. Former residents include George Bernard Shaw, Virginia Woolf and Lord Salisbury.

Gordon Square, WC1

A verdant alternative to neighbouring Russell and Bloomsbury squares, this quiet space is frequented by students from the surrounding colleges intent on loafing or exerting themselves with some light Frisbee action. One of Virginia Woolf's residences (the blue plaque is to be found at nearby Fitzroy Square), Gordon Square was also the epicentre of the Bloomsbury Group's literary activities.

Hanover Square, W1

Overlooked by the art deco presence of Vogue House, this shady spot behind Oxford Street unites fashionistas, shoppers and workmen looking for an impromptu lunchtime picnic spot – though at the time of writing, Crossrail was the dominant presence on the square. St George's, an 18th-century church to the south of the square, was once the most fashionable place in town to exchange your vows: George Eliot and Teddy Roosevelt were both married here.

Hoxton Square, N1

The square that spawned a thousand haircuts. Since the 1990s, this nocturnal green has been well known for its fashionable bars, clubs and contemporary art galleries. But the area's rambunctiousness was already being felt several centuries earlier: in 1598, playwright Ben Jonson killed actor Gabriel Spencer in a duel here, narrowly escaping a public hanging.

Lincoln's Inn Fields, WC2

This 17th-century square, laid out by Inigo Jones, is now a favourite spot for lunching lawyers from the Inns of Court. As well as the lawns, there are trees and tennis courts, in an area that's almost big enough to be considered a park. Sir John Soane's Museum (*see p26*) and the Royal College of Surgeons (*see p62*) face off across the greenery.

Fitzroy Square

580-583

Revisit Clerkenwell's radical roots

Now a trendily gentrified enclave for London's creative industries, Clerkenwell has travelled far from its time as a hotbed of radicalism. But much survives from the area's revolutionary heyday and you can still trace the footsteps of its radicals, rebels and reformers.

From the 18th century, the skilled artisans who lived and worked in the area met to discuss politics and far-reaching ideas of social justice in the coffee houses and inns around Clerkenwell Green, giving rise to the term 'Clerkenwell Radical'. The green became the focal point for demonstrations and mass meetings – such as that welcoming the Tolpuddle Martyrs (agricultural labourers transported to Australia for forming a trade union) on their return to Britain in 1836, after being pardoned.

Under the beady eye of the Old Court House on the green stands the Marx Memorial Library. It once housed a coffee house where radical organisations such as Karl Marx's International Working Men's Association met, and William Morris and Eleanor Marx addressed crowds from the building. In 1902-03, Lenin edited his revolutionary journal *Iskra* (*The Spark*) here in an office that is still preserved.

One of Lenin's favourite watering-holes was the nearby Crown Tavern, and an apocryphal story lingers that he met Stalin there for a quiet pint in 1903.

The struggles of Irish Nationalism came to London in 1867 at the House of Detention on Clerkenwell Close when a huge explosion – an attempt to free two jailed members of the Irish Republican Brotherhood (or Fenians) – killed six and injured 40, marking the diminution of working-class support for the Irish cause.

By the 1930s, the area, with its communist councillors and radical health programme, had become known as the People's Republic of Finsbury. You can see a legacy of this in one of London's finest modernist buildings, the Finsbury Health Centre (1935-38) on Pine Street, designed by Berthold Lubetkin and the Tecton architecture practice.

584 Check out the Mighty Wurlitzer

This Brentford-based collection of melodic curios provides a fascinating history of pre-electronic musical gadgetry and houses one of the largest collections of automated instruments in the world. Exhibits include ghostly self-playing pianolas, tiny Swiss musical boxes and the museum's grand centrepiece: the majestic 'Mighty Wurlitzer', which emerges from the orchestra pit of the 230-seat concert hall much as it once did in a 1930s picture house. Check the website for upcoming concerts.
Musical Museum *399 High Street, Brentford, TW8 0DU (8560 8108, www.musicalmuseum.co.uk).*

585 Celebrate Record Store Day

This annual celebration of independent record shops takes place in mid April across the UK, but the lion's share of the fun happens around London. Musos love the limited-edition vinyls and CDs sold in participating shops, but there's plenty of free events too, as the city turns into a hive of audio activity for the day. Bands and DJs perform in record shops, and various markets, pop-up bars and art exhibitions appear, as well as parties and club nights for beat-freaks. Berwick Street in Soho – a hub of London record shops – also puts on a free street festival with big-name bands playing short sets. You'll have forgotten what a digital download is by the end of the day.
www.recordstoreday.co.uk.

586

Pick up Time Out magazine

Time Out weekly magazine is completely free, and packed full of brilliant information about what to do, where to go and how to have fun in London. It's available on Tuesday mornings, distributed for free outside tube and train stations across the city. Don't miss it!

587 *Take a peek into Hell*

If you catch a double-decker bus on St James's, you can take a peek into Hell, the first-floor gaming room of aristocratic club White's (37-38 St James's Street, SW1) – where gauntlets were once thrown down for dawn duels and vast fortunes have been won and lost.

588 *Badger a beadle in the Burlington Arcade*

The Regency-era Burlington Arcade (www. burlington-arcade.co.uk) off Piccadilly is England's longest covered shopping street, Britain's first ever shopping arcade and the precursor of many similar oases of cashmere, jewellery and other classy craftsmanship throughout Europe. Upscale window-shopping is the order of the day here – that, and sneaking a peek at the top-hatted beadles, aka Georgian security guards.

589 *Explore Lesnes Abbey*

The ruins of Lesnes Abbey are an unexpected find in suburban south-east London, overshadowed as they are by tower blocks and beside a busy main road. The Abbey was founded in 1178 by Richard de Luci, a supporter of Henry II, in penance for the murder of Archbishop Thomas à Becket in 1170. A small Augustian foundation, after passing through various private hands it was bequeathed in the 17th century to Christ's Hospital, which sold it in 1930 to the London County Council. Nowadays, the Abbey's scant ruins are surrounded by attractive gardens, featuring a 17th-century mulberry tree, as well as the surprisingly extensive Lesnes Abbey Wood. Particularly delightful in spring, when the daffs and bluebells are in bloom, it's worth a visit at any time of year for its even more ancient fossil bed – it's not unusual to unearth 50-million-year-old shark's teeth and rare seashells from the Eocene period.

Lesnes Abbey *Abbey Road, Belvedere, Kent (8303 7777, www.bexley.gov.uk).*

590 *Revisit iconic scenes from London movies*

Starting out with a classic establishing shot, Lewis Gilbert's *Alfie* takes some beating for an iconic opening scene. The Tower of London is, of course, still a tourist attraction, and the Thames-side stretch overlooking the moat and ramparts is still a focus for buskers, artists, tat-floggers and thousands of happy snappers – if not quite Michael Caine's tourist photo scam.

David Lynch's *The Elephant Man* also used real London buildings to brilliant effect: squint up into the aerial walkways on a grey winter's day and it's almost possible to see Butler's Wharf on Shad Thames as the grim Dickensian world through which John Hurt shuffles. Likewise the façade of John Merrick's sanctuary, the Royal London Hospital on Whitechapel Road. Another 'slice of life' location well worth a visit is *Quadrophenia*'s pie and mash shop at the Goldhawk Road end of Shepherd's Bush Market, where mod Jimmy (Phil Daniels) meets greaser Kevin (Ray Winstone).

There's no more atmospheric a London film than Antonioni's *Blow Up*, and Maryon Park in Charlton is virtually unchanged since 1966, when the Italian director happened across the strange landscape of Cox's Mount and immediately moved the focus of his swinging London film away from the West End.

Another south-east London location associated with surreal violence is the notorious Thamesmead South estate, site of the slo-mo slicing 'tolchock' action between Alex and his three 'droogs' in Stanley Kubrick's *A Clockwork Orange*. Binsey Walk is the path in question, running at the side of the concrete Southmere Lake. Even four decades on, the walkways and tower blocks of the planners' dream have a faintly futuristic – and grim – feel about them.

Finally, no round-up of London film violence would be complete without a mention of *The Long Good Friday*. Sadly, there's no chance of visiting the Lion & Unicorn pub, because

it was built temporarily on the Wapping riverfront just along from the Town of Ramsgate pub (*see p268*). But the interior of St Patrick's Church on nearby Greenbank was used when gangster Bob Hoskins took his old mum to church, and the churchyard of St George in the East was where his Rolls-Royce got blown up. (Interestingly, the derelict location of the future Canary Wharf is visible when Hoskins takes to the Thames to view his proposed marina development.)

Grounds for a grand, all-encompassing conspiracy theory may be found in the fact that the Great Hall of Freemasons Hall (*see p21*), in Covent Garden was used as a ringer for the Kremlin in *From Russia With Love*. And there's yet more dastardly intrigue to be had at the Salisbury pub (*see p269*) in the heart of Theatreland on St Martin's Lane. It wouldn't be giving too much away to say that in the landmark 1961 gay thriller *Victim*, Dirk Bogarde is blackmailed over his sexuality – or that the true, scene-stealing star of the film is the pub itself, all glancing mirrors and art nouveau table lamps.

And finally to music. American documentary-maker DA Pennebaker ushered in a whole new era with the groundbreaking sequence he filmed for the opening of *Don't Look Back*, in which Bob Dylan flicks though cue cards scrawled with the lyrics of *Subterranean Homesick Blues*. It was a '60s high – ultra-cool and oft-copied – and these first shots of the coming video age were filmed, in 1965, in an alleyway called Savoy Steps, behind the Savoy hotel on the Strand.

It took Nic Roeg and Donald Cammell to signal the end of the '60s dream in *Performance*, in which Mick Jagger got to frolic with naked, drugged-up chicks, perform the cracking non-Stones tune *Memo to Turner* and swap personalities with psychotic hoodlum James Fox. It all happened (or was it just a bad trip?) behind the classical portico of 25 Powis Square, off the Portobello Road in Notting Hill.

591 Fill up a flagon of local ale

Hop Burns & Black on East Dulwich Road sells
three things: beer, hot sauce and vinyl, with the
former available to carry out in one-litre flagons
(what similar operations call a 'growler',
inevitably with a bit of puerile nudge-winkery).
Thanks to a nifty counter-pressure filling
machine, the grog stays fresh for weeks –
although with the breweries on offer including
London's finest, US legends and Kiwi trailblazers
such as Yeastie Boys, you'll do well not to see it off
in a single sitting. Flagons cost £6.50-£8, plus £3
bottle deposit.
Hop Burns & Black *38 East Dulwich Road, SE22
9AX (7450 0284, www.hopburnsblack.co.uk).*

592 Horse around with avant-gardists...

Since 1993, a former Horse Hospital (Horse
Hospital Colonnade, WC1N 1HX, 7833 3644,
www.thehorsehospital.com) near Bloomsbury's
Brunswick Square has been staging esoteric
arts events that range from rare film screenings
to gigs, from left-field theatre to seances and
strange pagan celebrations. Lots of the events
are free, and few – if any – cost more than a tenner.

593 ...or hang out at the Design Museum

For a former banana warehouse, the Design
Museum has come a long way – most of it
upwards. Conran & Partners' conversion was
described by one architecture critic in 1989 as
'cool and logical, a counterblast to the feverish and
feeble sub-vernacular styling which is almost de
rigueur in Docklands.' Well, quite our thoughts
exactly. Even the toilets are classy, thanks to
Australian design star Marc Newson. And it's
hardly necessary to look round the exhibits to
enjoy the place: have a coffee in the café and look
out over the river and Tower Bridge. But be aware
there's a time limit – in late 2016, the Design
Museum moves to the ex-Commonwealth
Institute building in west London.
Design Museum *28 Shad Thames, SE1 2YD
(7403 6933, www.designmuseum.org).*

594 *Call in at Dover Street Market*

Comme des Garçons' designer Rei Kawakubo's retail space combines the edgy energy of London's indoor markets – concrete floors, tills housed in corrugated-iron shacks, Portaloo dressing rooms – with a beautifully curated array of rarefied labels. True, it isn't the first place we'd direct the cash-strapped shopper to – you'll not walk out with any change from a tenner if you're hunting for clothes. But that doesn't mean you can't look. And what a space it is to look at: the theatrically designed displays give some of the capital's art galleries a run for their money and make for great browsing. If you really must buy something, nip into the Labour and Wait concession on the fourth floor for one of its cheaper items (some soap, say) or visit the Rose Bakery for a sit-down and one of its renowned carrot cakes.

Dover Street Market *17-18 Dover Street, W1S 4LT (7518 0680, www.doverstreetmarket.com).*

595 *Boost your brain power at a free public lecture*

British Academy

Organising public lectures for over a century, the British Academy persuades serious intellectuals (of the likes of Jonathan Bate and Mary Beard) to impart their wisdom. The series of endowed talks includes the annual Shakespeare Lecture on or around the Bard's birthday on 23 April. If titles such as 'Moral Panics: Then and Now' or 'From Shells and Gold to Plastic and Silicon: a Theory of the Evolution of Money' tickle your fancy, these mostly ticketless talks usually start at 5.30pm.
10 Carlton House Terrace, SW1Y 5AH (7969 5200, www.britac.ac.uk).

Gresham College

Gresham College was set up 400 years ago precisely to provide free lectures. There are eight permanent lecturers in disciplines ranging from geometry and commerce to (brilliantly) physic and rhetoric, who talk about anything from 'The Search for Other Worlds' to 'Are Normal People Sane?', as well as visiting speakers. Up to half a dozen lectures are held a week during term-time, mostly in the 90-seat Barnard's Inn Hall in Holborn; more popular lectures are sometimes forced to move elsewhere and may be ticketed.
Barnard's Inn Hall, EC1N 2HH (7831 0575, www.gresham.ac.uk).

National Gallery

The National Gallery runs several series of well-respected and informative free talks. These include lunchtime lectures (1pm Mon-Sat) on subjects such as 'Distant Lands, Uncharted Waters' (how can you paint an imaginary landscape?), as well as ten-minute talks (4pm Mon, Tue, Fri-Sun) that take a detailed look at a selected painting (perhaps Bronzino's *An Allegory with Venus and Cupid* or Degas' *Ballet Dancers*).
Trafalgar Square, WC2N 5DN (7747 2885, www.nationalgallery.org.uk).

Royal Institution of Great Britain

The hugely popular, flagship Christmas Lectures series is for paying punters only, but the superbly refurbished Royal Institution, established in 1799 to spread scientific knowledge among the masses, also runs a lively programme of free events. Regular monthly features include a book club, 'Fiction Lab', for which Dr Jennifer Rohn (founder of Lablit.com) leads discussions of great fiction with a scientific bent. The evening lectures generally cost £10 (£6-£8 reductions).
21 Albemarle Street, W1S 4BS (7409 2992, www.rigb.org).

Royal Society of Arts

In the business of promoting public thought for two centuries, the RSA runs over 100 lectures, talks, screenings and debates on a wide variety of subjects over the course of a year. Their 'Themes' strand has hosted speakers of the stature of Kofi Annan, Al Gore and Richard Rogers, while Thursdays offer a lunch-hour top-up of arts or politics, perhaps 'Living with a Black Dog' (on depression) or 'The Element' (on how to fulfil your creative potential). All events are free, but they're popular so you'll need to book well in advance – see the website for details. If you miss out, all events are audio streamed live and also available as podcasts afterwards.
8 John Adam Street, WC2N 6EZ (7930 5115, www.thersa.org).

University College London (UCL)

Ingest your sandwich and get some intellectual nutrition at the same time by attending one of UCL's 40-minute lunchtime lectures, intended to offer an insight into research carried out at the university. Lectures start at 1.15pm (days vary) and subjects range from the intriguing, 'The Man who Invented the Concept of Pi', to the abstruse, 'The Reception of Homer in Byzantium', via the plain scary, 'Physiology on Top of the World: Xtreme Everest'.
Darwin Lecture Theatre, Gower Street, WC1E 6BT (7679 9719, www.ucl.ac.uk).

596

Enjoy the view

Could this be the best view in London? Next to the Royal Observatory, the panorama from the summit of Greenwich Park is as splendid as anything you might see in the night sky. The genteel foreground, like something out of a period drama, makes a great contrast with the razzle dazzle of the Canary Wharf skyline.

597-603

Poke your nose into the City's livery halls

The City of London's 108 livery companies are the remnants of once-powerful guilds, or unions, for trades that mostly no longer exist. Many date back to medieval times, but most were formally established in the 16th century. Today, most of us would be hard pushed to describe exactly what a chandler does, never mind a fletcher or cordwainer; the relevance of a longbow maker and barber-surgeon is now, at best, symbolic, while the attraction of a decent currier is sadly illusory.

However, several of the worshipful companies still have a regulatory role and do a lot of fundraising for charity, pulling on their ruffles and big-buckled shoes for the annual Lord Mayor's Show. They also own a lot of property in the City. Most importantly, from our perspective, 33 of them have their own historic headquarters, or livery hall, secreted in some City backwater. It's fun to track them down – to spot and photograph their telltale ancient signs and coats of arms.

In terms of gazing at a secretive company's HQ façade, there are no greater thrills to be had than at the Cutlers' Hall (Warwick Lane, EC4M 7BR, 7248 1866, www.cutlerslondon.co.uk), which boasts a magnificent 3D terracotta frieze of cutlers going about their work. It's groovier than it sounds. Ditto, gazing through the outrageous ornamental gates of the Tallow Chandlers' Hall (4 Dowgate Hill, EC4R 2SH, 7248 4726, www.tallowchandlers.org) into the haunted courtyard, with its large Indian Bean tree.

Most livery halls are closed shops, though a surprising number are available to hire for functions, and some are occasionally open to visitors (call to check opening times). Top of the curiosities is at the Thames-side 18th-century Fishmongers' Hall (London Bridge, EC4R 9EL, 7626 3531, www.fishhall.org.uk), where, amid a jumble of precious loot, you'll find the preserved 12-inch dagger used by fishmonger-mayor William Walworth to stab Wat Tyler in the back and end the Peasants' Revolt of 1381. There's even a life-size wooden statue of the murderous Walworth, dagger in hand.

Meanwhile, the treasures at Butchers' Hall (87 Bartholomew Close, EC1A 7EB, 7600 4106, www.butchershall.com) include a key cupboard from Newgate Prison; Vintners' Hall (Upper Thames Street, EC4V 3BG, 7236 1863, www.vintnershall.co.uk) boasts the Swan Banner (they own the swans on the Thames – it's a long story), archaeological finds and a collection of bottles; and Mercers' Hall (Ironmonger Lane, EC2V 8HE, 7726 4991, www.mercers.co.uk) has a wonderful and expansive art collection, effectively lost to the world. The Renaissance-style Goldsmiths' Hall (Foster Lane, EC2V 6BN, 7606 7070, www.thegoldsmiths.co.uk) is probably the most open to outsiders' prying eyes, and stages regular free art exhibitions to promote both the history and modern-day work of jewellers, gold- and silversmiths.

Open House weekend (www.openhouse london.org.uk) in September always features several livery companies. In addition, every June/July, the City of London Festival (www.colf.org) uses some halls for events, while at this time others open their doors for architectural tours (and general nosying). In previous years, the secret courtyards, ballrooms, roof gardens and treasures of the Butchers', Drapers', Leathersellers', Painter-Stainers', and Watermen & Lightermens' halls (to name but a few) have all been opened up to the public.

604

Bag a vintage bargain

Brick Lane's vintage finds are hardly a secret, but that doesn't mean there are no bargains to be had. After window-shopping your way along the Bethnal Green Road end of the street and gazing at 1920s dresses priced at well over £200, try the simply named Shop (3 Cheshire Street, E1 6ED, 7739 5631), where the scarves, tea towels, aprons, '50s frocks and bolts of vintage fabrics and are much more agreeably priced. Staff are lovely too.

605-607

Wander, float or cycle along Regent's Canal

Opened in 1820 to provide a transport link between east and west London, Regent's Canal developed as a scenic public foot and cycle path in 1968. The route's industrial trappings have been transformed into a delightful green corridor over the decades since. Any stretch of the canal is worth a stroll or a cycle (bear in mind that you can't follow it between Angel and King's Cross), but the most popular patch is from Camden Lock west to Little Venice, passing Regent's Park and London Zoo. Narrowboat cruises also travel along the water in summer and on winter weekends. They depart from Camden Lock and cost around £9 for a single fare (Jason's Canal Boat Trip, 7286 3428, www.jasons.co.uk; Jenny Wren, 7485 4433, www.walkersquay.com; London Waterbus Company, 7482 2660, www.londonwaterbus.com).

608 *Watch glassblowers at work*

In the fiery workshop at Peter Layton's London Glassblowing studio, you can watch, mesmerised, as master craftsmen patiently and painstakingly create beauty out of molten silica molecules. Every object produced is unique and free-blown, and all are signed by their creators (there's currently a team of five working at the studio). This means, of course, that they don't come cheap (around £100 for a small perfume bottle and up to several thousand pounds for larger pieces) but the demonstrations themselves are completely free to watch – just drop in during working hours (but not between 1pm and 2pm). A word of warning: although there's no pressure to buy, the showroom next door is likely to prove a dangerous temptation.

London Glassblowing *62-66 Bermondsey Street, SE1 3UD (7403 2800, www.londonglassblowing. co.uk).*

Brought to books

Charlie Godfrey-Faussett suggests some places where you can borrow this book, along with many others, for free.

Who could disagree with Stephen Fry when he put public libraries firmly in his 'Room Lovely' on TV show *Room 101*? All that knowledge, all that power; the shelf-stacks packed with promising titles, each one quite possibly a key to wisdom, information or inspiration. All effectively ordered, categorised and indexed, quietly awaiting enquiry. And all for free. Though most libraries now offer internet access (usually also free) and various other local services, their essence remains that thrill of discovery and the firing of imagination going on gratis under one communal roof. (And when it comes to roofing, libraries often do it much better than many other municipal buildings.)

Few cities contain such a fabulous array of libraries as London: there's the mother of them all, the British Library at St Pancras; the more than 300 local authority lending and reference libraries spread across the capital; and then there are the delights of the city's individual, specialist,

independent and academic libraries – the Marx Memorial, the Women's, the Lindley, the Weiner and many others. All in all, if you haven't found what you're looking for in a London library, you probably haven't been looking for long enough.

The British Library (96 Euston Road, NW1 2DB, 0330 333 1144, www.bl.uk) is one of the most extensive research resources anywhere on the planet. One of five copyright libraries in the country (the others being the national libraries of Scotland and Wales, the Bodleian in Oxford, and Cambridge University Library) established by the Copyright Act of 1911, it receives a copy of everything published in the UK, as well as much more besides. Currently, it requires about eight miles of extra shelf space each year for its growing collection of some 14 million books. It's free to join, but you need to have a professional reason to gain access to the reference-only reading rooms. All other visitors are more than welcome at the great red-brick building at St Pancras,

Swiss Cottage Library

however. Much derided when it opened in 1997 after years of expensive delays, it is in fact a superb light-filled space inside, and special exhibitions (which usually cost less than £10 admission) draw on the library's remarkable holdings: in 2015, for example, it celebrated the 800th anniversary of the signing of the Magna Carta by displaying two of the four original 1215 Magna Carta documents alongside (loaned from the US) Thomas Jefferson's handwritten copy of the Declaration of Independence and an original copy of the US Bill of Rights. Another gallery contains a permanent free exhibition of some of the library's most precious treasures and displays, the likes of Shakespeare's First Folio, a Gutenberg Bible and Leonardo's notebooks – some extraordinary stuff, in other words.

Then there's the fantastic procession of public libraries in London. Many are the legacy of the Victorian drive to encourage self-help in the illiterate masses, but they've come a very long way since then. The City of London maintains several, but three are particularly noteworthy. Their flagship is the Guildhall Library (Aldermanbury, EC2V 7HH, 7332 1868, www. cityoflondon.gov.uk/guildhalllibrary), founded in the early 15th century by Dick Whittington and given its modern form in 1824 as a reference

library on 'all matters relating to the City, the Borough of Southwark and the County of Middlesex'. As such, its collections on the history and topography of the capital are exceptional, including maps dating from the 16th century and some 26,000 images of the City, viewable in its Print Room. This is also the place to see Lloyd's of London's historic marine collection of manuscripts relating to shipping; the wine and food libraries collected by André Simon, Elizabeth David and the Institute of the Masters of Wine, among others; and special collections devoted to Samuel Pepys, John Wilkes and Charles Lamb. At the same address, the City Business Library (www.cityoflondon.gov.uk/citybusinesslibrary) provides one of the most accessible and comprehensive practical sources of current business information in the UK. And the Barbican Music Library (Barbican Centre, EC2Y 8DS, 7638 0672, www.cityoflondon.gov.uk/barbicanlibrary) holds a huge number of recordings of all types of music (eight listening booths are provided), including the unique Music Preserved collection of recent live performances of classical music, as well as musical scores and books about music and musicians for both lending and reference.

The City of Westminster's libraries are also pretty special. Bang in the middle of the West

End, the Charing Cross Library (4-6 Charing Cross Road, WC2H 0HF, 7641 6200, www. westminster.gov.uk/libraries) is a public lending library that also serves Chinatown. It holds one of the largest collections of books in Chinese for loan in the country, has four Chinese-speaking staff, and stages a variety of China-related events. Nearby, just off Leicester Square, the Westminster Reference Library (35 St Martin's Street, WC2H 7HP, 7641 6200, www.westminster. gov.uk/libraries) is particularly strong in art and design and the performing arts. At the Westminster Archives Centre (10 St Ann's Street, SW1P 2DE, 7641 5180, www.westminster.gov.uk/ libraries), you can access www.ancestry.co.uk for free (for censuses from 1851 to 1901), as well as see illustrations dating back to the 16th century and search parish registers of baptisms, marriages and deaths.

Want to find out more about any given house, street, footpath or park in the mighty borough of Camden? Holborn Library (32-38 Theobalds Road, WC1X 8PA, 7974 4444, www.camden.gov.

uk/holbornlibrary), with its wonderfully helpful local studies centre, is the place to come. Staff will happily produce maps and resources relevant to your enquiry and point you in the direction of a variety of exhaustive card indexes.

Also in Camden, Swiss Cottage Library (88 Avenue Road, NW3 3HA, 7974 4001, www. camden.gov.uk) is worth a visit for its architecture alone. Designed by Sir Basil Spence, it's a wonderful modernist structure, looks a little like an enormous Rolodex, and was opened in 1964. It has a particularly strong psychology and philosophy collection.

Other public libraries around London have also pushed architectural boundaries: Peckham Library (122 Peckham Hill Street, SE15 5JR, 7525 2000, www.southwark.gov.uk) led the way with its colourful reading pods and glass walls. Opened in 2000 and designed by Will Alsop to undermine stuffy assumptions about libraries, it has become the busiest in Southwark. Tower Hamlets (www.towerhamlets.gov.uk) has gone a step further, ditching the word 'library'

Swiss Cottage Library

altogether, with their Idea Stores: Whitechapel Idea Store (321 Whitechapel Road, E1 1BU, 7364 4332, www.ideastore.co.uk) opened in 2005. Designed by conceptual architect David Adjaye, it has glass walls and rubber studded floors, and as well as books it boasts 'learning spaces' (and classrooms), a crèche, dance studio, complementary therapy room, café, baby-changing room and wheelchair-accessible toilets. Further east, is the even newer Barking Learning Centre (2 Town Square, IG11 7NB, 8724 8725, http://blc.lbbd.gov.uk), another award-winning new-build.

If other local authority libraries have struggled to become less, how shall we say, pedestrian, no such problem faces London's extraordinary collection of specialist and independent libraries. We highlight a handful here, while noting that, sadly, the most venerable of them all, the London Library (14 St James's Square, SW1Y 4LG, 7930 7705, www.london library.co.uk) costs £485 per annum to join, though it does offer free guided tours on some Monday evenings (reservations required).

If the muse takes you, then the Poetry Library (Level 5, Royal Festival Hall, SE1 8XX, 7921 0943, www.poetrylibrary.org.uk) could help harness your inspiration. Funded by the Arts Council, it's the major library of modern and contemporary poetry in the UK, and now holds some 100,000 books for loan and reference. Its sister in the visual arts is the National Art Library (Victoria & Albert Museum, Cromwell Road, SW7 2RL, 7942 2000, www.vam.ac.uk/nal). A reference library only, though with very well-appointed reading rooms, it's also the museum's curatorial department for the art, craft and design of the book. It holds fantastic documentary material on the fine and decorative arts of many different countries and periods. Simply register as a reader on your first visit if you want to investigate the collections.

Anyone interested in the art and design of books will benefit from a visit to the St Bride Printing Library (14 Bride's Lane, EC4Y 8EQ, 7353 3331, www.sbf.org.uk), which includes everything from typefaces to artefacts illustrating the history of printing, along with thousands of books and magazines. At present, the library is not generally open but access is still possible: phone if you're interested in visiting.

If you're more concerned with cultivating your garden, then the Lindley Library (80 Vincent Square, SW1P 2PE, 7821 3050, www.rhs.org.uk), the main library of the Royal Horticultural Society, is the place for you. It contains 22,000 botanical drawings, and some 50,000 books on gardening. Take along two forms of identification to register.

Meanwhile, all matters medical are comprehensively covered at the Wellcome Library (183 Euston Road, NW1 2BE, 7611 8722, www.wellcomelibrary.org), the UK's most important resource on the history of medicine, in all its grisly detail. Recently acquired are the pioneering notes of the great forensic pathologist Bernard Spilsbury.

For the more politically inclined, the Wiener Library (29 Russell Square, WC1B 5DP, 7636 7247, www.wienerlibrary.co.uk) is part of the Institute of Contemporary History and bills itself as 'the world's oldest holocaust memorial institution'. It was founded in 1933 by Alfred Wiener in order to record the persecution of Jews in Nazi Germany; all are welcome to search the shelves for modern European history and current affairs. Also founded in 1933, partly in response to Nazi book-burning, was the Marx Memorial Library (37A Clerkenwell Green, EC1R 0DU, 7253 1485, www.marx-memorial-library.org, open for guided tours only, 1-2pm Tue, Thur, £5) dedicated to the history of socialism and the science of Marxism. It was in this building that Lenin's *Iskra* magazine was printed before World War I.

Another hotbed of radicalism and freethinking is the Bishopsgate Library (230 Bishopsgate, EC2M 4QH, 7392 9270, www.bishopsgate.org.uk) which holds famous collections on London, labour, free thought and co-operation, and was founded in 1895 as part of the Bishopsgate Institute for the education of the working man. It's a reference library, restored in the 1990s to its original appearance, with research materials for local and family historians, as well as more general reference books and current national and local newspapers.

Finally, there is the Women's Library (LSE Library, 10 Portugal Street, WC2A 2HD, 7955 7229, www.lse.ac.uk/library), which contains the most extensive collection of works specifically relating to women's history in the country. As well as the reading room, there is a lively exhibition and events programme. Access here is free and open to everyone – just what libraries should be all about.

631

Celebrate the Thames

Without its river, London quite literally wouldn't exist, so it seems only right that there should be a proper celebration of the mighty Thames. This annual festival takes place throughout September and populates the area between Westminster Bridge and Tower Bridge with an assortment of movies, food stalls, sculptures, the odd bar and an eclectic musical line-up. There are also art events, concerts, talks, tours, boat races and more. Sail on the water, dance in the streets and take a moment to reflect on the river that brought London to the world, and the world to London.
Totally Thames *Mallside, Bargehouse, Oxo Tower Wharf, Bargehouse Street, SE1 9PH (www.totallythames.org). Free.*

632

Kick off with the women…

Women's football has really taken off over the past decade and there are now dozens of local teams looking for players. If you are interested, either contact the London County Football Association (11 Hurlingham Business Stadium, Sulivan Road, SW6 3DU, 7610 8360, www.londonfa.com) or visit the Football Association website (www.thefa.com/womens) to find a club that's convenient for you.

633

…or watch the professionals play

At a fiver a ticket to watch games in the FA Women's Premier League, it's cheaper than even non-league men's football (*see p36*), and yet professional women footballers are now playing at a seriously high (dare we say better?) standard. Most of London's pro clubs also have a women's team: Arsenal are far and away the best team, but Chelsea and Fulham also have Premier League sides.

634 *Help reach a Critical Mass*

Part political movement, part breezy bike ride, Critical Mass (www.network23.org/criticalmasslondon) is a global cycling organisation that aims to reclaim the roads for pedal-pushers. The website has links to cycling activism around the world as well as details of events in London – suffice to say, the vibe is fairly anti-motorised vehicle. The ride through the centre of town meets at 6pm on the last Friday of every month under Waterloo Bridge on the South Bank – if you want to take part, just turn up with a bike.

635-644 *Hear great bands for less*

Live music for less than a tenner? Bella Todd tours the town in search of the capital's best pub back rooms.

Amersham Arms

A roomy yet homely pub, the Amersham is something of a beacon for music fans navigating the unfriendly straits of New Cross Road. Its 300-capacity room plays host (usually Thursday to Saturday) to everything from big-name DJs to folk festivals and ukulele jams, but it's probably best loved (especially by the students from nearby Goldsmiths College) for pulling in well-known electro-pop acts including Ladyhawke and Hot Chip.
388 New Cross Road, SE14 6TY (8469 1499, www.theamershamarms.com). Free-£10.

Bedford

Gigs at this Tardis-like Balham pub take place in the sizeable 'globe theatre', a round space ringed by a balcony, and also in the 'ballroom' upstairs. The music policy is fairly middle of the road but there's an emphasis on breaking new talent – James Morrison and KT Tunstall both played here on the way up. What's more, there's no charge. Live music happens four nights a week (though comedy in the form of the Banana Cabaret takes precedence on Fridays and Saturdays). Names such as the Finn Brothers and Pete Townshend have played impromptu gigs here too.
77 Bedford Hill, SW12 9HD (8682 8940, www.thebedford.co.uk). Free.

Betsey Trotwood

Set over three floors, with a gig venue in the cellar and an acoustic room upstairs, this cosy Victorian pub hosts superior monthly alt-country and bluegrass nights (the latter in the form of an unplugged hoedown) and is a favourite with anti-folk heroes over from the States. It's also home to modern folk club the Lantern Society (on the first and third Thursday of the month), which commandeers the upstairs room for its candlelit harmonies.
56 Farringdon Road, EC1R 3BL (7253 4285). Free-£6.

Dublin Castle

Indie heaven in the stickiest, sweatiest sense, this Irish pub (or, more importantly, its back room) is slap bang in the heart of Camden Town and has seen more bands pass through its doors than its clientele have skipped hot dinners. Once Madness's second home, it's now the best place to go if your aim is to catch as many up-and-coming acts as possible (there are at least four bands a night) regardless of whether they're playing metal, psych-pop or techno-reggae. The day the Dublin Castle turns itself into a gastropub is the day the Rolling Stones take to their rocking chairs.
94 Parkway, NW1 7AN (7485 1773, www.thedublincastle.com). £4.50-£7.

Gladstone Arms

More like someone's candlelit front room than a venue, 'the Glad' in Southwark is often packed but always relaxed, with the chance to enjoy rootsy acoustic music (perhaps over a Pieminister pie and a game of chess) nearly every Wednesday, Saturday and Sunday. There's also a trad night on the last Monday of each month, and every Friday there are DJs playing soul, ska and rock 'n' roll from 7.30pm. Ellie Goulding and Noah and the Whale have played here, as have the Shortwave Set and Findlay Brown. A proper little charmer.
64 Lant Street, SE1 1QN (7407 3962, www.thegladpub.com). Free.

Haggerston

Formerly known as Uncle Sam's – and with a retro neon sign outside to prove it – this post-pub, pre-club venue, with its late licence, Hackney postcode, low-level lighting and leather sofas, somehow manages to straddle the divide between pretentious edginess and genuine good fun. Journey into Dalston for DJs and alt-ish bands on Saturdays and Sundays, but the jewel in its crown is 'Uncle Sam's Jazz and Blues', a weekly late-night Sunday session led by Alan Weekes' modern jazz quartet, where even the bar staff may take to the mic for the odd Billie Holiday classic.

438 Kingsland Road, E8 4AA (7923 3206, www.facebook.com/thehaggerston). Free.

Half Moon Putney

Well, where do we start? KD Lang made her UK debut here; Kate Bush played her first ever show here; Elvis Costello had a residency; Nick Cave played a surprise gig; and the well-kept Wall of Fame pays testimony to shows by everyone from the Rolling Stones and U2 to, er, Gay Dad. The Half Moon has been putting on bands since the 1920s, and seems to have a special pull on performers. There are concerts every night of the week, and the Monday night acoustic sessions have been going since the '60s. It's now owned by Geronimo Inns; good pub grub is served seven days a week.
93 Lower Richmond Road, SW15 1EU (8780 9383, www.halfmoon.co.uk). £2.50-£12.

Macbeth

An intimate hipster Hoxton boozer where all kinds of rock and indie acts play amid Renaissance-style paintings and some very

Amersham Arms

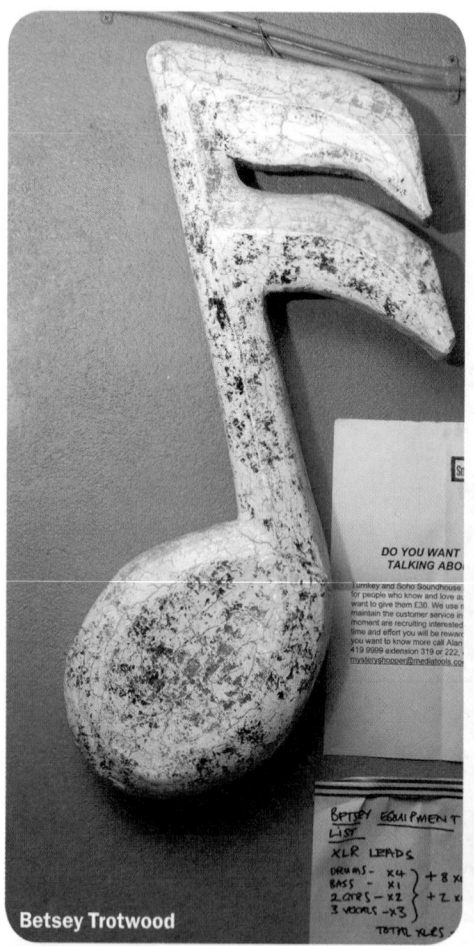
Betsey Trotwood

attractive tiling. Past performers have included
Florence and the Machine, Gang of Four and
Roots Manuva. There's no entrance fee charged
for the Monday jam sessions.
*70 Hoxton Street, N1 6LP (7749 0600, www.
themacbeth.co.uk). Free-£10.*

Old Blue Last
At times unbearably trendy (even more so since
NME voted it 'the coolest pub in the world'), this
shabby-looking Hoxton watering hole is highly
adept at generating a buzz. The Old Blue Last is
famed for secret performances by the likes of the
late Amy Winehouse and the Arctic Monkeys, but
it also runs a pretty hip live music ship the rest of
the time too. There are no frills here, and often
barely room to shake your hips, but when you're

enjoying early gigs by the likes of Kate Nash,
Dan Le Sac vs Scroobius Pip and Santogold,
who cares?
*38 Great Eastern Street, EC2A 3ES (7739 7033,
www.theoldbluelast.com). Free-£10.*

Slaughtered Lamb
The ground floor of this Clerkenwell fave, set
one block back from the main drag, is a trendy
drinking post for local office workers; down in
the basement – a cavern-like space packed with
mismatched sofas – it's a top spot for leftfield
acoustica and folky electronica. Accompany the
music with real ale, plus dishes such as fish finger
sandwiches or sausage and mash.
*34-35 Great Sutton Street, EC1V 0DX (7253 1516,
www.theslaughteredlambpub.com). £5-£10.*

645

Explore Pontoon Dock

Go on an urban adventure by taking the DLR to Pontoon Dock – where you'll find the industrial remnants of Silo-D and Millennium Mills. The ex-dock that could easily be mistaken for a sci-fi film set is, in fact, the remains of a 19th-century grain pumping station. The watery surroundings make it look as if it could once have been the scene of major nuclear activity or a space landing; and it has been the backdrop for multiple music videos including Coldplay's 'Every Teardrop is a Waterfall'; and was briefly the set for British TV series *Ashes to Ashes*.

646 *Respect your elders at the Age Exchange*

The Age Exchange centre in Blackheath (11 Blackheath Village, SE3 9LA, 8318 9105, www. age-exchange.org.uk) offers the senior citizens of south-east London a chance to meet, greet and wax nostalgic about the old days. But it also does much more than that, offering a range of arts and community services, especially for people suffering from dementia. As well as a community library and a theatre, there's also a museum decked out like a 1930s shop that showcases products of yesteryear: a wind-up gramophone, vintage records, retro clobber and wartime paraphernalia (from gas masks to ration books). It features regular exhibitions (an end-of-war tea party, a re-creation of London's docks) and invites schoolchildren to learn about the past. A nostalgia kick goes well with a nice cup of tea, served in the new café.

647

Wrap up warm and watch the Peter Pan Cup

Every Christmas morning in the frosty waters of Hyde Park's pond you can see members of the Serpentine Swimming Club (www.serpentine swimmingclub.com) thrashing it out for the Peter Pan Cup Christmas Morning Handicap Swim. The club requires participants to endure several months of winter training to help their bodies acclimatise – wetsuits are not permitted – as water temperatures rarely exceed 4°C. Every swimmer must be a club member and have competed in a series of competitions… and, last but not least, they must be sporting a Santa hat. Kicking off at 9am on 25 December on the south bank of the lake, it's great fun to watch from dry land in warm, snug clothes. For more open-air swimming places in the capital, *see p256*.

648 *Attend the olde Strawberrie Fayre in Ely Place*

This hidden little place – or Place – is the site of St Etheldreda's Church (14 Ely Place, EC1N 6RY, 7405 1061, www.stetheldreda.com), commended in Shakespeare's *Richard III* for its garden's fine fruit ('My Lord of Ely, when I was last in Holborn, I saw good strawberries in your garden there: I do beseech you send for some of them.'). In recognition of this, an annual Strawberrie Fayre is staged in late June (check the website for the exact date). There's plenty of traditional fun, games and strawberries, with all proceeds going to charity.

649

Sit on a ferryman's perch

Bankside was once London's pleasure quarter, where gaming, drinking and womanising could take place out of sight and mind on the far side of the river. On the corner of Bear Gardens (named for its bear pit), there's an ancient waterman's seat let into the modern wall, where boatmen once drummed up trade with their nudge-and-wink cry of 'Oars! Oars!'

650-659

Melissa Harrison,
Author, At Hawthorn Time

South London has some fantastic parks and green spaces, and Tooting Common is one of the best. It's not one of those manicured city parks with tidy flower beds and lots of signs telling you what not to do; instead, there's long grass that's great for wildlife, lovely old oak trees and lots of blackberries in autumn. Tooting Common's scruffy acres inspired parts of my first novel, *Clay*, and it features on the book's cover.

I first had a tipple in the Social (5 Little Portland Street, W1W 7JD, 7636 4992, www.thesocial.com) in 1999, and it's still going strong: what an achievement, especially in the West End. It's more than just a bar and music venue; on weekdays, there's coffee, hot dogs and free W-Fi for laptop workers, and one of London's best literary events, Faber Social, is held there too. No wonder its devotees feel such loyalty towards it: the Social really is built to last. Getting up at dawn is a tall order for most of us, but in spring birds sing at dusk too – the evening chorus – and it can be spectacular. April, May and June are the best months to seek a post-work symphony; pack a cardigan and a hip flask and head for a big green space such as Hampstead Heath or Wimbledon Common, or anywhere with lots of trees and thickety bits. As the sun sinks toward the horizon, thrushes, blackcaps, wrens, robins and warblers will belt out their bedtime songs; the hush when they stop – which can be sudden – is startling.

I have to declare an interest here: I've worked for dance music and club culture magazine Mixmag (www.mixmag.net) for many years. We pioneered the Lab LDN, the live-streamed office rave, with superstar DJs queuing up to play weekly late-afternoon sets in a club in the corner of our office. Check out Mixmag's socials to find out how to get your name on the list: there's free booze for guests, and the line-ups really are staggering.

Morden Hall Park (Morden Hall Road, SM4 5JD, 8545 6850, www.nationaltrust.org.uk/morden-hall-park) is like a little piece of deep countryside in the heart of the city. As you walk along the beautiful chalk stream that is the River Wandle, with kingfishers zipping past and brown trout in the shallows, you won't believe you're in London. There's a lovely rose garden too, and a fantastic horticultural centre and shop. Entry is free.

The Lambeth Country Show (http://lambethcountryshow.co.uk) is only held once a year – in Brockwell Park in mid July – but it's worth clearing your diary for: this free, two-day event is utterly, brilliantly bonkers. Part south London music festival (dub reggae, jerk chicken, roots and culture) and part agricultural show (sheepdog trials, steam tractors, home-made jam), 2015's event also featured disco legends Odyssey and medieval horseback jousting. Normal.

Hiding around the back of Angel Tube station, up two flights of stairs, is the Candid Arts Café (3 Torrens Street, EC1V 1NQ, 7278 9368, www.candidarts.com), a quirky, bohemian café attached to the Candid Arts Centre. Prices are decent for central London, and you can order beer or wine if you have food. The staff seem quite happy for you to while away an afternoon on one of the sofas with a book; it really does feel like a secret, hidden gem.

It's hard to overstate how important buying books in real bookshops is, or how much I enjoy doing so. We're in a use-them-or-lose-them situation – by which I don't mean going in to browse, then ordering from Amazon (monstrous!). Fortunately, an hour in a bookshop is a deeply pleasurable thing, and London still has some brilliant independents, including Big Green Bookshop (Unit 1, Brampton Park Road, N22 6BG, 8881 6767, www.biggreenbookshop.com) in Wood Green; Bookseller Crow (50 Westow Street, SE19 3AF, 8771 8831, http://bookseller crow.co.uk) in Crystal Palace; Review (131 Bellenden Road, SE15 4QY, 7639 7400, www.reviewbookshop.co.uk) in Peckham; and Slightly Foxed (123 Gloucester Road, SW7 4TE, 7370 3503, www.foxedbooks. com) in Kensington.

As well as books, the British Library (96 Euston Road, NW1 2DB, 0330 333 1144, www.bl.uk) houses a huge collection of recorded sound, including music, radio, oral history and wildlife. Some 100,000 recordings are available via terminals in the Reading Rooms; the rest can be accessed by appointment. If you're a writer, musician or do anything in the least bit creative, the Sound Archive is an unexpected source of inspiration.

At low tide, the Thames reveals areas of foreshore on which an ever-changing array of finds is washed up: bits of clay pipe, old coins, Roman pottery – if you go mudlarking, the fun is not knowing what you'll find. Always check the tide tables online, and remember you can't dig, or use a metal detector, without a licence, but you can pick up anything you see on the surface: clues to London's long and fascinating past.

660

Swap stuff

Call them what you like: swapping, swishing, or ditching 'n' switching events, where you exchange your clobber for someone else's – no cash required – are an excellent way to save money, the environment (it's recycling, see) and prevent wardrobe ennui. Of course, they're also a great way to meet total strangers. See http://swishing.com for a list of upcoming events.

The cheapest way to go about it is to hold your own clothes-swapping party. Like the 21st-century's answer to the Tupperware bash, you invite all your friends round, asking them to bring a bottle and the clothes they no longer want – then hope that someone else's cast-off is your own sartorial holy grail. And the rules are simple enough too: everyone brings a few items they're willing to relinquish and they can take home as much as they like. Reserving the best stuff before kick-off is frowned upon and, of course, remember your manners – all-out brawling is not in the spirit of swishing.

661 *Buy your lunch from an award-winning author*

A deliciously bucolic remnant of Old Spitalfields Market, upscale corner deli Verde & Co forms the ground floor of author Jeanette Winterson's restored Georgian home. Artfully presented – think linen-lined baskets of organic seasonal vegetables out front – and with an emphasis on Italian produce (to avoid competing with next-door Brit specialist A Gold), the fruit and veg on sale here is carefully selected by ex-St John chef Harvey Cabaniss. He clearly takes pride in his artisanal lunchtime sandwich menu: try the chorizo, gorgonzola and sweet chilli, the suckling pig and balsamic onion, or check the daily specials board.

Verde & Co *40 Brushfield Street, E1 6AG (7247 1924, http://verdeandco.co.uk).*

662

A miraculous vision in marble, the Shri Swaminarayan Mandir (8965 2651, www.mandir.org) is the biggest Hindu temple outside India. Fascinating architecturally and culturally, the Mandir is open to people of all faiths and none.

663

Visit the home of baseball

Baseball (unlike basketball) is a game of evolution rather than invention, and it may come as a surprise to learn that much of that evolving took place in Surrey rather than across the pond. Local records show that the game was played near Guildford in the 1750s, and there's even a reference to it in Jane Austen's *Northanger Abbey*. More than 250 years later, that tradition continues. The South London Pirates are one of the leading clubs in Britain's thriving baseball scene, competing in the National Baseball League from their home at Roundshaw Playing Fields. The Pirates also host the London Tournament every July, with 16 top teams enjoying a weekend of pitching, pinch hits and put-outs. All games are free to watch, and the season runs from April to September.

South London Pirates *www.southlondonpirates. co.uk.*

664
Get your hands dirty in a 17th-century knot garden

Next door to Lambeth Palace, the old parish church of St Mary-at-Lambeth and its churchyard are home to the Garden Museum (formerly the Museum of Garden History), which exhibits the works of various green-fingered luminaries in its beautifully refurbished galleries. Outside, a lovely churchyard garden laid out in a formal 17th-century knot garden design was the last resting place of the John Tradescants (father and son), gardeners to Charles I. If you are itching to share some of your horticultural knowledge or would like to learn more about the historic plant species growing here, why not volunteer your services to help tend the garden (it is run entirely by volunteers). Visit the website for more information and application details.

Garden Museum *Lambeth Palace Road, SE1 7LB (7401 8865, www.gardenmuseum.org.uk). £7.50.*

665-666
Wake yourself up at a market

Stir your stumps at the crack of dawn, or even earlier, and head for 'the largest fresh produce market in the UK'. New Covent Garden Market is open 3am-11am Monday-Friday, 4am-10am Saturday (most of the wholesale action is over by 8am), and claims to supply almost half of all the food that London likes to eat while it's out. Covering 53 acres, the market opened here in Vauxhall after moving from Covent Garden in 1974, and is about to be given a thorough makeover. Even if you're not buying (and there's plenty of opportunity to – whether you are thinking wholesale or not), your £5 entry fee (free if arriving on foot) guarantees a feel for the market's buzz, and there are plenty of market caffs where you can breakfast alongside the traders. In a separate building, the flower market offers the most spectacular profusion of plants for sale under one roof in the country. As well as supplying florists and flower-stall holders, it does brisk business with funeral directors, wedding planners and brides-to-be.

Sunbury Antiques market takes place on the second and last Tuesday of every month at Kempton Racecourse and features more than 700 stalls (350 indoor, 350 outdoor, with many traders coming from across the Channel). It opens at 6.30am, and if you're serious about your rummaging, you'll need a car – the trains don't start running until later, and it will be much easier to take your treasures home if you have your own transport. On the plus side, there's no entrance fee, and parking is free. The big appeal of the place is the vast variety of the stuff on offer, from old French maps and scores of stuffed owls to gargantuan Belgian farmhouse tables, vintage clothing to . Plus you can often buy in bulk – 20 science lab light-fittings, or 100 school chairs, for example. There's also the great atmosphere that comes from a jumble of different accents, a shared enthusiasm for unusual objects, and the solidarity of enduring an excruciatingly early start.

New Covent Garden Market *Nine Elms Lane, SW8 5NX (7720 2211, www.newcoventgarden market.com).*

Sunbury Antiques Market *Kempton Racecourse, Sunbury, TW16 5AQ (01932 230946, www.sunburyantiques.com).*

667 *Play poker*

Fancy your luck as a poker player? Whether you're a beginner, or looking for people to play with (in a friendly home setting or at a small-stakes tournament) or want to learn some new styles of poker, the London Poker Meetup group is the place. Find out more at www.meetup.com/london pokermeetup.

668
Eat bánh mì

Bánh mì, a delicious Franco-Viet baguette, is a big part of Vietnam's street-food culture, and increasingly a big part of London's food scene – popping up not only in market stalls, but in Vietnamese cafés and restaurants too. A great place to try one is City Càphê (17 Ironmonger Lane, EC2V 8EY, www.citycaphe.com – open Monday to Friday only). The 'classic pork' bánh mì comes with a succulent cold cut of pork, earthy liver pâté, fiery chilli, crunchy veg and fresh coriander, all in a light, crispy baguette.

669
Explore Kings Place

A key component of the ongoing regeneration of the King's Cross area, this major arts centre opened in 2008 to great fanfare and much critical acclaim. Incredibly, the airy modern building is home to the first new public concert hall to be built in central London since the Barbican Concert Hall opened in 1982. As well as offices (the *Guardian* newspaper is here), the building consists of a public open-plan ground-floor area with comfortable seating, a café and a restaurant, while the two lower levels house a gallery and two concert halls, whose acoustics can be adjusted for music or speech. There are classical, choral, jazz and folk concerts, with whole cycles dedicated to individual composers, as well as spoken-word evenings and events for children. All art exhibitions are free, while lectures and music events can be attended for just £9.50 if booked in advance online. Elegant inside and out, this is a great addition not only to King's Cross, but to London as a whole.

Kings Place *90 York Way, N1 9AG (7520 1490, www.kingsplace.co.uk).*

670-672
Get to know William Morris

Born in Walthamstow in 1856, Morris made it his mission to beautify the ends and means of mass production, most famously with his wallpaper designs inspired by natural forms, but more generally through a deep respect for craftsmanship and the dignity of labour.

In 1877, he rented a house on the lovely riverside path that runs from Hammersmith to Chiswick. He called it Kelmscott House after his manor in Oxfordshire, and died here in 1896. Now home to the William Morris Society (26 Upper Mall, 8741 3735, www.williammorrissociety.org, free), founded in 1955, the basement and coach house – containing a library and a variety of Morris memorabilia – can be visited from 2pm to 5pm on Thursdays and Saturdays.

Other key places in London associated with the pioneering socialist include the Red House (Red House Lane, Bexleyheath, Kent DA6 8JF, 8304 9878, www.nationaltrust.org.uk, £8), which Morris designed with architect Philip Webb and where he lived from 1860 for five years (before being forced to sell), and the wonderful William Morris Gallery (Lloyd Park, Forest Road, E17 4PP, 8496 4390, www.wmgallery.org.uk, free), where he lived as a teenager and which now exhibits his famous designs in fabrics, glass, tiles, wallpaper and furniture, as well as works by other Arts and Crafts designers such as Arthur Heygate Mackmurdo and William de Morgan.

673
Ogle classic cars in South Kensington...

In the various mews off the Old Brompton Road lie three of the world's top classic-car dealers: Peter Bradfield, 8 Reece Mews, SW7 3HE (www.bradfieldcars.com); Fiskens, 14 Queen's Gate Place Mews, SW7 5BQ (www.fiskens.com); Hexagon Classics, 6 Kendrick Place, SW7 3HF (www.hexagonclassics.com). Even if motors aren't really your thing, you'll be hard pressed not to drool over the Ferraris, Jaguars and Alfa Romeos, though your tenner won't be much use.

674
...or see a vintage car show

The free Regent Street Motor Show takes place on a Saturday in early November, the day before the Veteran Car Run from London to Brighton. It's a chance to gawp at some stunning examples of automotive technology and beauty: see http://regentstreetmotorshow.com for details.

675
Prove your superfan credentials at a Geeks Inc quiz

Running monthly quiz nights for trivia-lovers who don't care for the sports round, Geeks Inc theme each of their events around a TV show, film or game of the sort that can boast 'superfans'. There have been nights for those who know Sideshow Bob's shoe size, who can remember the name of Chandler's dad's drag act, who have read somewhere why Bubbles is called Bubbles, and many more. Round up whichever of your friends went halves with you on the box set and test out your obsessive sides. There are prizes to be won but, let's face it, you're only really in it for the glory. Details on http://geeksinc.co.uk.
Monarch, 40-42 Chalk Farm Road, NW1 8BG.
£3 per person or £15 per team of up to 6

676
Go Dutch

Dutch bars aren't unusual these days, but what they don't have is the century-old history of De Hems. This ornately fronted hostelry was first a refuge for homesick Dutch sailors, then an overseas base for the wartime Dutch Resistance. Now a convivial two-floor pub with a dark wood interior, its sturdy counters are lined with Grolsch Weizen and Kriek taps, with more unusual bottled beers such as Kwak, Vedett and Orval stored behind the bar. There are traditional Dutch bar snacks to enjoy too, such as *bitterballen* (deep-fried meatballs).
De Hems *11 Macdesfield Street, W1D 5BW (7437 2494, www.nicholsonspubs.co.uk).*

677-679
Get your skates on

Ice skating has become an expensive business, so it's good to know that there are some affordable options. At the Lee Valley Ice Centre (Lea Bridge Road, E10 7QL, 8533 3154, www.leevalleypark.org.uk), it's £8 to skate (plus £2 if you need to hire skates), while at the Sobell Leisure Centre (Hornsey Road, N7 7NY, 7609 2166, www.better.org.uk/leisure/sobell) a session costs £6.30 for non-members, with skate hire at £1.20. Replacing the previous 1930s rink and containing the only Olympic-sized ice pad in London, the new Streatham Ice Rink (390 Streatham High Road, SW16 6HX, 8677 5758, www.better.org.uk/leisure/streatham-ice) charges £7.20 plus £2 skate hire.

Streatham Ice Rink

680

Dance until the sun goes down

You'll find Northern Soul all-nighters taking place in Wigan, Manchester and indeed London, but newcomers to the music are better off starting with an all-dayer. As well as fantastic tunes, you can expect classic mod fashion and some truly remarkable dance moves.
Soul Nites All-dayers *www.soulnites.com. £10, £8 in advance.*

681

Discover Eadweard Muybridge at Kingston Museum

Kingston Museum is worth anyone's time – containing as it does a remarkably well-preserved Anglo-Saxon log boat – but for film buffs, it's an absolute must. The remarkable Eadweard Muybridge (1830-1903) was born in Kingston as plain Edward James Muggeridge, but changed his name to Muygridge then to Eadweard Muybridge (taking the spelling of his Christian name from the name of Eadweard the Elder on Kingston's coronation stone).

He headed for America hoping to find a market for his topical photographs and soon made a name for himself with his landscapes of Yosemite, cityscapes of San Francisco and work with moving images (in 1872, he was asked to photograph the racehorse Occident, belonging to a former governor of California, to prove that all four of the horse's feet left the ground at once when galloping – his experiments proved that they did).

At the museum in Kingston, there's a collection of his equipment and prints bequeathed by Muybridge. You can see two of the revolving slotted drums, or zoetropes, that he experimented with – they show an ostrich running and a man jumping up and down, as well as a phenakistiscope, one of the world's earliest moving picture devices. Muybridge's second zoopraxiscope, also on display here, was designed to project the movement and actions of various animals. The museum also holds one of only nine surviving copies of his 'Panorama of San Francisco', which is over 17 feet in length, and taken with a series of 13 cameras in 1878.
Kingston Museum *Wheatfield Way, Kingston upon Thames, KT1 2PS (8547 6440, www.kingston.gov. uk/museum). Free.*

682

Be a mystery shopper

Mystery shopping is probably the closest you are likely to get to being a secret agent (well, a sort of consumer sleuth anyway). Posing as a real customer, your mission, should you choose to accept it, is usually to check out customer service (sometimes in person, sometimes on the phone) and buy all manner of goodies incognito – some of which you may get to keep. With many big-name clients out there determined to maintain their high levels of service, you can find yourself in some exciting places (free flights are not unheard of) – and any expenses spent while on a case are reimbursed (you may also earn a small fee for completing an evaluation form). Start by registering online.
www.mystery-shoppers.co.uk.

Kingston Museum

The play's the thing

World-class drama doesn't have to mean top-end prices.
Daisy Bowie-Sell explains how to bag theatre tickets for less.

One of the most common laments you'll hear from the would-be theatregoing community relates to the expense of the tickets. And yes, it's true: if you turn up to a box office kiosk trying to buy a ticket to catch the latest Hollywood starlet as they're bathed in the bright lights of the West End, you will almost have to take a mortgage out for the privilege. But with a little careful planning and brain work, you can still catch some of the most dynamic, world-class – and potentially still celebrity-filled – drama in London.

Day seats, preview and standing tickets, and booking ahead are all ways of seeing West End shows for much less, while many smaller theatres allocate specific dates as cheap ticket nights. Many of the venues that produce some of the most interesting and thought-provoking work in London offer pay-what-you-can nights – an excellent chance to catch what could be the next big thing, for whatever shrapnel you happen to have in your pocket.

Pay-what-you-can

Pay-what-you-can means just that: you pay what you can afford and it's entirely at your discretion: some punters pay a pound, some pay full price, but a fiver or so is a good average. All the theatres below offer this deal on certain nights – although you may need to be quick off the mark to take advantage. Keep your ear to the ground or, more usefully, your finger on the mouse.

The always surprising Battersea Arts Centre, (Lavender Hill, SW11 5TN, 7223 2223, www.bac. org.uk), housed in a beautiful Grade II-listed building that was originally Battersea Town Hall, has championed the idea of the 'Scratch' performance. Performers stage a work-in-progress show to a live audience, who contribute what they can to the cost of a ticket. The standard will vary wildly, but the work on offer – anything from site-specific pieces in secret corners of the building to storyteller extraordinaire Daniel Kitson's new show – is usually right on the cutting edge of the country's experimental theatre scene. 'Since 2000, Scratch has been at the heart of theatre-making at BAC. By taking a punt with pay-what-you-can tickets, audiences catch a glimpse of fresh ideas, and artists enter into a conversation with their audiences. It's a process that's unpredictable, exciting and often a little bit magic,' says BAC artistic director David Jubb.

Hackney's Arcola Theatre (24 Ashwin Street, E8 3DL, 7503 1646, www.arcolatheatre.com) has been growing steadily in repute since it opened in 2000. The programming is varied, from comedy through to classics, and is staged by both new and established practitioners. The Arcola offers a limited number of pay-what-you-can tickets on most Tuesdays for shows in both Studio 1 and Studio 2; you can buy them, in person, from 6pm of the evening of the performance, but arrive early, especially once reviews are out, as queues can be long.

Finsbury Park's swish Park Theatre (Clifton Terrace, N4 3JP, 7870 6876, www.parktheatre. co.uk) has been impressing critics and punters since it opened in 2013. The theatre operates pay-what-you-can on matinées for both its 90-seat and 200-seat spaces. As usual, you have to turn up in person at the box office – from an hour before the show.

Early-bird and preview tickets

Making sure you're the first in line when tickets go on sale (whether that is in front of a screen or an actual person) is another way to get your cultural kicks on a limited budget. Again, you need to be prepared (following the theatre on Twitter really helps here), but being quick off the mark will give you all the more time to look forward to the upcoming thrill. Seats are often easier to come by – and a huge amount cheaper – during previews, the week before the reviews come out.

Arcola Theatre

Though the well-established and respected Gate Theatre (11 Pembridge Road, W11 3HQ, 7229 0706, www.gatetheatre.co.uk) in Notting Hill, known for some of the most exciting international writing around, has stopped its pay-what-you-can night, they still offer a couple of excellent deals. The intimate but flexible space above the Prince Albert pub seats about 75 people and on preview nights and at Saturday matinées, tickets cost £10.

The 251-seat Donmar Warehouse (41 Earlham Street, WC2H 9LX, 0844 871 7624, www.donmar warehouse.com) may be one of the smallest theatres in central London, but it is definitely one of the best. It has staged everything from all-female productions of Shakespeare to musicals, and new writing to old classics; and starry actors such as Tom Hiddleston, Jude Law, Nicole Kidman and Judi Dench have all trodden its boards. Unlike many of its West End neighbours, the Donmar is a subsidised theatre and therefore offers some juicy deals. Don't miss its Barclays Front Row tickets – two weeks before a performance date, two-thirds of the front row go on sale, online and over the phone, for just £10.

Josie Rourke, the Donmar's artistic director, says: 'Barclays Front Row is also about making sure Donmar tickets are always on sale. It amounts to over 300 tickets a week, and more than two-thirds of those £10 tickets are being bought by people who are coming to the Donmar for the first time. It's cheap, high-quality, weekly tickets in the heart of the West-End.' The Donmar also usually sells a limited number of standing tickets at the back of the circle (£7.50) on the day of the performance.

At Islington's King's Head Theatre (115 Upper Street, N1 1QN, 7193 7845, www.kingshead theatrepub.co.uk), a tiny space tucked away at the back of a Victorian boozer, all tickets are £10 for previews. Artistic director Adam Spreadbury-Maher has recently focused on wily revivals of old classics – such as *Rocky Horror* follow-up *Shock Treatment* – and new plays.

Lunchtime shows

A few London fringe theatres run regular lunchtime shows. The Bridewell (7353 3331, www.sbf.org.uk), a theatre in a converted Victorian swimming pool near Fleet Street, holds Lunchbox theatre – emerging talent and classic short plays that last about 45 minutes; you can even bring your own picnic. Tickets can be bought online or on the day at the box office; prices vary but you'll usually pay under £10.

Opened in 2012, the brand-new St James Theatre (12 Palace Street, SW1E 5JA, 0844 264 2140, www.stjamestheatre.co.uk) has become known as a strong receiving house. The main theatre has 312 seats; the 120-seat studio stages musical revues, song cycles, gigs and cabaret. Lunchtime theatre here, popular with a local office crowd, usually happens in the last two weeks of the month. Shows last about 50 minutes and cost £10 in advance, or £12 on the door.

Standing, standby, restricted view and other deals

The Royal Court (Sloane Square, SW1W 8AS, 7565 5000, www.royalcourttheatre.com) is Britain's leading national company dedicated to new writing, usually of the very highest quality. It was here in 1956 that John Osborne's *Look Back in Anger* was first performed, marking the beginning of a new wave of British theatre. The space is great, with a big restaurant and bar in the basement. It operates £10 Mondays, where all tickets for both spaces (Jerwood Theatre Upstairs,

Bridewell Theatre

Jerwood Theatre Downstairs) cost £10. Tickets are available from 9am online.

Also, if you're prepared to stand, four tickets for Downstairs are available for a paltry 10p. These go on sale an hour before the show starts, but check in advance because they are subject to availability and are usually restricted-view. (It's worth noting that other theatres sell standing tickets 'in the slips' too, but a lot of them don't advertise the fact, so do enquire at the box office.)

At the National Theatre (South Bank, SE1 9PX, 7452 3000, www.nationaltheatre.org.uk), you can buy standing tickets on the day for £5, if all other tickets have been sold. At Shakespeare's Globe (21 New Globe Walk, SE1 9DT, 7401 9919, www.shakespearesglobe.com), you can feel like an Elizabethan peasant by parting with a fiver to be a groundling and stand in the pit. Prices for the Almeida (Almeida Street, N1 1TA, 7359 4404, www.almeida.co.uk) in Islington start at £10, though they are mainly restricted-view. As for West End shows, try for standby seats or the cut-price ticket kiosks or, if you have good eyesight and don't mind heights, sit in the gods.

One of the capital's best fringe theatres is Southwark Playhouse (Newington Causeway, SE1 6BD, 7407 0234, www.southwarkplayhouse.co.uk), now happily ensconced in its new home in Elephant & Castle. The theatre has two spaces

and the shows in both are usually well worth checking out. Preview tickets cost £10, but the theatre also has a pay-as-you-go subscription: pay £50 and get to book five tickets to five shows at any point in the run.

The award-winning Bush Theatre (7 Uxbridge Road, W12 8LJ, 8743 5050, www.bushtheatre.co.uk), recently relocated to an old library in Shepherd's Bush, has long been committed to showcasing promising new writing and boasts an impressive list of alumni, including Stephen Poliakoff, Mike Leigh and Jim Broadbent. The Bush has a multi-buy offer that pushes the price down if you purchase three tickets to three different shows at the same time. The three-for-two offer is only on top-price tickets and isn't valid on previews or matinées.

If you're under 26, always ask whether theatres do deals – such as the Young Vic (66 The Cut, SE1 8LZ, 7922 2922, www.youngvic.org) in Waterloo. If you live near a specific theatre, there may be special deals for locals: for example, the Lyric (King Street, W6 0QL, 8741 6850, www.lyric.co.uk) in Hammersmith offers two free tickets per show to borough residents.

Finally, it's always worth looking at the theatre section of *Time Out* magazine (free, of course), not only for the latest reviews and listings, but also for two-for-one ticket offers and other deals.

699 *Birdwatch*

Despite warnings of declining populations and lack of habitat, there's still a surprising amount of birdlife to appreciate in London – around 300 species of bird have been identified in the last few years, including large birds such as herons, cormorants, falcons and sparrowhawks. Even without a pair of binoculars (you'll have to pay more than a tenner for those), there's still a lot you can do to maximise your chances of getting some interesting sightings.

With the help of the RSPB's free guide to birds or a well-illustrated field guide, you may soon be ticking off species (such as tits, thrushes and finches) from your twitcher list before you've even left your back garden, but the best sites are obviously places where there's a lot of vegetation. In the centre of town that means parks, where you can see species such as woodpeckers, redwings and fieldfares (in hard winters), goldcrests and wrens, as well as water birds such as great crested grebes. Also try wilder areas such as Rainham Marshes, Brent's Welsh Harp Reservoir, Sydenham Hill Wood, the Lee Valley Park and – just 25 minutes by train from central London – the London Wetland Centre in Barnes (www.wwt.org.uk), an international award-winning visitor attraction, considered the finest urban site in Europe for wildlife spotting. The Centre is home to some rare and beautiful birds, including bitterns, redstarts, kingfishers, skylarks, red shanks and golden plovers.

If you want to learn more, you could always join a group – try the East London Birders Forum (www.elbf.co.uk), the London Natural History Society (www.lnhs.org.uk) or your local RSPB group (www.rspb.org.uk).

700 *Take a day-trip to Portugal*

The Portuguese population is around 50,000 in Lambeth – that's nearly one in every five residents of the borough – and on 10 June (or the nearest weekend, if it falls on a weekday), there's a celebration of all things Portuguese in the 'Little Portugal' area that surrounds Kennington Park. Expect live fado (and other music) and numerous seafood stalls selling *bacalhau* (salted cod).

701-710 *Follow a London blog...*

A Little Bird
www.a-littlebird.com
A carefully curated run-down on the hottest shops, exhibitions, pop-up projects and more.

Dave Hill's London Blog
www.theguardian.com/uk/davehillblog
Scrutinising London politics.

Diamond Geezer
www.diamondgeezer.blogspot.com
One of London's key bloggers.

The Great Wen
www.greatwen.com
From London's worst statues to weird museum exhibits, Peter Watts certainly has an eye for the unusual.

London Reconnections
www.londonreconnections.com
Heaven for transport geeks: everything from rolling-stock plans to major infrastructure work.

London Review of Breakfasts
www.londonreviewofbreakfasts.blogspot.co.uk
Breakfast places of all sorts, from Acton to West Hampstead, investigated by very readable reviewers.

Spitalfields Life
www.spitalfieldslife.com
The 'Gentle Author' has attracted a cult following from across the globe for his offbeat, well-written articles on the East End past and present.

Tales of the City
www.mel-talesofthecity.blogspot.co.uk
Nature in the city, lovingly and authoritatively described by *Clay* author Melissa Harrison.

Time Out London Blog
www.timeout.com/london/blog
The ultimate guide to eating and drinking, clubbing, fashion, the arts and more in London. We would say that, of course.

Tired of London, Tired of Life
www.tiredoflondontiredoflife.com
Not sure what to do in the city? TOLTOL's daily posts provide varied suggestions.

711

...or check out a quirky London website

www.britishpathe.com
Archive newsreel footage, from spaghetti-eating contests to pre-war Soho.
www.classiccafes.co.uk
Great archive of 1950s and '60s caffs.
www.hidden-london.com
Undiscovered gems – and a neat place-names pronunciation guide.
www.londonremembers.com
Definitive site for London memorials.

712

Visit the Photographers' Gallery

The Photographers' Gallery, just off Oxford Street, is London's largest public gallery dedicated to photography – in fact, when it was founded in 1971 (in Covent Garden), it was the first such establishment in the world. It has three floors of galleries devoted to British and international photography, plus the Studio Floor – a space for talks, events, workshops and free film screenings – a camera obscura and Touchstone, a changing display of a single photographic work. Annual highlights include the Deutsche Börse Photography Prize exhibition. The building also holds a bookshop, a print sales room and a street-level café.
Photographers' Gallery *16-18 Ramillies Street, W1F 7LW (http://thephotographersgallery.org.uk).*

713

Drink in the gardens at the Chumleigh café

In the otherwise slightly barren surrounds of Burgess Park, the quaint Chumleigh almshouses

(now used as conference facilities) and magnificent gardens come as a pleasant surprise. The latter captures the spirit of five distinct gardening styles – Islamic, English, African/Caribbean, Mediterranean and Oriental. You'll find some unusual plant species here as well as two ponds: one for wildlife, the other a more formal, mosaicked Islamic-style affair. Another garden area north of the café is being landscaped by Groundwork London with a playground and walks. You can feast on some hearty snack fare (and roasts on Sunday) and Fairtrade drinks in the cheerful café (located between the Mediterranean and Islamic gardens), with its bright colours, samba music and peaceful outdoor seating.
Chumleigh Gardens *Burgess Park, SE5 0RJ (7740 8070).*

714

Listen to world music at SOAS

Want to expand your musical horizons? Without paying a penny? Then head to the world music concerts organised by SOAS, University of London, which specialises in the study of Asia, Africa and the Near and Middle East. North Indian dhrupad, a classical vocal genre dating from the 15th century, is just the tip of the musical iceberg. How about hearing a master of the Middle Eastern lute-like oud, or watching an expert play the Afro-Cuban batá drums? There might be exorcistic salpuri dance from Korea; Pontic lyre sessions; Argentinian chacarera, candombe, zamba and chamamé dances; the maqam music of the Uighurs; Judeo-Spanish Ladino song; or seprewa sounds from the Ashanti region of Ghana. The concert season runs from October to May, with concerts – all free – starting at 7pm, usually on a Tuesday, Wednesday and/or Friday. You can't book, so you'll need to turn up in good time, and even then there might be a crush at the door.
Brunei Gallery Lecture Theatre, SOAS *University of London, Thornhaugh Street, Russell Square, WC1H 0XG (7898 4500, www.soas.ac.uk/concerts).*

715 Visit the Serpentine Sackler Gallery

Zaha Hadid remodelled what was a 19th-century gunpowder depot to transform it into the Serpentine Sackler Gallery. Opened in 2013, the handsome, Grade II-listed yellow-brick building is in a plum position on West Carriage Drive in Kensington Gardens. It also contains the Magazine café-restaurant, beneath Hadid's swooping white tent-like roof. A short stroll away is its parent, the Serpentine Gallery; both galleries specialise in international contemporary art, architecture and design. Admission is free. See www.serpentinegallery.org for more details.

716 Learn karate...

Karate is an exciting blend of kicks, punches and knee and elbow strikes – and is as popular as ever. Guided by *sensei* Linda Marchant, a 7th dan black belt and former world champion, the structured programme of tuition at Tooting Karate Club includes short sequences to allow you to practise defence and attack techniques with your partner, but without the risks that are involved in free fighting. Class prices for adults start at £10 (£6 for children).
Tooting Karate *1st Floor, Gap Bridge House, Gap Road, SW19 8JA (07771 932963, www.southwestlondonkarate.co.uk).*

717 ...or kick-boxing

The Martial Arts Place – with *dojos* (teaching centres) in Swiss Cottage and Stoke Newington – teaches a form called *mo-gei-do*, meaning 'the way of no boundaries'. It's a combination of European and Eastern techniques, including karate and boxing. Kick-boxing is an excellent all-round fitness workout and is as popular with women as it is with men. You can book a trial class for £10.
Martial Arts Place *88 Avenue Road, NW3 3HA (7586 1222); Unit 2, Victorian Grove, 35-39 Stoke Newington High Street, N16 8DR (7254 0332); www.themartialartsplace.com.*

Serpentine Sackler Gallery

718

Turn your garden into a nature reserve

There are more that three million gardens in London – that's a whole lot of habitat for the capital's wildlife to take refuge in. As well as managing over 50 London-wide reserves, the London Wildlife Trust is on a mission to get gardeners to turn their backyards into more inviting environments for plants and animals. It suggests planting mixed hedgerow and broad-leafed trees to create more shade, buying drought-resistant plants that are less water-hungry, digging ponds to provide further habitat diversity and a place for animals to drink and bathe, and sticking compost on the roof of your shed to create a living roof and provide more space for plants to grow. Visit the website for more information.
London Wildlife Trust *7261 0447, www.wildlondon.org.uk.*

719

Dust off your crest at the College of Arms

The Court of the Earl Marshal in the College of Arms is the 17th-century, wood-panelled headquarters of the royal heralds, guardians of the right to bear arms (of the heraldic variety). If you ask to speak to the officer-in-waiting, one of the qualified genealogist heralds, pursuivants or officers-in-arms, they may be happy to explain their function for free, especially if there's a chance of them later being able to undertake research into your ancestors and whether or not they carry a coat of arms (for a fee). The College can also arrange for the examination of pedigrees and prepare heraldic artwork.

Recent grants of arms include those to Loyd Grossman, who chose a polar bear for his crest, and the motto 'If not now when', and to Sir Christopher Frayling, former rector of the Royal College of Art, who, perhaps equally inexplicably, chose a dodo for his crest, three owls on his arms, and a cactus for his badge.
College of Arms *Queen Victoria Street, EC4V 4BT (7248 2762, www.college-of-arms.gov.uk)*

720-729

Drink in a pub with a real fire

The height of civilisation – and all yours for the price of a pint. We recommend the following:

Anglesea Arms 35 Wingate Road, W6 0UR (8749 1291, www.angleseaarmspub.co.uk).
Antelope 76 Mitcham Road, SW17 9NG (8672 3888, http://theantelopepub.com).
Clapton Hart 231 Lower Clapton Road, E5 8EG http://claptonhart.com).
Crooked Billet 14-15 Crooked Billet, SW19 4RQ (8946 4942, www.thecrookedbillet wimbledon.com).
Earl Spencer 260-262 Merton Road, SW18 5JL (8870 9244, www.theearlspencer.com).
Fire Stables 27-29 Church Road, SW19 5DQ (8946 3197, www.firestableswimbledon.co.uk).
Golden Heart 110 Commercial Street, E1 6LZ (7247 2158).
Grand Union 45 Woodfield Road, W9 3BA (7286 1886, www.grandunionlondon.co.uk).
Holly Bush 22 Holly Mount, NW3 6SG (7435 2892, www.hollybushhampstead.co.uk).
Three Kings of Clerkenwell 7 Clerkenwell Close, EC1R 0DY (7253 0483).

730-732

Play bar billiards

Providing an ideal, and not arduous, workout to accompany a pint, bar billiards involves sinking balls in holes of varying difficulty, without knocking down the skittles that protect the most high-scoring holes. A time limit is set on each game (eventually, a bar drops inside the table preventing any more balls returning to be replayed), so, unlike billiards and snooker, even clueless novices know they won't be stuck at a game for hours. There are bar billards at the Pembury Tavern (90 Amhurst Road, E8 1JH, 8986 8597, www.individualpubs.co.uk/pembury), Dog & Bell (116 Prince Street, SE8 3JD, 8692 5664) and King Charles I (55-57 Northdown Street, N1 9BL, 7837 7758). Games cost £1.

A few of my favourite things

733-737

Tessa Watt,
Author,
Mindful London

Walking along one of London's old canal towpaths feels like entering into the slower pace of a different era: a watery haven from asphalt and traffic, yet completely urban. Regent's Canal, almost two centuries old, is a ribbon of quiet water linking some of London's most lively neighbourhoods. I enjoy the two-mile section starting near Angel tube station at Colebrooke Row, N1, which winds by old industrial buildings, new architecture, gas works, locks and houseboats. Just before Kingsland Road, there's a cluster of canalside cafés. End the walk at Hackney's Broadway Market, with its food market on Saturdays and promenade of quirky independent cafés, pubs, bookshops and vintage clothes shops.

Another watery walk, this time in south London, is the Wandle Trail (www.merton. gov.uk), which also makes an excellent, mainly traffic-free cycle route. This 12-mile route follows the River Wandle from its mouth at the Thames in Wandsworth, and heads south-east towards Croydon, taking in green spaces and hidden parts of the city. Highlights en route include Merton Abbey Mills (www.mertonabbeymills.org.uk), a former textile works that once housed William Morris's factory, and now has a weekend arts and crafts market, places to eat, a children's theatre and even pottery classes. There's also Morden Hall Park (www.nationaltrust.org.uk/morden-hall-park), a tranquil National Trust estate. Wilderness Island near Carshalton is a haven for dozens of bird species.

If you're walking along the Thames Path (www.nationaltrail.co.uk/thames-path), there are many historic pubs, all of which pack out on warm evenings. But if you can come on a quiet weekday, there's nothing more relaxing than sitting with a drink by the river. The Mayflower (117 Rotherhithe Street, SE16 4NF, www.mayflowerpub.co.uk) claims to be the oldest pub on the River Thames, standing near the moorings from which the pilgrims set sail in 1620. The current pub dates from the 18th century, with comfortable nooks and crannies, oak beams and wooden panelling. The deck has a heated outdoor marquee area with views up towards London Bridge and the Shard, and across to the wharves of Shadwell and Wapping.

When I find myself in the City, I often pop into one of the many beautiful churches – it's a wonderful way to regain a sense of stillness and space, even within a hectic day. St Stephen Walbrook (39 Walbrook, EC4N 8BN, http://ststephenwalbrook.net) was the parish church of the great 17th-century architect Sir Christopher Wren and is considered by many to be his finest work. You step inside to be bathed in space and light, in a vast, perfectly proportioned classical space; white everywhere, with light from clear glass windows. Light pours down through the dome's central lantern on to a massive stone altar by sculptor Henry Moore, surrounded by curved pews. There are regular free lunchtime organ recitals and classical music concerts.

For me, meditation is the key to finding a sense of balance within the busyness of the big city. I learned to meditate at the London Shambhala Meditation Centre (27 Belmont Close, SW4 6AY, 7720 3207, www.shambhala.org.uk). You can drop in any Monday or Wednesday evening for free meditation instruction and a friendly welcome at this Clapham-based centre, part of the global Shambhala network. The beautiful meditation hall has high ceilings and white walls with vivid Tibetan banners. While it has roots in Buddhism, Shambhala has a strong tradition of teaching meditation as a natural human skill that anyone can learn.

738

Take a tour round the pet cemetery in Hyde Park

A century before Stephen King's creepy cat, Church, scared us silly by clawing his way back from the dead in *Pet Sematary*, the Victorians, obsessed with death and mourning, were laying their dear-departed mutts and moggies to rest in this macabre little corner of Hyde Park. It started with Cherry, a Maltese terrier, in the 1880s and the last interment was in 1967. George Orwell described it as 'perhaps the most horrible spectacle in Britain', and while we wouldn't go that far, it's certainly a spooky spot, hidden behind the railings at Victoria Gate on the Bayswater Road. If you fancy a fright, visit at twilight and you might agree with Mr King's assertion that 'sometimes dead is better'.

739

Visit Bermondsey's Fashion & Textile Museum

British designer Zandra Rhodes is known for her outlandish use of colour, and so it comes as little surprise when you catch sight of the gaudy pink and orange façade of her brainchild (now run and co-owned by Newham College). As well as housing permanent exhibits by Rhodes, the Fashion & Textile Museum – a short stroll from London Bridge station – also has a changing programme of exhibitions (these usually showcase British designers), runs courses for both fashion students and businesses, and holds a series of fashion-related events and talks (many of which cost less than a tenner – see the website for details).

Fashion & Textile Museum *83 Bermondsey Street, SE1 3XF (7407 8664, www.ftmlondon.org). £8.80, £5.50-£6 reductions.*

740

Pay your respects at
Nunhead Cemetery

*Tree-filled Nunhead Cemetery
(entrances on Limesford Road or
Linden Grove, SE15 3LP, 7732-
9535) is a nature reserve and a
maze of Victorian statues with
fine views from its highest points.*

741-747 ...then pay some more at London's other great graveyards

Abney Park

If ivy-clad sculpture is your thing, then head to this cemetery in Stoke Newington. A series of atmospheric, rambling walks takes you past the last resting place of William Booth, founder of the Salvation Army, whose massive headstone assures us that he has not died but been 'promoted to glory'. Further on, you'll see monuments to slavery abolitionists and missionaries, as well as music hall stars.
Stoke Newington High Street, N16 0LH (7275 7557, www.abneypark.org).

Brompton Cemetery

Full of magnificent Victorian monuments, Brompton Cemetery has seen many of the great and the good laid to rest within its boundaries, not least among them suffragette Emmeline Pankhurst. And it's said that many of the names you'll see here inspired Beatrix Potter, who lived nearby – look out for Jeremiah Fisher, Peter Rabbett, Mr McGregor and Mr Nutkins.
Fulham Road, SW10 9UG (7352 1201, www.royalparks.org.uk/parks/brompton-cemetery).

Bunhill Fields Burial Ground

Tucked away off City Road (near Old Street tube) is another atmospheric oasis of eternal peace. Used as a nonconformist – and therefore unconsecrated – cemetery from the late 17th century to the middle of the 19th, it features the graves of such notables as poet and mystic William Blake, John 'Pilgrim's Progress' Bunyan, some assorted lesser Cromwells, Thomas Hardy, Daniel Defoe and Susannah Wesley – mother of John Wesley, the founder of Methodism.
38 City Road, EC1Y 1AU (7374 4127, www.cityoflondon.gov.uk).

Highgate Cemetery

The fame of many of Highgate Cemetery's 'residents' makes this a popular visitor attraction and explains the entry fees (East Cemetery £4; West Cemetery, by guided tour only, £12). But with its angels, shrouded urns, broken columns and dramatic tombs, this is a delightfully atmospheric place to wander. The checklist of celebrated graves includes Christina Rossetti, Michael Faraday, Karl Marx and George Eliot. Both sites are closed during funerals, so call ahead to check before you visit.
Swain's Lane, N6 6JP (8340 1834, www.highgate-cemetery.org).

Kensal Green Cemetery

Kensal Green Cemetery hides its fair share of notable figures behind its neoclassical gateway. It's particularly strong on 19th-century intellectuals – towering examples of which include Isambard Kingdom Brunel, William Thackeray, Anthony Trollope and Wilkie Collins – but don't forget to visit the grave of Charles 'the Great' Blondin whose high jinks on a tightrope above Niagara Falls way back in 1859 put David Blaine to shame.
Harrow Road, W10 4RA (8969 0152, www.kensalgreen.co.uk).

Tower Hamlets Cemetery

Though the gravestones here may be a little light on famous names, Tower Hamlets Cemetery has a serene charm all of its own – an expanse of calm just off the busy Bow Road. You'll find 31 acres of beautiful woodland and meadow, making it a much-needed green heart in the middle of the East End.
Southern Grove, E3 4PX (8983 1277, www.fothcp.org).

West Norwood Cemetery

West Norwood cemetery in south London, in the borough of Lambeth, with its impressive Gothic Revival architecture, holds memorials to Mrs Beeton, Sir Henry Doulton, Dr William Marsden, Baron Julius de Reuter, Charles Spurgeon and Sir Henry Tate.
Norwood Road, SE27 9JU (7926 7999, www.lambeth.gov.uk, www.fownc.org).

748 Visit Trinity Buoy Wharf

Once a ship- and buoy-maintenance depot, Trinity Buoy Wharf has had many different incarnations over the years and now it's a centre for the arts and creative industries. With spectacular views over the Thames and with Canary Wharf twinkling in the background, the site is home to exhibitions and performance venues, and houses what is probably London's smallest museum – a former docker's hut dedicated to 19th-century scientist Michael Faraday. Old shipping containers that have been revamped and painted bright colours are used for artists' studios.

The Wharf is also home to London's only lighthouse (there are great views from the top) and the mesmerising *Longplayer* Tibetan bell sound installation (http://longplayer.org): Jem Finer's 1,000-year-long musical composition has been playing since 31 December 1999 and should continue, without repetition, until the year 3000. It's open to the public at weekends.
Trinity Buoy Wharf *64 Orchard Place, E14 0JY (7515 7153, www.trinitybuoywharf.com). Free.*

749

Create a Spark

Tired of listening to celebrity self-publicity? Well, Spark (www.sparklondon.com) is your chance to star – along with other 'ordinary people' – in your own tragicomic story. Creator Joanna Yates explains that Spark is the place to hear and tell true stories. Performers – including teachers, car dealers, mothers and barristers – stand up in front of an audience and spill their beans. Each show is loosely structured around a theme (such as 'mistaken identity' or 'under the influence') and individual stories are (perhaps advisedly) limited to five minutes. After the show, audience and performers mingle for a drink and a chat. Tickets are £4; see the website for venues.

750-751 *Watch short films*

Short-film screenings are thriving in London. The capital offers a variety of venues and festivals where audiences can enjoy anything from quirky music videos and short stories to animations and documentaries – and not necessarily in a traditional cinema setting.

The good folk behind Future Shorts (www.futureshorts.com) have taken it upon themselves to create a culture around the medium of short films. They're not afraid to take film out of the cinema and have previously let their reels loose in galleries, bars and clubs (such as Fabric, where they showed *Metropolis*, with a band re-scoring the film), and a cave in Cornwall while on tour with the Guillemots. 'We want to change the way people watch short films and to create an immersive experience,' says Future Shorts founder and director Fabien Riggall. Films are grouped by theme, so around Valentine's Day, for example, you'll see 90 minutes' worth of shorts from all over the world, each showing different interpretations of love.

The team is also behind Secret Cinema (www.secretcinema.org – although this costs more than £10), a regular event that invites people to a secret and often bizarre venue to watch a film (are you up for spending an evening in a five-star hotel car park?).

And there's also the London Short Film Festival (LSFF, www.shortfilms.org.uk), set up in 2004, which runs over ten days each January in some of the city's best cinemas, and brings together excellent contemporary talent.

752 *Moonwalk*

A charity marathon walk held each year in aid of breast cancer research, Moonwalk is for the hard core. Yes, a 26.2 mile walk through London is doable – but try doing it sleep-deprived in the dead of night, wearing a lavishly embellished bra. The shenanigans start at midnight and places get sold out fast, so book early. Register on www.walkthewalk.org.

753 Have a Friday Night Skate

This weekend warm-up skate around town is one of London's best free nights out. Open to rollerskaters (in-line and quad varieties both welcome) of all ages and levels, the evening kicks off every Friday at 8pm. Hundreds of individuals (many of them clad in Lycra) bunch together, racing, socialising and rolling along to tunes pumped out by a boombox taped to an accompanying bike. The route (which changes every week) is between ten and 15 miles long, with things getting more intense in the second half as the pace picks up for the serious skaters. Afterwards, everyone usually piles into the nearest pub for a well-deserved pint. The skate starts at the Wellington Arch, Hyde Park Corner; see www.lfns.co.uk for details.

Family fortunes

Riding the DLR, splashing in fountains, picnicking with llamas –
there's a wealth of budget family fun to be had in the capital, says
Ronnie Haydon.

London has an embarrassment of riches for the thrifty family. You only need the price of a travelcard, a packed lunch and a following wind to spend the whole day freely entertaining your children. Museums, galleries, parks, gardens, farms, dancing fountains and prancing minstrels await their pleasure.

A Travelcard is your ticket to all the free fun that London can offer. Just experiencing big red buses (old-fashioned Routemasters still operate on route 15), trains and trams is a treat for the very young, especially those deprived darlings who don't ordinarily travel on public transport. The range of vehicles you can hop on and off using your Travelcard is wider than in any other city. Choose your means of transport: bus, tube, DLR (Docklands Light Railway), Overground, train, tram or riverboat (where you'll get a discount).

A pleasant overview of that excellent source of free entertainment, the South Bank, is afforded by the commuter/tourist bus RV1. The clue's in the name. It takes you past some great riverside sights – the London Eye, National Theatre, Royal

Festival Hall, Tate Modern – on its route from Covent Garden to Tower Gateway. You could use it on a fun-filled self-guided tour starting at Covent Garden Piazza, where crowds gather for the street entertainers on a daily basis, then on to the River Stage outside the National Theatre (7452 3400, www.nationaltheatre.org.uk), which has a free summertime arts programme (July to mid September) showcasing the best street theatre, circus, music, art and dance from all over the world. Then you can stroll all the way along the South Bank to see what else is going on. If it's hot, the dancing fountains outside the Royal Festival Hall are a source of pure pleasure for children. Take a change of clothes and tempt them out of the water for a South Bank picnic in Bernie Spain Gardens nearby. Also take a moment to look in on the Clore Ballroom in the Royal Festival Hall (0844 875 0073, www.southbankcentre.co.uk) while you're promenading: this is often the site for free school holiday events, such as treasure trails, storytelling and some quite bizarre performances.

Discover the Story Centre

Angel Theatre

The RV1's terminus at Tower Gateway will lead you to your next fun transport option – the DLR. Happy is the child who baggsies a front seat on these driverless trains. They love to pretend to be the driver and enjoy the swoops down the humpy track that leads to Docklands. Stop off at Canary Wharf for an ogle at the shiny tower blocks around Canada Square and the various neat little gardens, pontoons and public art, then hop back on to the DLR and continue your journey.

If you take the southerly branch towards Lewisham, you can get down on the farm in the heart of the city at Mudchute City Farm (7515 5901, www.mudchute.org, free), one

of the most rewarding of London's bumper crop of agricultural idylls. This is the only place in the city where you can picnic with llamas. Other animals grazing and rootling – with skyscrapers as their backdrop – include ponies, poultry, sheep, goats, pigs and cattle. The Mudchute Kitchen is plump with homemade cakes and delicious savouries, if your budget will allow. For a list of London's other city farms, see p107.

The next DLR stop from here is Island Gardens, by the river. If you fancy a trip south, take the Greenwich Foot Tunnel (a spooky experience if ever there was one) under the river and emerge at Greenwich, to visit one of the best free museums in the city, the National Maritime

Museum (8858 4422, www.rmg.co.uk), which has art activities and storytelling for children. If the weather's good, don't miss the chance to enjoy the airy heights of Greenwich Park and the Royal Observatory courtyard (8858 4422, www.rmg.co.uk/royal-observatory, free), where costumed storytellers often hold forth during the school holidays. The Meridian Line here is the classic photo opportunity.

If you choose to travel north on the DLR from Docklands, you can stop off at Stratford for the varied delights of the Queen Elizabeth Olympic Park (0800 0722 110, www.queenelizabeth olympicpark.co.uk; see p241). Also in Stratford is the Discover the Story Centre (8536 5555, www.discover.org.uk, £5), which, although it has an admission charge for the indoor story-building centre, has a lovely little garden with a space ship, slides and willow tunnel that kid adore. It's a splendid place for a picnic too.

Back in town, the DLR links up with the Jubilee line of the tube system, the most modern and attractive line. It'll take you to London Bridge, where several overground trains an hour can whisk you to Forest Hill and the most original – and one of the best – free museums in town: the Horniman Museum & Gardens (8699 1872, www.horniman.ac.uk). Here, there's always something going on in the school holidays: summer sees wildlife art activites in the extensive, beautifully managed grounds and woods, and open-air shows in the bandstand. If the weather's iffy, take time to enjoy the music rooms and yet more arts-based fun inside this quirky museum. The Aquarium (£3.85 adult, £1.65 child) here is fantastic fun, with mesmeric jellyfish, graceful seahorses and loads of variations on the Nemo theme.

If the children are keen to sample every form of public transport in the city, be prepared to fit in a tram ride – down in deep south London. Take a train from Forest Hill to East Croydon, from where you can pick up a tram to Wimbledon, an oft-neglected London outpost but an essential stop-off point for families because of the excellent children's theatre, the Polka (8543 4888, www.polkatheatre.com). You don't have to buy tickets for a show to enjoy spending time in the indoor and outdoor play areas, the super little café and at the teddy bear collection.

From the Polka, the fastest way into town again is by tube from South Wimbledon station. Get out at London Bridge and walk westward along Bankside to Tate Modern (7887 8888,

www.tate.org.uk, free). Smart arty programmes for children can be found here; check online for details of children's multimedia guides, activity packs and the under-fives play zone. Once you've done the Modern, you can float off to older sister Tate Britain on Damien Hirst's dotty Tate Boat – with a Travelcard it costs just £4.75 for adults and £2.40 for children. Tate Britain provides kids with the Art Trolley at the weekends, which is laden with a wide variety of make-and-do ideas.

If you want to take in a show in the evening, a just-a-tenner artistic treat not to be missed (if your party consists of just one adult and one child) is Friday Fives at the Little Angel Theatre in Islington (7226 1787, www.littleangeltheatre.com), where all tickets for the 5pm Friday performances cost just a fiver. This diminutive but legendary arts venue (the only permanent puppet theatre in London), is an atmospheric place to take in a show, particularly around Christmas time.

Bear in mind that packing a picnic is essential if you're going to spend the day in London with the children without spending more than a tenner. With so many museums and galleries to explore, the kids are going to fade fast without one. And we haven't even mentioned the big three: Science (7942 4000, www.sciencemuseum.org.uk, free), Natural History (7942 5000, www.nhm.ac.uk, free) and Victoria & Albert (7942 2000, www.vam.ac.uk, free) museums, all of which have a busy school-holiday programme of events for younger visitors. Also, in good weather there's nothing better than relaxing in the park with your lunch. Hyde Park and Kensington Gardens (0300 061 2000, www.royalparks.org.uk) are your best bet, mainly for the excellent Diana, Princess of Wales Memorial Playground and for paddling in the Memorial Fountain, by the Serpentine. Most big museums have a picnic room too, so food brought from home can still be eaten in comfort even if the weather's foul.

Still, if you've forgotten to bring a picnic or fancied treating everybody, and there's just one adult and one or two children to feed, you can just about do lunch for under a tenner. The Deep Blue Café in the Science Museum offers a good children's set meal; some places in Chinatown offer budget lunch deals; as do, of course, the Pizza Huts and McDonald's of this world. However, in order to keep within the budget, it means everyone has to settle for tap water. Sometimes it's hard to be a parent.

777-781

Take advantage of the capital's free festivals

Who says festivals have to happen in leafy green fields in the middle of nowheresville? London's streets might not be paved with gold, but in the summer they are a hive of free musical and cultural activity.

Big Dance
This week-long dance party encourages all ages to get fit in toe-tapping fashion. You can get your jig on at hundreds of events. In the past, these have included tango demos on the tube, performances in Oxford Street shop windows and alfresco shows in Regent's Park.
Various venues (www.bigdance.org.uk). July.

London Jazz Festival
The London Jazz Festival continues to stretch its elastic definition of jazz, so an excitingly eclectic and top-notch line-up is guaranteed. Not only that, but LJF has now expanded out of its original central London bases such as the South Bank and Ronnie Scott's to embrace far-flung venues across the capital, from Finchley's Artsdepot to Blackheath Halls. Many tickets are under a tenner and there's an amazing range of free events – a great opportunity to discover different jazz genres.
Various venues (www.londonjazzfestival.org.uk). Nov.

London Mela
Dubbed the Asian Glastonbury, tens of thousands flock to Ealing for this exuberant celebration of Asian culture – contemporary and traditional. Garage beats play happily alongside traditional Qawwali, and you'll also get an opportunity to check out innovative commissioned projects (such as a collaboration with Circus Space that brought Indian dancers together with aerial performers). As well as the music and dance, there are also bustling bazaars and tasty food stalls.
Gunnersbury Park, W3 (www.londonmela.org). Sept.

London Mela

More London

Stroll down to City Hall and the outdoor riverside Scoop amphitheatre for a diverse range of alfresco events over the summer months. July brings live coverage of the season's key sporting action (Wimbledon, Tour de France, cricket, golf); August turns all theatrical (2015 involved reworkings of Roman and Greek dramas); while September offers film screenings (favourites for all the family, from *Paddington* to *The Sound of Music*). There's bound to be something to please. *City Hall, SE1 (www.morelondon.com). June-September.*

River Stage

The National Theatre takes the action outdoors in summer with this packed programme of cultural riverside events on the South Bank at weekends. The entertainment is a playful mix of music, dance, DJs, circus acts and street theatre. *Theatre Square, South Bank, SE1 (www.national theatre.org.uk/riverstage). Late July-Aug.*

More London

782
Ride the old Routemaster...

The old Routemasters, with their hop on, hop off back door, still run on the no.15 heritage route, from Charing Cross to Tower Hill and back.

783
...or a Santander bike

Casual users can hire a bike by going to a docking station, touching the 'hire a cycle' icon and inserting a credit or debit card. The machine will print out a five-digit code for you to tap into the docking point of a bike, which releases the machine. £2 buys 24-hour access, and the first 30 minutes are free. See https://tfl.gov.uk for more details.

784
Serve yourself a pint

At the Thirsty Bear (62 Stamford Street, SE1 9LX, 7928 5354, www.thethirstybear.com), drinkers can pour their own pints from iPad-controlled pumps at each table.

785
Take a closer look at the Albert Memorial

The overblown Gothic Revival wonder that is the Albert Memorial, opposite the Royal Albert Hall in Kensington Gardens, was opened to public view 11 years after the premature death, from typhoid, of Queen Victoria's beloved Prince Consort in 1861. At 176 feet tall, it's a shrine to the certainties of the Victorian age – and definitely worthy of closer inspection.

Surrounded by Empire and all its achievements in microcosm – four continents, frozen life-size models representing the industries and the respected professions of the day – a 14-foot figure of Albert sits amid a fantastic sparkling shed of jewels, polished stones and glass, surmounted by four brightly coloured mosaics of the arts, an angel-strewn spire and a golden cross. It's as kitsch as anything you're ever likely to lay eyes on.

Stand and stare, and you'll soon find hidden wonders: a marble camel and bison; models of Native Americans; voluptuous Miss Asia and her elephant; as well as a 'hive' of industry. If you want to know more, tours are held every first Sunday of the month from March to December; they cost £8, and pre-booking is not required.

Homeslice

786-788
Enjoy Italian fizz on tap...

Prosecco on tap is a growing trend in London's bars. Though, according to the Prosecco DOC Consortium, true prosecco (which is produced in the Conegliano-Valdobbiadene region in north-east Italy, near Venice) must be served in a glass bottle. The on-tap Italian fizz that we Brits have become so fond of is made from the same grape as prosecco, but because it's served on tap, it can't officially be called prosecco.

Whatever the name, enjoy a glass or two at Soho's Mele e Pere (46 Brewer Street, W1F 9TF, 7096 2096, www.melee pere.co.uk), Covent Garden's Homeslice (13 Neal's Yard, WC2H 9DP, 3151 7488, www.homeslice pizza.co.uk) – whose menu cleverly skirts the issue by advertising the on-tap frizzante as 'prosecco by any other name') – and Shoreditch's Crown & Shuttle (226 Shoreditch High Street, E1 6PJ, 7375 2905, http://crownand shuttle.co.uk).

789-791
... or drink champagne

Bars selling champagne aren't rare, but a classy joint offering fizz for under a tenner is a less common occurrence. Here are a few of our favourite spots for bubbly.

Sit amid the wood-panelled surrounds of the bar at the City branch of steak specialist Hawksmoor (10 Basinghall Street, EC2V 5BQ, 7397 8120, www.thehawksmoor.com) and sip champagne for £9 a glass. In Soho, long-established wine bar Shampers (4 Kingly Street, W1B 5PE, 7437 1692, www.shampers.net) lists a glass of champagne for £7.95. And while the surroundings may not be as glam, it's hurrah for Amuse Bouche (51 Parsons Green Lane, SW6 4JA, 7371 8517, www.amuse bouchelondon.co.uk), the Fulham champagne bar where the house bubbly starts at £7.50 a glass, and there are more than ten champagnes offered by the glass.

792 Do the Docks

It's a shame so few tourists make their way any further east than the pub-, restaurant- and shopping-happy St Katharine's Dock, close by Tower Bridge. A mere ten-minute walk away on Wapping Wharf there are whole streets of waterfront wharves prospering as flats, but still full of atmosphere with their stock-brick pavement arcades, deep-water inlets, old gantries, river stairs and lookouts.

For example, from next to the Town of Ramsgate pub (62 Wapping High Street, E1W 2PN, 7481 8000, www.townoframsgate.co.uk), take the historic Wapping Old Stairs down to the Thames foreshore – make sure the tide's out, and don't wander too far – to explore the site of the old Execution Dock, marked with an 'E' on the pierhead façade. This is where the East End river pirates – known variously as Heavy Horsemen, Mudlarks and Scuffle Hunters – were chained and washed by tides in punishment for robbing an impressive 50 per cent of the Docks' spices, tea, butter, tobacco, tropical woods and coal. That was until the West India Dock Company began defending their new, stoutly fortified premises with cannon.

793 Watch a Bollywood film at the Boleyn Cinema

A beacon of charm amid fast-food shops on Barking Road in Newham, this ornate picture palace screens a strict diet of Indian Bollywood blockbusters (£5).
Boleyn Cinema 7-11 Barking Road, E6 1PW (8471 4884, www.boleyncinemas.com).

794-800
Visit the city's best beer shops

Twickenham's Real Ale Shop (371 Richmond Road, TW1 2EF, 8892 3710, www.realale.com) sells around 100 beers, ales, ciders and perrys, including bottle-conditioned varieties that are as close as the home-drinker can get to cask ale flavour without installing handpumps in their kitchen. Even better, you get 500ml sizes of most

bottles for around £3. Beer Boutique in Putney (134 Upper Richmond Road, SW15 2SP, 8780 3168, www.thebeerboutique.co.uk) has a carefully selected range of Trappist, Belgian, fruit and pilsner beers; London ales are well represented too. Drink of Fulham (349 Fulham Palace Road, SW6 6TB, 7610 6795, www.drinkoffulham.com) has an exceptional range of brews (more than 500) from around the world. At Camden's Kris Wines (394 York Way, N7 9LW, 7607 4871, www.kriswines.com), ales are arranged by country of origin and range from Odell's 90 Shilling ale (from the States) to bottles from Manchester's Marble Brewery. Handily placed for all those BYO Vietnamese restaurants is Amathus (303 Old Street, EC1V 9IA, 7729 2111, www.amathusdrinks.com), a Hoxton off-licence that keeps all its beer in the fridge, including ales from the Kernal and Meantime breweries. Caps & Taps (130 Kentish Town Road, NW1 9QB, www.capsandtaps.co.uk) is a craft beer specialist in Kentish Town. It's a tiny place but it sells around 300 beers from around the world. Look out for relative rarities: Burning Sky Cuvée from Sussex, Stone Old Guardian from Southern California, and Barrel-Aged India Hells Lager from nearby Camden Brewery. Fans of esoteric US beers are particularly well served. From Tuesday to Saturday, the Utobeer stall in Borough Market (Unit 24, Middle Road, SE1 1TL, 7378 6617, www.utobeer.co.uk) sells hundreds of different beers from all over the world.

A few of my favourite things

801-808

Erik-lee Briscoe,
Performance coach

My favourite park in London is also my 'office': Hilly Fields Park, between Ladywell and Brockley in Lewisham. It has its own mini Stonehenge, a great café and me! I train athletes: runners, footballers, boxers, all sorts. My company (www.team6.fitness) is focused on movement training, so my clients receive a full-body workout using weights, punchbags, the VertiMax, Slam balls, battle ropes and more. I set up every morning: I'm a familiar face round here.

My life is all about sport, so I enjoy going to Ladywell Running Track (Ladywell Arena, Silvermere Road, SE6 4QX, 8314 1986, www.fusion-lifestyle.com) and talking to the other coaches. A lot of my athlete clients train at the track on Tuesdays and Thursdays, so I can see how they're running too.

My other favourite park is Mountsfield Park in Catford. It has a new community garden, great children's playgrounds, and is home to Lewisham People's Day every July – one of south-east London's biggest free festivals.

When I'm not working, I love being near the river. The Trafalgar Tavern (Park Row, SE10 9NW, 8858 2909, www.trafalgartavern. co.uk) in Greenwich is a marvellous old pub. You can sit outside by the Thames and have a great dinner – the steak and chips is excellent – and some Meantime Wheat beer, then work it all off by taking a brisk riverside stroll to the Thames Barrier (see p254) listening to the seagulls calling, and looking out for cormorants and herons.

I also love taking boat trips up the river. Thames Clippers (www.thamesclippers.com) are just brilliant: they're a fine way to impress visitors and a very swift way to travel east to west. You get a discount with an Oyster card or Travelcard.

I like to eat well (it's essential in my game), and love a little café near my home in Forest Hill. Called My Jamii (3 Honor Oak, SE23 1DX, 3581 6234, www.myjamiicafe.com), it's part of a not-for-profit scheme for young people aged 17-23 who are struggling to make a living in these austere times. It has a simple, really good menu for breakfast and lunch (including Brick Lane bagels), and the food sets you up for the day. I like its mission: 'Great coffee and homemade food with a slice of dignity for young people.'

Once in a while I get to the theatre to see a play or musical. I adored *The Lion King* (www. thelionking.co.uk), which has been playing at the Lyceum Theatre in Covent Garden for years. Fantastic dancing and costumes, and I really appreciated the way the audience got involved with the action.

When I go to the cinema, it's usually to the big, nine-screen Odeon at Surrey Quays (Redriff Road, SE16 7LL, www.odeon.co.uk). I love action films, with loads of stunts and explosions – I just can't resist all the *Mission Impossible* films.

809

Yodel!

Since 1967, Joseph, with the help of his lederhosened lads and dirndled lasses, has been providing an impressively high-camp version of Austrian hospitality in this cellar venue. The likes of David Walliams, Elle McPherson and Kate

Moss have descended the stairs to this basement restaurant – along with countless stag nights and work parties: and we're pretty sure they didn't come for the bratwurst. It's the floorshow of yodelling, cowbells and accordian-accompanied singalongs that keeps the place packed. A meal would cost around £25-£30 per head (reservations are recommended), but you can squeeze in at the tiny bar and wet your whistle for under a tenner. You might even be persuaded to belt out to a few tunes from *The Sound of Music*.
Tiroler Hut *27 Westbourne Grove, W2 4UA (7727 3981, www.tirolerhut.co.uk).*

810 *Experience some animal magic*

A visit to Battersea Dogs & Cats Home offers an amazing opportunity to explore the famous south London kennels and cattery, and learn about the charity that cares for the capital's lost and abandoned cats and dogs. Admission costs just £2 per adult, and visitors can take a tour and meet some of the residents. It's not a petting zoo, though – instead, you'll find out the stories behind the animals, learn more about responsible pet ownership and have the chance to buy treats for any forlorn faces that steal your heart. There's also a gift shop and a courtyard café, from where you can watch owners being reunited, and rehomers leaving for their new home. While you're there, look out for a pair of unadorned gateposts. The two beautiful cast-iron dogs that once decorated them have been lost over the years – probably the only two mutts the Home hasn't been able to help.

Battersea Dogs & Cats Home *4 Battersea Park Road, SW8 4AA (0843 509 4444, www.battersea.org.uk).*

811

Hula-hoop!
Of all the retro crazes that have come back – from neon to knitting – hula-hooping is the most fun, not to mention the best for your waistline. Hula-hoop guru Anna Drury (http://annathehulagan.com) has developed quite a following for her classes – light-hearted, sociable occasions; perfect for those who want to work out in an atmosphere more 'Flashdance' than Fitness First. Call 07545 499618 to book.

812
Walk the Jubilee Walkway...

Pity the taxi drivers. London is a colossal patchwork rug of a city, and even long-term residents find it tricky to gain an understanding of how its various districts stitch together. The tube map might be a design classic, but those linear patterns and handy spacings bear little relation to things at ground level – the average street layout in the *A-to-Z* is cartographic spaghetti.

The Jubilee Walkway, then, offers a dual function: meaningful exploration for newcomers to the city and a refresher course for those who call it home. Just as important, though, is the fact that it's a great walk. Initially created to celebrate the Queen's Silver Jubilee in 1977, the route has since been honed and enlarged to provide a pavement-pounding 15-mile loop through some of the centre's more absorbing pockets. You'll get your fair share of postcard sights – Big Ben, the Tower et al – but you'll also get a genuinely enlightening look at London in its various guises: old and new, hushed and chaotic, grand and grotty.

The 'official' starting point is Leicester Square, although in our view it makes more sense to begin with the stretch between Lambeth and Tower bridges – it's the only section south of the river and a view-packed hors d'oeuvre for what's to follow. Then it's over the water into St Katharine Docks, across into the Square Mile and on to the Barbican before winding back down to St Paul's. Then, head along Fleet Street, up into Holborn and hard north to St Pancras, at which point the route plunges back through Bloomsbury and Covent Garden, touching St James's and heading on into Westminster and Lambeth. Easy.

There are metal 'Jubilee Walkway' sign-plates embedded in the pavement at regular intervals, although if you'd rather not stare down at your feet all day you'd do well to pick up a dedicated map beforehand (see www.tfl.gov.uk). The route can be done in a full day but it's a fair trek, so many choose to split it over two or three days. It can be whatever you make of it – a history tour, a photographic walk or even the mother of all pub crawls. And the beauty lies not in the classic set pieces but in the finer details: the architectural quirks, the sense of ages gone by, the stately calm of backstreet Bloomsbury, the suit-and-tie mêlée of St Paul's, the sheep of Coram's Fields and the pelicans of St James's Park.

Potential pit-stops are countless, and a big part of the fun – the route passes some of the best cafés, museums, shops, pubs and galleries that London has to offer – but we'd cherry-pick the following: the madcap interior design at Sir John Soane's Museum (13 Lincoln's Inn Fields, WC2A 3BP, 7405 2107, www.soane.org); an arthouse flick at the Brunswick's Curzon Bloomsbury cinema (0330 500 1331, www.curzoncinemas.com); a pint in Victorian opulence at the Princess Louise (208-209 High Holborn, WC1V 7EP, 7405 8816, http://princesslouisepub.co.uk); then head over to Monmouth Street, where you'll find boutiques aplenty along with caffeine stalwart Monmouth Coffee House (27 Monmouth Street, WC2H 9EU, 7232 3010, www.monmouthcoffee.co.uk). Finally, walk to Cecil Court (www.cecilcourt.co.uk), off Charing Cross Road, and have a browse through its antiquarian bookshops.

813

...and then the Jubilee Greenway

This walking and cycling route, completed in 2012, marks the Queen's Diamond Jubilee. It's exactly 60 kilometres (37 miles) long – one kilometre for each year of Her Majesty's reign – and is waymarked with distinctive glass pavement slabs. The start (at Buckingham Palace) links in with the Jubilee Walkway, and section one runs through the heart of London up to Little Venice, but some of the later sections are arguably more interesting, as they offer a route into less-visited parts of town. Section four, for example, leads east through Victoria Park along the Greenway (above the city's main sewerage system) past the Queen Elizabeth Olympic Park and Abbey Mills Pumping Station to Beckton.

You can download maps and route descriptions pointing out sights of interest – as well as a congratulatory certificate once you've completed the walk – from https://tfl.gov.uk.

814

Browse the Petrie Museum with a torch

While the British Museum's Egyptology collection is strong on the big stuff, we love the Petrie for its focus on the minutiae of ancient life. Set up in 1892 by eccentric traveller and diarist Amelia Edwards, the museum is named after Flinders Petrie, one of the indefatigable excavators of ancient Egyptian treasure. With around 80,000 objects, it's one of the world's greatest collections of Egyptian archaeology. Borrow a torch from staff and explore the gloomy Second Gallery (dimly lit for conservation purposes). Shine your light into old-fashioned glass cases housing all manner of everyday items, including the world's oldest tunic (a 5,000-year-old linen dress), tools, cosmetics (kohl pots, combs) and – Hurrah! Just what you need to complete the Indiana Jones fantasy – human remains in a pot (a 4,000-year-old male skeleton).
Petrie Museum of Egyptian Archaeology *University College London, Malet Place, WC1E 6BT (7679 2884, www.petrie.ucl.ac.uk). Free.*

815

Tower over the city atop Westminster Cathedral

Often overlooked in favour of the more famous Westminster Abbey, Westminster Cathedral is spectacular in its own bizarre way. Looking like a wedding cake with a stick of rock stuck on the side, this neo-Byzantine confection – finished in 1903 – has incredible views from the four-sided viewing gallery 210 feet up in the bell tower. The bell's inscription reads, 'While the sound of this bell travels through the clouds, may the bands of angels pray for those assembled in thy church.' Don't worry about aural assaults, though: the public aren't allowed in while the bell is being rung. Access (by lift) costs £6, £3 reductions.
Westminster Cathedral *Victoria Street, SW1P 1QW (7798 9055, www.westminstercathedral.org.uk).*

816

Watch Scene & Heard

Scene & Heard is an unusual and inspiring theatre trip. Based on New York's similar 52nd Street Project, it's a scheme that was set up a decade ago to encourage and challenge – emotionally and creatively – disadvantaged children from the Somers Town area south of Camden Town. The kids, all aged between nine and 15, write a short play and are then united with a dramaturge, a director and two actors – all of whom are professionals. The result is an often hilarious, heart-warming and hugely impressive piece of theatre, proving that children have a lot to teach us about imagination and clarity of vision. Performances are held at Theatro Technis, and are endorsed and attended by many well-known faces; donations are appreciated.
Theatro Technis *26 Crowndale Road, NW1 1TT (7388 9009, www.sceneandheard.org). Free.*

817 *Check out the Thames Barrier from all angles*

The Thames Barrier has saved the city from watery catastrophe nearly 90 times since its construction in the early 1980s. It's also a fantastic sculptural presence on the river that's worth travelling to see. Ideally, a visit should be timed to see it in action – you can find out when that is from the Information Centre.

One approach is via Charlton train station (from Charing Cross or Cannon Street) followed by a ten-minute hike up Anchor & Hope Lane, then right along Nagasaki Walk and Hiroshima Promenade. Alternatively, take the DLR to Pontoon Dock, which is set in the lovely Thames Barrier Park, from where there are superb views of the structure.

You can also check out the east side of the barrier from the Woolwich Free Ferry (8853 9400) – just hop back on the DLR for a couple of stops to King George V, from where it's a short walk south to get to the ferry.

Alternatively, and for perhaps the most amazing views, visit Greenwich Yacht Club (0844 736 5846, www.greenwichyachtclub.co.uk) on their club night – after 8pm on a Tuesday. Their clubhouse is on the river a few hundred yards upstream from the barrier. Of course, come the flood, they'll be OK on their boats.

Thames Barrier Information & Learning Centre *1 Unity Way, SE18 5NJ (8305 4188, www.gov.uk/ the-thames-barrier). £3.75.*

818-825 Listen to free lunchtime recitals

Robin Saikia spends his lunch hours listening to sublime music in lovely churches – for next to nothing.

Listening to live classical music in London can be an expensive pastime, but there are several churches around town hosting astonishingly good recitals where you'll come away with change from a fiver. At most of the venues mentioned below, events are free but donations are always appreciated.

The Church of St James's, Piccadilly (197 Piccadilly, W1J 9LL, 7734 4511, www.sjp.org.uk) offers a holy grail of free recital programming with its 50-minute concerts every Monday, Wednesday and Friday at 1.10pm. The suggested £3.50 donation is well worth paying for concerts that routinely include – and this is taken from the running order for one month alone – works from the likes of Bach, Chopin, Rachmaninoff, Beethoven, Glinka, Janáček, Fauré and Ravel.

St Martin-in-the-Fields (Trafalgar Square, WC2N 4JJ, 7766 1100, www.stmartin-in-the-fields.org) hosts a popular programme of music (from Franck and Parry, Mozart and Gershwin, for example) at its free lunchtime recitals at 1pm every Monday, Tuesday and Friday. For a concert in such a magnificent church, the suggested donation of £3.50 is a snip – and the money goes towards the church's continuing renewal programme.

There are free lunchtime recitals too at St Paul's, Covent Garden (Bedford Street, WC2E 9ED, 7836 5221, www.actors church.org), known to Londoners as the Actors' Church on account of the many thespians interred or commemorated here. The recitals are usually held on Thursdays and Fridays, but check the website before you turn up.

The City is a particularly rich source of music thanks to its abundance of churches. Tiny St Olave's Church (Hart Street, EC3R 7NB, 7488 4318, www.sanctuaryinthecity.net), is the burial place of Samuel Pepys and his wife Elizabeth, and also one of very few medieval churches still standing in London (it dates from around 1450). Lunchtime recitals are held here at 1.05pm on Wednesdays and Thursdays, ranging from piano soloists to assorted vocalists and small ensembles.

At St Lawrence Jewry (Guildhall Yard, EC2V 5AA, 7600 9478, www.stlawrence jewry.org.uk), there are piano recitals on Mondays and organ concerts on Tuesdays – both at 1pm. The church is the official church of the Lord Mayor of London and of the City of London Corporation. Not far away, lovely Wren church St Martin-within-Ludgate (40 Ludgate Hill, EC4M 7DE, 7248 6054, www.stmartin-within-ludgate. org.uk) has classical recitals most Mondays at 1.05pm. Note that most churches in the City don't host concerts during August.

In addition to a busy calendar of lectures, seminars and exhibitions, Southwark Cathedral (London Bridge, SE1 9DA, 7367 6700, http://cathedral.southwark. anglican.org) has an impressive musical programme. As well as the free organ recitals on Mondays, there are other classical recitals on alternate Tuesdays – check the website for details.

Finally, don't forget that there are free organ recitals at Westminster Abbey (Dean's Yard, SW1P 3PA, 7222 5152, www.westminster-abbey.org) every Sunday evening from 5.45pm to 6.15pm. The Harrison and Harrison organ, built in 1937, is a magnificent beast and, if you're lucky, you could hear it being played by the Abbey organist, James O'Donnell, one of the finest musicians in Britain.

Cheap chills

*In freezing December weather, **Annie Dare** plunges headlong into London's outdoor swimming pools.*

Iceland's financial collapse, in the summer of 2008, was a surreal demonstration of the start of the global recession. In its wake, shocked Icelanders, noted the BBC, distracted themselves by attempting a little submersion of their own: in November, Reykjavik harbour (at 3.5°C) was bobbing with unprecedented numbers of swimmers, up by more than 300 per cent since the start of the banking crisis that had caused monthly job losses of 5,000. Observers saw a direct correlation between the crash and the soaring attendance levels, as people took drastic measures to forget their economic woes. Now that Britain's economy has also suffered, have more Londoners taken the plunge too?

It is a cold white morning. People are stomping their feet at Gospel Oak's bus stops, exhaling breath plumes. Up on Hampstead Heath, a series of terriers wear tartan gilets and some hockey lads lazily jog round goalposts in an attempt to keep warm. On the brick ledge encircling Parliament Hill Lido (Parliament Hill Fields, Gordon House Road, NW5 1NA, 7485 3873, www.cityoflondon.gov.uk), a troop of pigeons have puffed out their feathers so hard that you can't even see their necks. Their bird eyes follow the figures of bobble-hatted humans bounding beneath them. At the water's edge, a small group dressed in fleeces traces the slow arc of a martial arts sequence. Behind, as a peptalk draws to an end, a crowd in swimming caps and Speedos suddenly breaks apart, towels are flung off shoulders and feet move fast, like children's, towards the pool's edge. With 'Two widths minimum!' as our only requirement, on the count of three, we're told, we are to jump into the December water. This is the December Dip at Parliament Hill Lido of the Outdoor Swimming Society (www.outdoorswimming society.com) and the goose-bumped bodies have been gathered here by its high priestess, Kate Rew, as part of a crusade to reconnect Britons – and today, Londoners in particular – with nature by way of water.

Standing on the brink, strangers giddily swap stories and the line of people sways with excitement; thighs jog in trepidation, toes are dipped into the freezing meniscus, ice drops are dribbled on to the backs of necks. Then, on three, a hundred or so ragtag swimmers jump into the

Serpentine Swimming Club

pool, more or less instantaneously. I see the tall man next to me power away in a front crawl. Then I realise that I'd be close to having an out-of-body experience, were it not for the acute lightning-rod sensations running through the cavity of my belly and around my chest. I didn't realise shock had a physical expression, but it does, and it is this that is now stabbing up and down my legs and arms, scything at my pelvis and ribs. It is masochistically fun. Around me, people laugh and yell, frantically front- and back-crawling, and quite forget who, and where, they are – apart from the near-cardiac arrest sensations.

After 90 seconds – for me, at least – it's over. A few stalwarts swim on, gently gliding to and fro. But most are quickly wrapped up in towels, whooping, comparing notes on pain and invigoration, eyes bright as they surge towards the queue for hot chocolate and mince pies.

The popularity of outdoor swimming in Britain predates the current testing economic times. The empassioned writing of the late environmentalist Roger Deakin was a key catalyst. His 1999 book *Waterlog: A Swimmer's Journey Through Britain* galvanised people to use swimming outdoors as an expression of anarchic delight in the natural world. Rew is one of a handful of new evangelists to follow in his slipstream.

While the OSS's new recruits shudder and chat at the pool's margins, a handful of men and women are nonchalantly stripping off and plopping into the water to do unhurried laps. Members of Parliament Hill's local swimming fraternity, they greet each other with a familiar, if a little staccato, bonhomie, and there's some friendly bragging about the natural beauty of various British swimming sites, recent swims and friends' attendance levels.

Among them is Frank Chalmers, a daily swimmer at the lido, but whose spiritual home is Ye Amphibious Ancients Bathing Association on Scotland's River Tay. Chalmers, who is writing a book about cross-Channel swimmers, has notched up a few remarkable dips since taking up outdoor swimming in the run-up to his 40th birthday: for example, the four-hour swim he made across eight treacherous miles in high seas (temperature 12°C) off the coast of Scotland, and the 'unnavigable' whirlpool he braved between two Hebridean islands (famously taken on by George Orwell's brother-in-law, drenched in sheep fat, in the 1940s). 'This is where it starts,' he nods knowingly towards the glacial lido. 'Next thing you know, you'll be down at Dover Sands and training for the Channel.'

'By swimming throughout the seasons, you get to know a small area in a very intimate way.'

The next day in Gospel Oak, it's another ghostly pre-dawn. Past brambles and under the canopies of ancient trees are two beautiful, and altogether more solitary, swimming wildernesses. Mallards scud low across the limpid swell of Highgate Men's Pond (7485 4491) – a spartan mirror of water to swim in – and crows, seagulls

and magpies caw and hop unperturbed under the trees. At the end of a lane past a further tangle of bush and briar, bullrushes sway around Kenwood Ladies' Pond (7485 4491), a popular summer Shangri-La for many Londoners; however, at this time of year you can count on swimming with maybe two or three ladies, and seldom more than ten.

Margaret Hepburn has been swimming on the Heath since 1946, and has just had her morning dip. Her father-in-law, a free-spirited Scot, once led midnight swimming expeditions to the Heath's ponds during the summer, but she herself joined the cold-water swimming minority when her husband's health began to falter 20 years ago. 'I began getting up early and swimming regularly, creeping away silently with the dog. The people at the pond were so supportive, and kept saying "See you tomorrow". That's when it became a habit. Having done one winter, I just kept it up. You come out physically feeling better, it makes your joints looser, and you've let go of things mentally. I'm of a sanguine temperament, but for some people it is something akin to therapy.'

Jane Shallice, chair of the Kenwood Ladies' Pond Association (www.klpa.org.uk), has been swimming here since she came to London after university in 1964. She only started to swim during the winter when she retired in 2000, and explains that being ringside to a particular part of the Heath is an inextricable part of the appeal of year-long outdoor swimming. 'By going throughout the seasons, you get to know a small area in a very intimate way: which trees lose which buds, when the catkins come. You become very, very conscious of the surroundings.' Here, then, wild swimming is about holding a deep reverence for nature. Under your toes, fish are teeming, while grebes, herons and swans float above. Today, Shallice lasted seven minutes in the 4°C pond, and emerged feeling invigorated – and incredibly privileged. It's a privilege Shallice doesn't take for granted. The issue of funding never goes away (the Corporation of London has maintained the facilities since the demise of the GLC) and the KLPA has to be vigilant against threats from developers.

Conversely, these straitened times could represent a real opportunity for the advocates of outdoor swimmers. The London County Council engineered the last great lido-building programme in the 1920s and '30s, during the Depression, to provide working-class leisure facilities. Many closed during and after the 1980s (58 to date) and now London has just 12 outdoor swimming venues left.

Janet Smith, who swims at London's oldest pool, Tooting Bec Lido (dating from 1906), is also the author of *Liquid Assets*, a paean to Britain's outdoor swimming pools and an elegy for those that have already closed. She argues that if the government is to meet its pledges for swimming pool provision, resurrecting lidos would be a cost-effective way of doing so. 'They are cheaper to build: you build less. The great lido boom of the 1930s, which followed the great crash, came under the government policy of work projects as a scheme to give the unemployed a job and to build facilities for the benefit of families afterwards. Possibly... high unemployment could provide an opportunity for similar buildings.' She points to the successes of campaigns to reinstate London Fields and Brockwell Park lidos, both of which were the subject of vigorous campaigning on the part of their local communities and are now finding favour with a new generation of swimmers.

It's a sentiment echoed by the River & Lake Swimming Association (www.river-swimming.co.uk), which says cash-strapped local authorities should stop subsidising swims at pools and instead reverse restrictions that overzealous interpretations of health and safety directives have imposed on outdoor swimming in lakes. 'There'd be no heating bill to pay.'

Other outdoor-swimming fans argue it's not just cost-effective: beyond the act of swimming itself, the hardship and adrenaline associated with cold-water swimming keeps morale up. As Smith sums up: 'There's a very high feel-good factor for swimming in the open air. It appeals to people's current desire for simplicity. It makes a great contrast to our stressful, complicated working lives to wind down with a swim outdoors. It gives a sense of freedom and liberation you simply don't get in an enclosed building. And the common devotion to a lido is quite a bond.'

Enthusiasts are also proudly egalitarian. Smith talks of the 'incredible spectrum' of people who swim together as part of the South London Swimming Club (www.slsc.org.uk) in Tooting Bec. Meanwhile, on the south shore of Hyde Park's Serpentine lake is the Serpentine Lido, home of the year-round Serpentine Swimming Club (www.serpentineswimmingclub.com).

Sir Anthony Cleaver (former chairman of the Nuclear Decommissioning Authority) is bounding towards the changing rooms just as a fellow member lowers himself off the jetty, fresh from his shift as a night porter. A 24-year-old visiting American student, who is training to swim the Channel, remarks that the comradeship is what binds her to the pond. 'I was also taken aback,' she says. 'You hear so much talk about the English class system. Here, you get a total cross-section of society, and a really strong sense of community.' '£20 a year,' beams the club secretary, her pen poised over a spiral-bound notebook as she tries to sign me up for membership and record the latest heats in the club's handicapped winter series. A flock of swans flies low over the horizon. 'The cheapest annual sports membership fee of anywhere in London, and we'll throw in a cup of tea too.'

London's lidos and ponds

Brockwell Lido
Brockwell Park, Dulwich Road, SE24 0PA (7274 3088, www.brockwell-lido.co.uk). £5.95.

Charlton Lido
Hornfair Park, Shooters Hill Road, SE18 4LX (8856 7389, www.better.org.uk/leisure/charlton-lido). £6.

Hampstead Heath Ponds
Hampstead Heath, NW5 1QR (7485 3873, www.cityoflondon.gov.uk). £2.

Hampton Heated Open Air Pool
High Street, Hampton, TW12 2ST (8255 1116, www.hamptonpool.co.uk). £6 peak; £5 off-peak; £6.90 Sat, Sun.

London Fields Lido
London Fields Westside, E8 3EU (7254 9038, www.better.org.uk/leisure/london-fields-lido). £4.80.

Park Road Lido
Park Road, N8 8JN (8341 3567, www.fusion-lifestyle.com). £5.60.

Parliament Hill Lido
Hampstead Heath, Gordon House Road, NW5 1NA (7485 5757, www.cityoflondon.gov.uk). £6; £2.50 winter or early morning.

Serpentine Lido
Hyde Park, W2 2UH (7706 3422, www.royalparks.org.uk). £4.80; £4.10 after 4pm.

Tooting Bec Lido
Tooting Bec Road, SW16 1RU (8871 7198, www.wandsworth.gov.uk). £7.80; £5.20 after 6pm.

835

Play fives

Similar to squash but played on smaller, oddly shaped courts and with the use of a gloved hand rather than a raquet, fives is a sport indelibly linked with the public schools in which it originated (Winchester, Eton and Rugby). However, that doesn't mean it's elitist. You can play the Eton version (sloping walls, split-level floor, no back wall and a buttress known as a 'pepperpot') on four purpose-built courts at Westway Sports Centre in Ladbroke Grove. Small group or private tuition is available, after which you can pay a £5 registration fee then book a court for £6-£8 per hour or test your skills in tournaments and leagues.

Westway Sports Centre *1 Crowthorne Road, W10 6RP (8969 0992, http://sports.westway.org/outdoor-sports).*

836 Get up early to see the deer in Richmond Park

The park opens at 7am (7.30am in winter), and there are around 630 red and fallow deer roaming freely within its grounds. See www.royalparks.org.uk for more on the deer.

837

Inspect (but don't lie on) Freud's couch

Sigmund's family home is preserved as it was when he died – and as his previous house was when he fled Vienna in 1938 (he had written down the position of everything in his study, so it could be recreated in London). The centrepiece of the museum is Freud's library and study; check out his collection of Greek, Roman and oriental antiquities, along with the famous couch – such a surprisingly inviting and comfortable-looking piece of furniture, piled with cushions and a lush persian rug, it's a shame you're not allowed to lie on it.

Freud Museum *20 Maresfield Gardens, NW3 5SX (7435 2002, www.freud.org.uk). £7.*

838

Volunteer in a charity shop

Although you won't be paid (unless you become a manager – and even then we're hardly talking big bucks), time spent working in charity shops is nevertheless rewarding. First, there's the warm glow you'll get from doing something worthwhile and helpful. And second, chances are you'll get first dibs on all the items that get donated, which could be anything from Moschino dresses to rare vinyl. For your nearest shop, see www.charityretail.org.uk.

839

Watch Tower Bridge opening

Long before it was a tourist landmark, Tower Bridge was a dazzling feat of engineering. Unveiled in 1894, it still thrills when its bascules swing into action. Watching it work its magic, one can understand why London was once the most technologically advanced city in the world. The Tower Bridge Exhibition, meanwhile, spells out the history, but the highlight (in every sense of the word) is the walk along the top tier of the bridge – now with the added thrill of a glass floor. Check the website to see when the bridge opens (which it does around 1,000 times a year).

Tower Bridge *SE1 2UP (7403 3761, www.tower bridge.org.uk). £9; £8 online.*

840

Join the Fight Club

For blood, sweat and tears, and plenty of raw, unadulterated testosterone, watch East End bruisers punch each other's lights out in the unreconstructed surroundings of York Hall in Bethnal Green (5 Old Ford Road, E2 9PJ, 8980 2243). The professional fights command prices of up to £100 a ticket, but on amateur night (usually held once a month), tickets are usually only a tenner.

841 Celebrate London's canals

Decked out in bunting and flowers, more than 100 colourful narrowboats assemble in the pool of Little Venice to celebrate Canalway Cavalcade, a free, three-day boat bash that takes place every May. There are food and craft stalls, kids' activities, bands, a real-ale bar and boat trips. The beautiful illuminated boat procession on Sunday evening is a must-see.

Little Venice *Between Blomfield Road, Warwick Avenue & Warwick Crescent, W9 2PB (www.waterways.org.uk).*

842 Hang out at the bar of the Theatre Royal Stratford East

Never mind the performances on stage, check out the free ones seven days a week in the bar. As well as a diverse roster of musical performances –including Funky Fridays, when DJs play reggae, hip hop, funk and soul – the bar also hosts comedy nights every Monday. And, of course, (inexpensive) food and drinks are available too.

Theatre Royal Stratford East *Gerry Raffles Square, E15 1BN (8534 0310, www.stratfordeast.com).*

Theatre Royal Stratford East

Bar Italia

843-852 *Have a proper cup of coffee in the West End*

Bar Italia
When in Soho… do as the Romans (and other Italians) do and head to Bar Italia if you're in need of a short, sharp caffeine hit. The macchiato is all toffee richness, the dab of creamy foam smoothing the bitterness of the Italian-style blend produced by former neighbours Angelucci Coffee. *22 Frith Street, W1D 4RF (7437 4520, www.baritaliasoho.co.uk).*

Espresso Room
A tiny coffee bar opposite Great Ormond Street Hospital that punches above its weight, with Square Mile beans and quality soup, sandwiches and cakes. Pleasant, intelligent staff offer a glass of water with the brews and are happy to grind bags of beans for customers to take home. *31-35 Great Ormond Street, WC1N 3HZ (www.theespressoroom.com).*

Fernandez & Wells
The baristas here work their magic by way of textbook-perfect crema served at the just the right temperature, and cappuccinos on which the foam stands proudly several millimetres above the cup rim – the mark of an expert indeed. Sit at a window seat and, in true Italian coffee-drinking tradition, people-watch in style. *73 Beak Street, W1F 9SR (7287 8124, www.fernandezandwells.com).*

Lantana
This airy space is ideal for a quiet morning with the paper. The Australian proprietor, Shelagh Ryan, has chosen what she calls the 'coffee super-couple' to create her brews: Monmouth beans and a La Marzocco espresso machine. *13 Charlotte Place, W1T 1SN (7637 3347, www.lantanacafe.co.uk).*

London Review Cake Shop
Books, newspapers and magazines are strewn about this sun-filled room. Monmouth beans are used and cakes are sourced from independent producers. The room, with its communal table, is perfect for literary chinwagging. *14-16 Bury Place, WC1A 2JL (7269 9030, www.londonreviewbookshop.co.uk/cake-shop).*

Milk Bar
The espresso (made from Square Mile Coffee Roaster beans) melds seamlessly into the thick, cashmere-soft layer of foamed milk creamed with microscopic bubbles. Everything – from the charming, mellow baristas to the ever-changing art on the walls – exudes a certain cool. *3 Bateman Street, W1D 4AG (7287 4796, www.milkbarsoho.co.uk).*

Nordic Bakery
The cappuccino served amid Scandinavian warehouse design is strong and sturdy, much like the cup it comes in – and the cocoa dusted on top is smooth and bitter. You won't find sugar on the table, nor will sachets be presented on your serving tray – welcome to coffee purism. *14A Golden Square, W1F 9JG (3230 1077, www.nordicbakery.com).*

Rapha CC
The café area occupies a little less than half the floor space of this smart cycle clothing shop, and is a remarkably relaxing place, largely because of the chatty but efficient staff. The house espresso blend comes from Workshop, and there are guest beans as well. A haven near Piccadilly Circus. *Brewer Street, W1F 9ZN (7494 9831).*

Sacred
At this 'Southern Hemisphere' café, creative beatniks stake out the sofas and down ethical espressos (made from fairtrade beans, blended in-house) under the mindful eye of a stone Buddha. Rather fitting, considering their almost-evangelical attitude to promoting good coffee. *13 Ganton Street, W1F 9BL (7734 1415, www.sacredcafe.co.uk).*

Timberyard
Branching out from its Shoreditch original, Timberyard brings its brand of Wi-Fi and caffeine to Theatreland, putting on a splendid show of strong brews, great bakes and light bites. Baristas deliver A-grade, big-on-floral-flavour coffees using Has Bean's signature Jabberwocky blend. *7 Upper St Martin's Lane, WC2H 9DL (https://tyuk.com).*

853

Remember the Winchester Geese at Crossbones Graveyard

At 7pm on the 23rd day of every month, a group, loosely collected under the banner 'Friends of Crossbones' and led by local Southwark playwright and historian John Constable, gathers outside the iron gates of an unprepossesing Transport for London storage lot on Redcross Way, SE1. They are here to honour the memory of the 'Winchester Geese' – prostitutes who were given a licence to work in the area by the Bishop of Winchester (this part of London being under his – let's call it, 'liberal' – jurisdiction). Eventually closed in 1853, once it was 'completely overcharged with dead', Crossbones Graveyard was an unconsecrated burial ground dating from the medieval period and used for disposing of people not considered fit for Christan burial.

Each month, candles are lit; flowers, ribbons, notes and other memorial tokens are tied to the gates; poems are recited – and gin is poured on the ground in tribute to the fallen ladies' favourite tipple. As well as this monthly get-together, each Halloween sees performances from the Southwark Mysteries, an epic cycle of poems and mystery plays written by Constable and inspired, he says, by the spirit of a Winchester Goose who first visited him on 23 November 1996 on Redcross Way. Check the website for Halloween performance venues. *www.crossbones.org.uk.*

philanthropist and pioneer of affordable housing, George Peabody, holds court at the Royal Exchange, EC3, in the heart of the City. His statue is by WW Story and was erected in 1869, the year of his death.

More famously, in Grosvenor Square, W1, the statue of Franklin D Roosevelt by Sir William Reid Dick was unveiled by his wife in 1948, three years after his death. It was paid for with 200,000 donations of five shillings each, apparently raised in a single day, from grateful Brits. Also in the square, Dwight D Eisenhower, Allied Commander during World War II and 34th president of the United States, was sculpted by Robert Dean in 1989. In 2011, a statue of Ronald Reagan was unveiled to mark the centenary of his birth.

A fine bust of John F Kennedy overlooks Marylebone Road, NW1, near Regent's Park tube. It was made by Jacques Lipchitz, unveiled in 1965 by Bobby and Edward Kennedy, and paid for by £1 donations from 50,000 readers of the *Daily Telegraph*. And finally, nearby at 84 Hallam Street, off Great Portland Street, a blue plaque acknowledges that flat no.5 was the home (1938-46) of the legendary World War II broadcaster for CBS Ed Murrow.

863
Deliver a speech at Speakers' Corner

See www.speakerscorner.net for a list of illustrious past orators.

854-862
See Americans in London

Every patriotic American, and quite a few others besides, might want to track down some of the monuments to their illustrious countrymen scattered around London. And it won't cost them a dime.

Abraham Lincoln has just risen to his feet in Parliament Square, SW1, to hold forth in fine democratic style. You'll find an even older father of the nation, Captain John Smith, first governor of Virginia, next to the St Mary-le-Bow Church on Cheapside, EC2, in the City. He was created by Charles Rennick in 1960. George Washington's likeness stands proudly in front of the National Gallery; it was presented by the Commonwealth of Virginia in 1921. The great American

864
Dodge bullets in Pickering Place

Down the side of Berry Brothers wine merchants (3 St James's Street, SW1A 1EG) is a rare surviving timbered passageway, dating back to 1730. As you duck through, the warped and crooked wainscoting draws you into the quiet of gas-lit Pickering Place, site of the last duel ever to be fought in London. Fittingly, a plaque at the alley entrance proclaims the 19th-century site of the Republic of Texas embassy.

865-867

Eat old-school sweets

The realisation not only of the owner's but also many other people's long-held dreams, Hope & Greenwood is a proper, old-fashioned sweet shop that opened its doors to a grateful local clientele in East Dulwich a decade ago, and now has a branch in Covent Garden. Those yearning for cola cubes, sherbert pips and rosy apples won't be disappointed. Just off Oxford Street, Mrs Kibble's Olde Sweet Shoppe is a handy source of clove rock, liquorice twists and swirly lollipops. For a different confectionery vibe, try Cybercandy, which stocks a range of sweets from all over the world – perfect if you're a US national craving a Hershey Bar or you need some Hello Kitty Candy.

Cybercandy
3 Garrick Street, WC2E 9BF (0845 838 0958, www.cybercandy.co.uk).

Hope & Greenwood
1 Russell Street, WC2B 5JD (7240 3314, www.hopeandgreenwood.co.uk).

Mrs Kibble's Olde Sweet Shoppe
4 St Christopher's Place, W1U 1LZ (7734 6633, www.mrskibbles.co.uk).

Hope & Greenwood

868-876

Drink in some history

What's the strangest, most historic watering hole in all London? To locals and visitors of a certain disposition, it's a hotly debated question (in a casual, leaning-on-the-bar, giving it the large opinion after four pints kind of way). So, for argument's sake, here's our must-sample 'rub-a-dubs' to set you on the right road to an unforgettable knees-up – especially if you manage to crawl round them all in one go.

When it comes to layer upon layer of atmospheric history, the waterfront Town of Ramsgate (62 Wapping High Street, E1W 2PN, 7481 8000, www.townoframsgate.co.uk) takes some beating. This was once Captain Bligh and Fletcher Christian's local, pre-mutiny. The cellars were at one time fitted with shackles for drunks in the process of being press-ganged. From the tiny Thameside patio, you look out directly on to Execution Dock and Wapping Old Stairs, where Captain Blood was nabbed making off with the Crown Jewels. In the panelled bar, 'Hanging'

Judge Jeffreys was spotted dressed as a woman as he tried to escape England in 1685. The Bloody Assizes' hardliner's local was actually the 16th-century Prospect of Whitby (57 Wapping Wall, E1W 3SH, 7481 1095, www.taylor-walker. co.uk), five minutes downriver, where a dangling noose marks his memory. There's also a 400-year-old flagstone floor, London's last pewter bar and a smashing hoard of antique seafaring knick-knacks.

Directly over the river in Rotherhithe is the Mayflower (117 Rotherhithe Street, SE16 4NF, 7237 4088, www.mayflowerpub.co.uk), whence local skipper Christopher Jones carried the Pilgrim Fathers to America in 1620. The rickety wooden terrace over the river is recommended.

Off Borough High Street, near London Bridge, lies the National Trust-owned George Inn (George Inn Yard, 77 Borough High Street, SE1 1NH, 7407 2056, www.nationaltrust.org.uk/george-inn), London's sole remaining galleried coaching inn, handily positioned just down the road from what was then London's only bridge. Just a third of the rebuilt 1676 structure survives, but there's still a wonderfully creaky atmosphere that evokes the pilgrims, travellers and theatre

Mayflower

Prospect of Whitby

players who have crowded the cobbled courtyard over the centuries.

Moving across the river into the City, you can find the tiny Mitre Tavern (1 Ely Court, EC1N 6SJ, 7405 4751, http://yeoldemitreholborn.co.uk) down an alley between Hatton Garden and Ely Place. Built in 1547 as a London base for the servants of the Palace of the Bishops of Ely, until recently this pub was officially considered to be part of Cambridgeshire, and therefore became a regular loophole refuge for thieves escaping the frustrated City police. The recently deceased tree built into the wooden frontage is said to have been used as a maypole by Elizabeth I.

Meanwhile, although the Viaduct Tavern (126 Newgate Street, EC1A 7AA, 7600 1863, http://viaducttavern.co.uk) stands right opposite the Old Bailey (once Newgate Prison), it features a landlady's token kiosk aimed at preventing staff thievery. Its cellars boast four vaulted, barred cells from the long-gone Giltspur Street Compter debtors' prison.

Over in the West End, the Salisbury (90 St Martin's Lane, WC2N 4AP, 7836 5863, www. taylor-walker.co.uk) is even more magnificently showy. All cut-glass chandeliers and eye-catching mirrors, with fabulous light fittings decorating the bar, it's a Victorian art nouveau gin palace that manages to mimic the experience of walking directly into your great gran's jewellery box.

Down on Millbank, the cells in the cellar of the riverfront Morpeth Arms (58 Millbank, SW1P 4RW, 7834 6442, www.morpetharms.com) remain an intriguing mystery. Now the neighbour of Tate Britain, this was once the site of the miserable Millbank Penitentiary megastructure, to which the pub cells are supposedly related. However, hard fact on the subject seems to be as scarce as the long-rumoured tunnels linking the pub, prison and foreshore.

Finally, a change of pace up at the Spaniards Inn (Spaniards Road, NW3 7JJ, 8731 8406, www. thespaniardshampstead.co.uk), effectively a wood-beamed and -floored country pub in zone 3, knee-deep in Dick Turpin 'lookout' legends and a full set of Romantic ex-locals in the form of the poets Shelley, Keats and Byron. It's great for Hampstead Heath, and the garden is heaven on a sunny summer afternoon.

877

Tour Wilton's Music Hall

Wilton's Music Hall (Graces Alley, E1 8JB (7702 2789, www.wiltons.org.uk) is one of the world's oldest and last-remaining grand music halls. Built by John Wilton in 1858, it still has a programme of plays, concerts and performances. You can also tour the Grade II-listed building, in which a great many of the original Victorian features remain intact. Tours cost £6.

878

Chill in St Pancras's Crypt Gallery

Under the watchful gaze of the caryatids of St Pancras Parish Church, young, emerging artists exhibit their work in what used to be the last resting place of the local Bloomsbury gentry back in the 1800s. Opened as an exhibition space in 2002, the Crypt Gallery's echoing corridors, low ceilings and uneven cobbled floor are constant reminders of the building's past, but despite being chilly and a little damp, it avoids being too creepy, thanks to some soft lighting and almost no trace of its former occupants. In fact, the musty alcoves now act as enclosures for individual artworks: paintings, installations and sculptures, whose inspiration is often the setting itself. The gallery hosts a year-round programme of group shows that rotate frequently and are often curated by the artists themselves, so opening times may vary.
St Pancras Church *Euston Road, NW1 2BA (7388 1461, www.cryptgallery.org.uk). Free.*

879 *Walk a ley line*

Regardless of your views on paranormal energy fields, walking a ley line through London's backstreets is a great way to explore the hidden city and a neat medieval antidote to the 21st-century world. Follow in the footsteps of Alfred Watkins – who first defined leys as prehistoric sighting lines conceived from high viewpoints and maintained by ground-level markers – by grabbing a map, drawing a straight line from St Martin-in-the-Fields in Trafalgar Square to Arnold Circus in Shoreditch, and walking the Strand Ley – roughly two and a half miles (as the crow flies). The line spookily falls through three other City churches (St Mary le Strand, St Clement Danes and St Dunstan-in-the-West) before finishing up at the Victorian bandstand in Arnold Circus in the grand Victorian Boundary housing estate.

880 *Watch classic films for free*

A high-tech peep show for the capital's cineastes, the British Film Institute's Mediatheque on the South Bank offers the chance to explore the entire digitised National Film Archive for free. Users are given their own private booth in which they can browse hundreds of British films and TV shows, from David Lean's *Brief Encounter* to Shane Meadows' *Dead Man's Shoes*. Check out the monthly updated Pandora's Box collection, an oddball mix of celluloid quirks. It includes a 1920s shock drama about STDs and what are thought to be among the first words ever recorded on film: a cheeky Alfred Hitchcock toying with Anny Ondra, the Czech-Polish star of his 1929 thriller *Blackmail*.
BFI Mediatheque *BFI Southbank, Belvedere Road, SE1 8XT (7928 3232, www.bfi.org.uk).*

881 *Make the most of your time*

The Worshipful Company of Clockmakers, one of the City of London's historic livery companies, was founded way back in 1631: it's the oldest surviving horological institution in the world. Take heed of its motto – *Tempus Rerum Imperator*, Latin for 'Time is the ruler of all things' – and don't waste a second in going to look at its outstanding collection of clocks, watches and other timepieces, now in a brand-new home on the second floor of the Science Museum (Exhibition Road, SW7 2DD, 0870 870 4868, www.sciencemuseum.org.uk).

882 *Learn about plants*

Budding botanists should visit the South London Botanical Institute (323 Norwood Road, SE24 9AQ, 8674 5787, www.slbi.org.uk), tucked away near Tulse Hill railway station. Founded in 1910, the institute is open on Thursdays (and Saturdays in summer) and has a library full of old botanical books, a herbarium and a lovely garden – all of which can be visited for free. Look out for children's activities in the school holidays, and occasional lectures and workshops.

883 *Swim outside in King's Cross*

Fans of open-air swimming, rejoice! Set behind King's Cross station is a new swimming hole – the first man-made, freshwater bathing pond in the UK, no less. It's actually an art installation, created by Ooze Architects and artist Marjetica Potrc, designed to bring the rural into the urban – which it does very successfully. Chemical-free (so no nasty, eye-stinging chlorine), it's a pleasant place for a (somewhat chilly) dip, with changing rooms, showers and a viewing platform for non-swimmers. But it's only a temporary affair, in operation until 2016 (possibly longer). Swimming times are from 6.30am to dusk daily, and you'll need to book a session (two-hours maximum, £3.50-£6.50) in advance online.

King's Cross Pond Club *20 Canal Reach, entrance on Tapper Walk, N1C 4BE (www.kingscrosspond.club).*

884

Get out of town

Despite soaring rail fares, there are still places you can get to from London for less than a tenner that really do feel like they're a world away (rather than just at the end of a commuter line). The train stations listed below all cost less than £10 to reach, if you travel at off-peak times (after 10am Mon-Fri and all day at the weekend).

Coulsdon South station (£6.90) is less than 30 minutes from London Bridge or Victoria, but you'll soon be walking in unspoilt country, in particular the belt of ancient hedgerow (home to more than 20 different tree varieties) and Farthing Down, designated a Site of Special Scientific Interest.

From Marylebone station, the village of Great Missenden (sometime home of both Roald Dahl – his house is now a museum – and Robert Louis Stevenson) is around 40 minutes away (£9.30). Nestled in a valley in the Chilterns, it makes a great starting point for walks. Maps and routes are available from www.chilternsaonb.org.

The dormitory town of Oxted in Surrey is half an hour from both London Bridge and Victoria stations (£9.40) and a good jumping-off point for walks on the North Downs. We recommend walk no.2 from the reliable Saturday Walkers Club – one of many free downloadable walks (www.walkingclub.org.uk).

Purfleet in Essex is within walking distance of the RSPB reserve Rainham Marshes, where you can spot all manner of wading species as well as the odd peregrine falcon. It takes about half an hour from Fenchurch Street station (£7.60).

885

Keep the party going

With the east London party scene having now firmly made its way up the Kingsland Road into the Turkish heartland of Dalston, it was inevitable that at some point the two cultures would come together. There are a number of small Turkish pool and snooker halls dotted along Stoke Newington Road, but Efes Snooker Club is the largest and best known. Its late opening hours mean that on Thursday to Saturday nights it's jam-packed full of partygoers looking for somewhere to carry on after the surrounding pubs have shut. There are pool and snooker tables, some arcade machines and a lot of voguing, plus, on Wednesday and Thursday nights, Plonk crazy golf (£7.50 per person). **Efes Snooker Club** *17B Stoke Newington Road, N16 8BH (7249 6040).*

886

Chow down at Kerb

King's Boulevard is a recently constructed walkway leading north from King's Cross and St Pancras stations to Granary Square and the relocated Central Saint Martins College of Art. At its north end on Cubitt Square, from Mondays to Fridays (noon-2pm) you'll find a huddle of food vans serving lunch. They all belong to the Kerb collective (www.kerbfood.com), founded by Petra Barran and Giles Smith. Part of the appeal is that the vendors rotate. You might find a line-up that includes Luardo's burritos, dispensing from a bright pink retro van; Anna Mae's variants on mac 'n' cheese; and Tongue 'n Cheek selling Italian-style ox cheek burger with polenta. Most of the dishes cost around a fiver, and are filling, and there are parasols and plenty of seating – perfect if the sun is out and the wind not whistling by too hard. Check the website for that day's featured vans, and also for Kerb's other locations around town.

887 *Visit William Blake country*

Across the road from North Lambeth tube is a plaque marking the sometime home of William Blake, the writer, artist and rebel of the Romantic age. Until recently, this was the only evidence of Blake's presence in Lambeth, despite him spending ten productive years living and working in what, in his time, was a 'new suburb'. Today, Blake is finally getting some recognition in south London with the help of Southbank Mosaics and the William Blake Heritage Project.

Blake always wanted his works enlarged and put on the streets where the public could see them, and it seems that he's finally getting his wish: on the brick walls of the railway bridge running over Centaur Street and low enough for you to be able to touch, Southbank Mosaics have replicated several of his artworks. including his haunting vision of God, *The Ancient of Days*. There are now 28 mosaics mounted here – they're part of a mosaic walk around Waterloo that you can download from the group's website.

You can also learn how to make mosaics out of ceramics, glass, marble and found materials in the group's studio in St John's Crypt in Waterloo, under the guidance of artistic director David Tootill. Once you've got the hang of it, you can help out on one of their numerous projects. *www.southbankmosaics.com.*

Geffrye Museum

888

Trace the New River

The New River was constructed in the early 17th century to bring fresh water into London from Hertfordshire. Designed by Hugh Myddelton – commemorated with a statue on Islington Green – and some 20 miles long, it was the first fresh water supply of its type in the city, and most of its route can still be walked, courtesy of Thames Water.

In Islington itself, where it has been covered over in most parts, the council has constructed a lovely sliver of a park along a half-mile open stretch: New River Walk runs from Canonbury Road (near Essex Road station) upstream to St Paul's Road, where the river disappears beneath Wallace Road and Petherton Road. A small section of it can also be seen further north in Clissold Park, where it has been converted into a duck pond in front of the café.

Back nearer Highbury, as it winds its way behind ranks of gentrified mansions, the walk along the river park can easily include a diversion to Canonbury Square – once home to George Orwell (no.27B) and also Evelyn Waugh (no.17) – or even the Estorick Collection of Modern Italian Art (no.39A). The maintenance of the waterway is undertaken by the New River Action Group (http://newriver.org.uk), which also runs occasional guided walks.

889

Save on interior design fees at the Geffrye Museum

The Geffrye, housed in a set of converted almshouses, is a quite marvellous physical history of the English interior. It recreates living rooms through the ages – from refined Georgian drawing rooms to cool Stateside-style 'living spaces' beloved by local Shoreditch DIY-obsessives. If you can't afford an interior designer, this is the perfect place to steal ideas. There's also a series of lovely gardens designed on similar chronological lines (open April to October). Special exhibitions are mounted throughout the year – the Christmas one, when the rooms are decorated in period style, is always a winner.

Geffrye Museum *136 Kingsland Road, E2 8EA (7739 9893, www.geffrye-museum.org.uk). Free.*

890

See deep space in Hampstead

The capital's would-be astronomers may think of Greenwich as the ultimate place to star gaze in London – or they may not bother at all, given the city's light pollution – but Hampstead's observatory, with its six-inch Cooke refracting telescope, opens up the night sky to both curious beginners and keen amateurs. Located at the highest point of London, on a clear night it allows fascinating views of not just the moon, but also planets, stars and double stars (such as Alpha Centauri), as well as eclipses and comets when they occur. The observatory is open to the public on Friday and Saturday nights and on Sunday during the day – but only if the sky is clear. Visits are free. It's run by the Hampstead Scientific Society charity, and a member is always on hand to help navigate visitors round the sky. If you're interested in becoming a member, take a look at the website.

Hampstead Observatory *Entrance on Lower Terrace, by Whitestone Pond, NW3 (www.hampstead science.ac.uk). Closed mid Apr-mid Sept.*

891

Get on board a barge

This multi-tasking 1930s Dutch grain barge has been converted into a floating bar-restaurant and performance venue, moored on the Thames at Nine Elms. Once used to transport German tanks during World War II, it now hosts a wide range of events, from gigs and theatre to comedy and cabaret – note that some of them break the £10 barrier. See the website for details of what's on, and to check in case the barge is hired out for a private event.

Battersea Barge *Nine Elms Lane, SW8 5BP (7498 0004, www.batterseabarge.com).*

892

Get the real deal at Ridley Road Market...

While so many markets go trendy and/or upscale, Ridley Road in Dalston has hung on to its roots. It is gloriously cheap: fresh fruit and vegetables sold in giant buckets go for a quid a throw, and the fresh red snapper is the cheapest you'll find this side of Billingsgate. Whether it's watch straps, giant snails or saucepans you need, there's sure to be someone flogging them for next to nothing. Conclude your visit with a wander round Turkish superstore TFC – the on-site bakery is particularly tempting.
Ridley Road Market *Ridley Road, E8 2NP (www.ridleyroad.co.uk).*

893-897

...or at other long-established street markets

There are thriving old-fashioned outdoor markets in most corners of London, where you can pick up fruit and veg, household goods, clothing, shoes, fabrics, cosmetics and perfume, flowers and more at bargain prices.

Head south for Brixton Market, a true classic, which takes over the streets around Brixton tube/train station. It's open daily except Sundays, and African and Caribbean produce is, not surprisingly, to the fore. Also south is East Street Market (closed Mondays), located off the Walworth Road near Elephant & Castle. One of London's oldest traditional markets, in business since the 1880s, it's still very much a locals' affair.

North are two options. Despite being located in the heart of upmarket Islington, Chapel Market (open daily except Mondays) is a distinctly ungentrified affair, while Walthamstow Market is supposedly the longest outdoor market in Europe, stretching for more than half a mile along the pedestrianised High Street. It's particularly raucous on Saturdays, and closed on Sundays.

West, in Fulham, is North End Road Market (closed Sundays), relatively small but still busy with stalls that have been in the same family for generations.

Brixton Market

Royal Gala
Golden Delicious
Red Delicious

Fresh Prawns
9.00
2.20
Octopus
3.50
Snappers
1.95

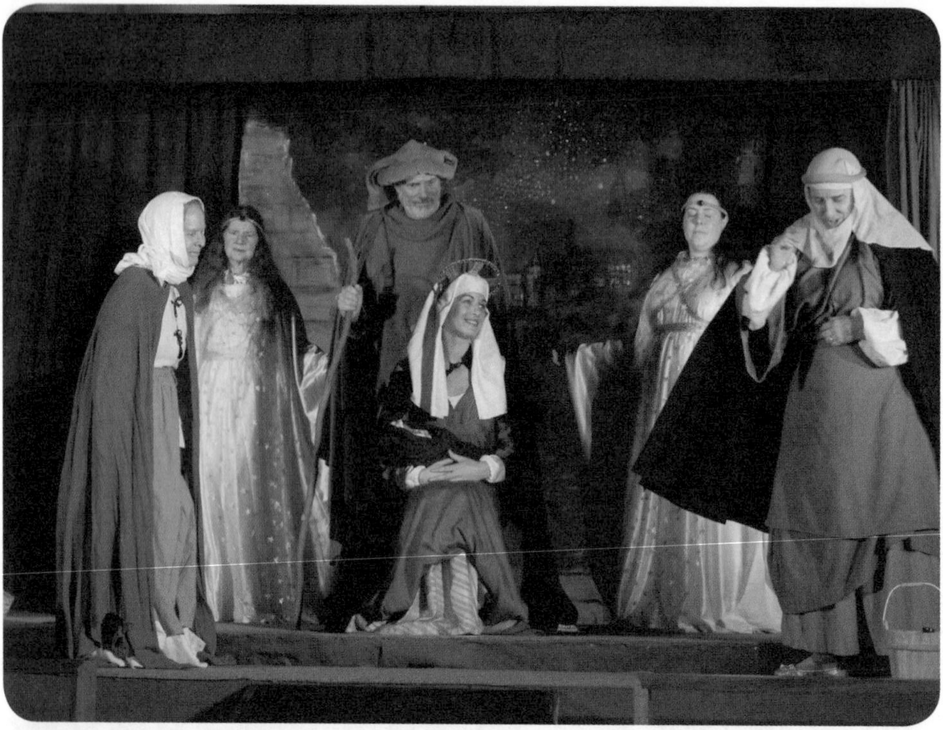

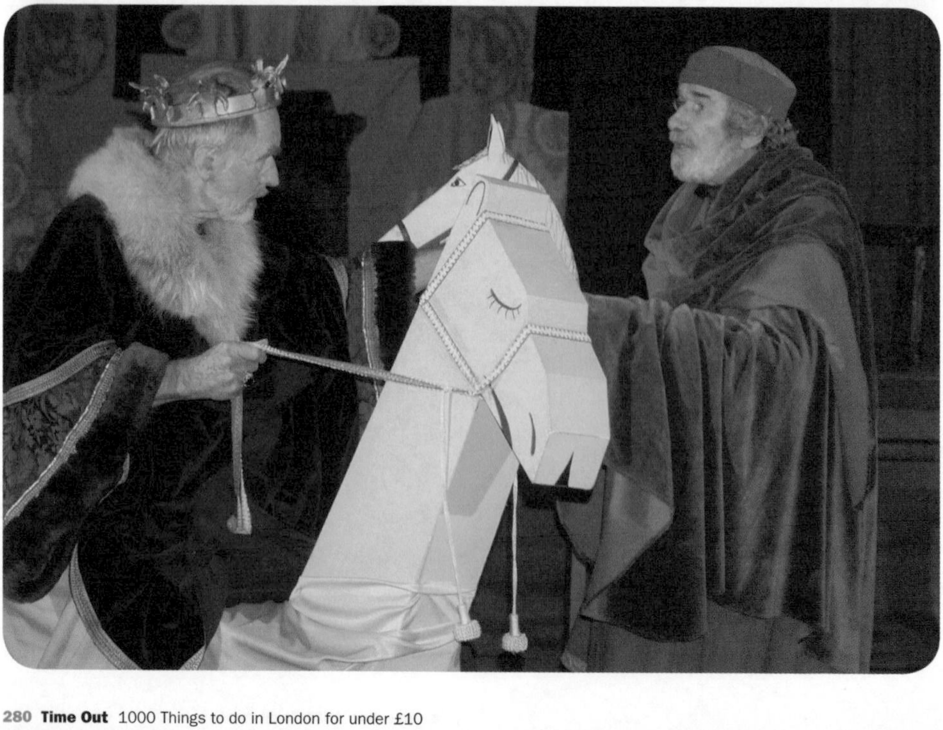

898

Cheer, boo and hiss at a Mystery Play

For the last few years, the walls of Hawksmoor's St George-in-the-East (Cannon Street Road, E1 0BH, www.stgite.org.uk) in Shadwell have served as a backdrop for medieval Mystery Plays given a new lease of life by venerable amateur drama group the Players of St Peter (www.theplayersofstpeter.org.uk). Back in the 15th century, the plays, which could go on for as long as 20 hours, were performed in the streets of London by guildsmen and craftsmen on pageant wagons that were moved around the streets, each company or guild performing a different play. Based on biblical texts, the plots range from the story of Creation to the Last Judgment. These days, having tweaked the language just a bit, the Players select scenes from the plays and edit them to form an Advent production. They tell the story of the birth of Christ right through to the Ascension.

Watching the performers dressed in elaborate and lovingly crafted costumes that resemble those originally worn in the 15th century, the audience is transported back to medieval London. 'We don't use any materials that wouldn't have been used originally,' says Edward Weedon, stage manager and bit-part actor in the productions. 'Even our stage hands are in costume.' The scene from the Shepherds' play features an excellent and very life-like sheep, while the shepherds themselves sup on 'a sheep's head soused in ale' (actual sheep's head not included).

Members of the audience are encouraged to join in with the performance: make sure you hiss and boo at the bad guys (that's Satan and his helpers) and clap and cheer on the good (Christ and Mary). With 50 volunteers involved in each production every year, the Players (founded in 1946) welcome new members. The entrance fee to the productions costs £6 and all profits from the venture go to the church fund. You'll find more information on the Players's website.

899

Wander through Canary Wharf's new greenery

Canary Wharf's Crossrail station won't actually have any trains running through it until 2018, but the perks it's bringing to the area are already starting to flourish – this one literally. Designed by Foster & Partners, the Crossrail Place roof gardens are covered almost entirely by a lattice of timber and air-filled plastic cushions that opens in the centre to allow a bit of the actual natural world in, come rain or shine. In the 19th century, trading ships that had travelled all over the world would use the area's docks, and the planting has been chosen to reflect this exotic bit of history; many of the species chosen are indigenous to countries the traders would have visited. The development will also house four floors of shopping, restaurants and leisure facilities, and the gardens will be used for concerts and other events, but we're sure the locals will most appreciate the plants.

900

Be a (French) philosopher at Café Philo

If the level of discourse at the watercooler is getting you down, you can always spend your Saturday mornings exercising the little grey cells by debating the philosophical question du jour at the Institut Français' Café Philo. The informal gathering is open to all – and, as was the case in ancient Athens, philosophy degrees are definitely not required. Just roll up at the Institut's classy art deco premises in South Kensington at 10.15am for a prompt 10.30am kick-off. The discussion (which alternates between French and English each week – check which one it is before you go) bounces back and forth between the participants until about noon. Haven't got much to say? No problem. Just sit back and listen – there will be plenty who do.

Institut Français *17 Queensberry Place, SW7 2DT (7871 3515, www.institut-francais.org.uk). Contact Christian Michel (cmichel@cmichel.com) to book a place. £2.*

901
Follow the Artangel

Londoners generally consider themselves spoilt when it comes to art shows, but they have Artangel to thank for some of the bolder exhibitions in the capital. Working with a range of different artists, the production company (not a gallery in itself) stages one-off projects in temporary spaces around the city, placing priority on powerful concepts. Anything goes – thousand-year musical compositions, detritus sculptures, or re-created battles between miners and police – and they're often free to view. One of the most popular was Roger Hiorns' extraordinary copper sulphate crystalline installation *Seizure* in a derelict council flat near Elephant & Castle.

Artangel *7713 1400, www.artangel.org.uk.*

Seizure

902 Visit the eighth wonder of the world

The grand entrance hall of the Thames Tunnel can be found at the Brunel Museum in Rotherhithe. Built by the father-and-son team of Marc and Isambard Kingdom Brunel, the subterranean chamber – half the size of Shakespeare's Globe – was hailed as the eighth wonder of the world when completed in 1843. Isambard held probably the world's first underwater dinner party here, complete with 50 guests and tunes from the Coldstream Guards. There are plans to convert the hall into a gallery performance space. Guided tours (£10) take place three times a week (11am Monday, 4.30pm Wednesday, 10.45am Sunday).
Brunel Museum *Railway Avenue, SE16 4LF (7231 3840, www.brunel-museum.org.uk).*

903-904 Celebrate the great British bacon butty

The bacon butty is more than just a sandwich. It is a British institution. The St John Bread & Wine's version has become the stuff of sandwich lovers' legend – thick Gloucester Old Spot bacon sandwiched between chargrilled slices of home-baked white loaf, served with a months-in-the-making in-house ketchup. So if you can't afford

St John at lunch or dinner (and let's face it, a meal here doesn't come in at under a tenner), you can have the experience at breakfast, over a pot of tea and a meticulously created example of one of Britain's crowning culinary glories. The treat is now also served at weekends at the St John offshoot in Maltby Street.
St John Bread & Wine *94-96 Commercial Street, E1 6LZ (7251 0848, www.stjohngroup.uk.com).*
St John Maltby Street *41 Maltby Street, SE1 3PA (7553 9844, www.stjohngroup.uk.com).*

905 Brush up your Polari

Hosted by author and journalist Paul Burston, 'London's peerless gay literary salon' attracts a truly mixed crowd of all ages, from 18 to 70. There are different guest authors each month (Neil Bartlett, Stella Duffy, Christopher Fowler, Ali Smith and Will Self have all graced the stage). Readings are followed by a book signing, courtesy of Foyles bookshop. As well as authors, there have been performances from singers such as David McAlmont and Marcus Reeves, and cabaret from the likes of David Hoyle and Michael Twaits. No wonder the *New York Times* called Polari 'London's most theatrical literary salon'. There's also a bar. Tickets tend to sell out fast, so book early to avoid disappointment.
Polari *Southbank Centre, SE1 8XX (0844 875 0073, www.southbankcentre.co.uk). £5-£7.*

Polari

906-910 *Celebrate New Year*

Baishakhi Mela

Pohela Boishakh (Bengali New Year) happens in Bangladesh on 14 April, but its London incarnation isn't celebrated here until the second Sunday of May. The main thrust of this vibrant, cross-cultural event is a grand street procession and party in the heart of the East End's buzzing Banglatown. Food, rather than alcohol, is central to festivities, and many of the curry houses bring their kitchens on to the (pedestrianised) streets to offer samples of their native cuisine.

For the most authentic, head towards the smaller cafés such as Meraz (56 Hanbury Street, E1 5JL, 7247 6999, www.merazcafe.co.uk). Finish with a trip to traditional Bangladeshi sweet shop Madhubon (42 Brick Lane, E1 6RF, 7655 4554, http://modhubonbricklane.co.uk) for some jalebis (deep-fried orange sugar spirals) or rasgullas (soft, spongy balls).

Chinese New Year

Based on the lunar and solar calendar, the date of this festival ranges from late January to mid February and usually coincides with the capital's annual China in London festival. Flagship events include a parade of contemporary arts and traditional lion dance across the West End and a spectacular fireworks display in Leicester Square. Fortunately, the Chinese haven't installed their own version of a western-style midnight countdown piss-up – rather, celebrations are spread out across the restaurants and bars of

Diwali

Soho and Chinatown, which are adorned with low-slung lanterns and *duilián* (paper banners). For Chinatown on a budget, try Baozi Inn (25 Newport Court, WC2H 7JS, 7287 6877) for satisfying noodles, dumplings and featherlight 'dragon' won tons.

Diwali

This five-day 'Festival of Lights' is celebrated in October and is one of the most important religious occasions for Hindus, Jains and Sikhs. Trafalgar Square usually plays host to a day of lively festivities that typically involves traditional prayers and a moving and tranquil lamp-lighting finale (known as *aarrti*). But by far the best celebration is at the celestial Shri Swaminarayan Hindu Temple (*see p210*) in Neasden, where thousands of Londoners queue to enter the grand prayer hall to see a kaleidoscopic display of over 1,000 artisanal vegetarian dishes known as an *annakut*.

Alternatively, head to Ealing Road in Wembley, a unique hub of Indian shops and cafés. One of the best budget meals here is at Sakonis (129 Ealing Road, HA0 4BP, 8903 9601, www.sakonis.co.uk), which is always heaving with local Gujju families. Try the masala dosa or dahi wada – and don't expect to pay much for it.

Nowruz

Iranian New Year lands on 21-23 March on the Gregorian calendar and is best celebrated in London's little Middle East – Edgware Road.

The street is home to a large number of the capital's Arabic and Iranian population, and a variety of languages, including Farsi, can be heard outside the street's many kebab shops and shisha lounges. Persian New Year here can feel like a central Tehran bazaar.

For some of the cheapest and most authentic cuisine, head to Patogh (8 Crawford Place, W1H 5NE, 7262 4015). It doesn't stand on ceremony – the decor is basic, the menus laminated and main courses come served on simple metal plates. Try starters of freshly baked persian bread with *masto khiar* (yogurt with cucumber and mint), *masto musir* (yogurt with diced shallots) or houmous, followed by lemon and saffron-marinated chicken or lamb kebabs. The fact that no alcohol is served is not only in keeping with the native tradition, but another let-off for the wallet – though you can always bring your own.

Russian 'Old' New Year

The Soviet Union adopted the Gregorian calendar in 1918, but Russians still celebrate 'Old New Year' (that is, New Year according to the Tsarist calendar), which falls on 13-14 January. The Russian Winter Festival no longer takes place in London; instead, look out for the Russian Sun Festival (www.maslenitsa.co.uk) in February, celebrating the start of spring. The week-long extravaganza includes music, food, art, literature, kids' entertainment and usually an event in Trafalgar Square.

Chinese New Year

911-920 *Get your mojo working*

Ronnie Scott's main stage may be prohibitively expensive these days, but that's not to say that there are no London venues catering to the hard-up jazzer – far from it. Here are ten to try.

Boat-Ting

A jazz session based on a boat. Held on the first Monday of the month, Boat-Ting has established itself at the best weird-yet-wonderful, free jazz/poetry night in town – all for £8. Featuring three off-kilter combinations of cello/voice/guitar/bass/drums/laptop each night, the bizarre but friendly atmosphere is enhanced by poetry readings. *Temple Pier, Victoria Embankment, WC2R 2PN (8133 6045, www.boat-ting.co.uk).*

Bull's Head

A venerable Thames-side pub that won a reputation for hosting modern jazz in the 1960s, but today specialises in mainstream British jazz and swing. It's now part of the Geronimo Inns chain and has had a revamp, but the back-room jazz club is as reliable as ever, with gigs nightly. *373 Lonsdale Road, SW13 9PY (8876 5241, www.thebullshead.com).*

Charlie Wright's Music Bar

A newly refurbished jazz bar in the heart of trendy Hoxton, Charlie Wright's (founded 1992) has established itself as one of the most exciting new-jazz venues in the capital. London's equivalent of New York's legendary 55 Bar, this is very much a 'players' club, attracting a new generation of jazz virtuosos, as well as quite a few international heavyweights, both in the diverse modern jazz programme and also at its high-energy late-night jam sessions. *45 Pitfield Street, N1 6DA (7490 8345, www. charliewrights.com).*

East Side Jazz Club

This lovely, atmospheric pub venue in Leytonstone has consistently booked big jazz names from the UK scene for its monthly gigs. Yet the USP here is seeing the likes of Acoustic Ladyland's Pete Wareham playing 'straight ahead' jazz without any postmodern irony in a relaxed 'pick up' band setting. *Tommy Flynn's, 692 High Road, E11 3AA (8989 8129, www.eastsidejazzclub.blogspot.com).*

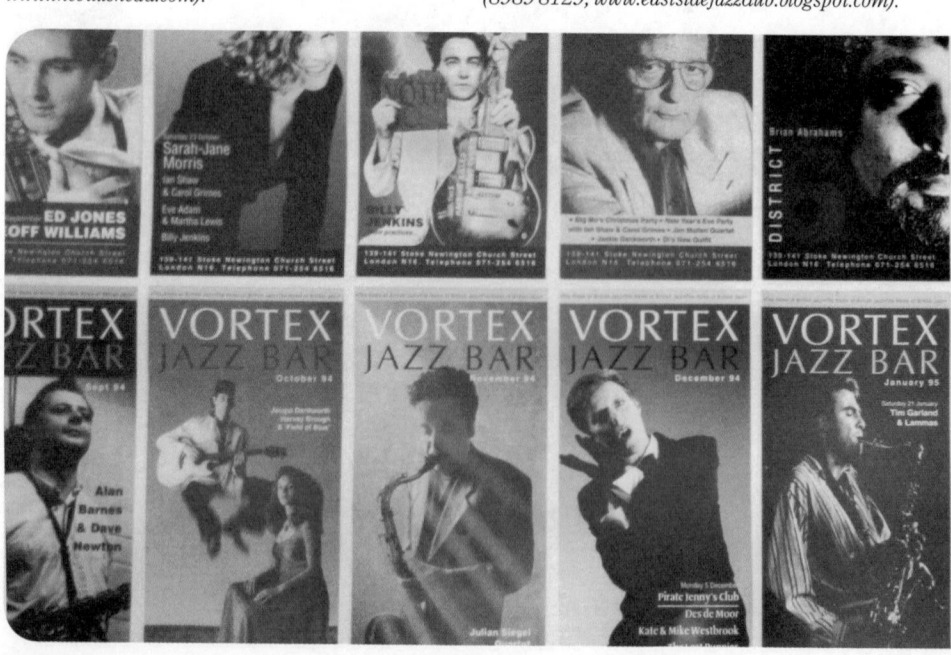

Jazzlive @ the Crypt

There's something both magical and mysterious about walking into this basement jazz club, situated under an imposing church a stone's throw from the centre of Camberwell. Attracting a loyal and knowledgeable jazz audience, this charming, quirky venue hosts many high-calibre (and often cutting-edge) jazz and world music acts. The no-nonsense food is a real plus, as is the well-stocked (and cheap) bar.
Crypt, St Giles Church, 81 Camberwell Church Street, SE5 8RB (www.jazzlive.co.uk).

Ronnie's Bar, Upstairs at Ronnie Scott's

Once destined to be an exclusive members' bar under the old management regime, this is now the hippest late-night hangout in central London thanks to the club's new, inclusive attitude. With its plush decor and funky vibe, general admission is a steal. Musicians can get in for free on the now-packed Jazz Jam nights, while themed vocal, Latin and funk jazz nights make up a lively late-night weekly programme (free-£10). There's even a regular live improvised tap-dancing event. Expect to queue if you arrive late.
47 Frith Street, W1D 4HT (7439 0747, www.ronniescotts.co.uk/ronniesbar).

606 Club

The 606 is still run by flautist/saxophonist Steve Rubie (who took over in 1976). As well as retaining its original street number (its first home was on the King's Road), it's also hung on to its intimate but swinging atmosphere. Programming mainly classic hard bop jazz artists such as sax greats Peter King, Bobby Wellins and Mornington Lockett, the club also features fine blues, soul and funk artists. Note that on Friday and Saturday nights, the entrance fee rises to (just) more than £10.
90 Lots Road, SW10 0QD (7352 5953, www.606club.co.uk).

Spice of Life

Another stalwart of London's Soho music scene, the Spice has been around for more than 60 years, taking in blues, funk and trad jazz (with a regular Friday afternoon big-band session). It's also nurtured many of the new generation of jazz musicians, and there are jazz sessions every Wednesday and Thursday nights.
6 Moor Street, W1D 5NA (7437 7013, www.spiceoflifesoho.com).

Upstairs at the Ritzy

Brixton's beautiful Ritzy cinema is further enhanced by a well-designed upstairs café area that offers an intimate space for a huge selection of often free music nights – as well as jazz, there's blues, roots, reggae and more, plus regular album launches. Look out for Cool Struttin' (afternoon of the third Sunday of the month); full listings on Facebook.
Brixton Oval, Coldharbour Lane, SW2 1JG (0871 902 5739, www.picturehouses.com).

Vortex

Widely regarded as London's hippest jazz club, this cosy venue puts on the cream of today's contemporary jazz scene. While international luminaries such as Tim Berne, Vinicius Cantuaria and John Taylor have all played at Vortex, the imaginative and eclectic nightly programme ensures speculative visits are rewarded with a diverse selection of artists from the top drawer of the jazz spectrums.
11 Gillett Square, N16 8AZ (7254 4097, www.vortexjazz.co.uk).

921-924

Get some wickets

London landmarks such as White Conduit Street in Islington, Lincoln's Inn Fields and, of course, Lord's, are key locations in cricket's venerable history. However, until recently the game was almost extinct in inner London (though a common sight out of the city and more bucolic areas such as Kew). Things only began to improve when the charities Cricket 4 Change (www.cricketforchange.org.uk) and Capital Kids Cricket (www.capitalkidscricket.org.uk) started campaigns to restore the game to urban areas. You'll now find thriving cricket leagues in Regent's Park and Victoria Park, with many inner-city schools involved. See the websites for more details.

Club cricket remains, on the other hand, quintessentially suburban. The sport is organised on a county basis, and top clubs play in Premier Leagues where recreational and professional teams compete. The season runs from late April to mid September and games are free for spectators, plus there's usually a bar to help jolly the afternoon along. For all the details of both clubs and fixtures, consult the following websites: Essex League (www.essexcricket.com), Middlesex League (www.middlesexccl.com), Kent League (www.kcl.uk.net) and Surrey Championship (www.surreychampionship.com).

If you're after something more bucolic, simply head off into the countryside around the capital. You won't have to go far before you find a village green with two sets of stumps pitched – and possibly even a welcoming pub on the corner.

The following are all good grounds within London where you can catch matches:

Wanstead & Snaresbrook Cricket Club (Essex)
Overton Drive, E11 2LW (8989 5566, www.wanstead.hitscricket.com).
Blackheath Cricket Club (Kent)
Rectory Field, Charlton Road, SE3 8SR (8858 1578, www.blackheathcc.com).
Finchley Cricket Club (Middlesex)
East End Road, N3 2TA (8346 1822, www.finchleycricket.co.uk).
Dulwich Cricket Club (Surrey)
Burbage Road, SE24 9HP (7274 1242, www.dulwichcc.com).

925-926

See (bits of) Buckingham Palace

The State Rooms and garden of Buckingham Palace cost more than £10 to see and they're only open in August and September. However, throughout the year two lesser known, and in some ways more rewarding, bits of the Queen's official London residence can be visited – each for less than a tenner.

The Royal Mews (admission £9) are the Queen's stables (and garage), complete with Georgian riding school and magnificent horses, as well as a pungent saddlery, impressively sumptuous state carriages and the odd customised Rolls-Royce (aka Her Majesty's motor). The Queen's Gallery (£10), erected in the 1950s on the ruins of the palace's bomb-damaged private chapel, and recently renovated at great expense, shows changing selections from the Royal Collection of fine art, sculpture, furniture and porcelain.

Royal Mews & Queen's Gallery *Buckingham Palace, SW1A 1AA (7766 7301, www.royalcollection.org.uk). Combined ticket £17.10.*

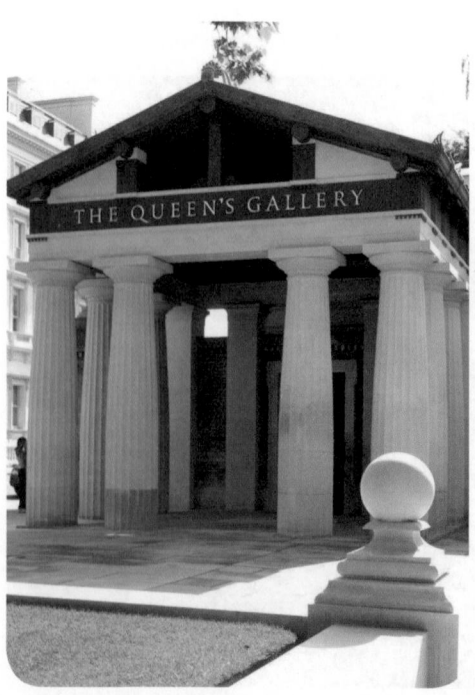

927-930 Indulge in tea and cake

Tea at the Ritz and other 'ritzy' London hotels will set you back anything up to £40. Here we pick some of our favourite tearooms where you'll come away with change from a tenner.

Bea's of Bloomsbury

Dusky blue walls and plush velvet chairs add a glamorous contrast to the bakery that sits at the back of this friendly café. Teas from prestige specialist Jing (earl grey, english breakfast, green tea and a couple of herbal options) are offered alongside excellent coffee and chai lattes made with Cordon Bleu-trained Bea's own concoction of organic darjeeling tea and spices. Cakes are in the French and American traditions: chocolate truffle, cheesecakes, red velvet and pretty cupcakes. Bea's now has branches in Farringdon and by St Paul's Cathedral.
44 Theobald's Road, WC1X 8NW (7242 8330, www.beasofbloomsbury.com).

Le Chandelier

Both tea and cake are in plentiful supply at Le Chandelier. More than 30 varieties of loose-leaf tea by Jing are stacked in jars, while the cakes cause passers-by to ogle through the window. Piled high and wide, they cover the gamut of confections from cupcakes and brownies to billowing meringues and grown-up cheesecakes, and are ordered daily from various local suppliers. The scones, however, are baked in-house. The salon setting – a sort of grand French, British and Middle Eastern fusion – is a suitably special backdrop.
161 Lordship Lane, SE22 8HX (8299 3344, www.lechandelier.co.uk).

High Tea of Highgate

Tea cosies illustrated with dogs, hearts and Union Jacks, cow-shaped milk jugs, cute aprons, porcelain jelly moulds and bags of humbugs provide a colourfully retro take on the traditional village tearoom in this most traditional of London villages. You can hear the hand-mixer whirring away behind the counter as owner Georgina Worthington whips up a fresh victoria sponge or carrot cake. A cream tea costs £6.95.
50 Highgate High Street, N6 5HX (8348 3162, www.highteaofhighgate.com).

Orange Pekoe

A pretty tearoom huddled neatly among the boutiques of Barnes, just a stone's throw from the river, Orange Pekoe has a shop boasting over 100 high-quality teas. Owner Marianna Hadjigeorgiou uses teapots with a removable filter, so you can brew your tea to the perfect strength. There are some spectacular cakes and very popular savoury dishes, and the cream tea (£8.95) includes two big, warm own-made scones – one sultana, one plain.
3 White Hart Lane, SW13 0PX (8876 6070, www.orangepekoeteas.com).

Bea's of Bloomsbury

931

Watch fireworks all year round
Why limit fireworks viewing to the Fifth of November? Other pyrotechnic highlights of the capital's calendar include Diwali, Chinese New Year, the Lord Mayor's Show and, of course, New Year's Eve on the river.

932

See the poetry in modern architecture

The heart of the City doesn't necessarily feel like the most auspicious spot for a poetic experience, but if you sit on the stone benches that circle the base of the 'Gherkin' (30 St Mary Axe, EC3A 8EP) that is exactly what you'll have. Incised on each bench, one line at a time, is *An Arcadian Dream Garden* by eccentric, neoclassical-modernist Scottish artist Ian Hamilton Finlay. Could he have been thinking about the Gherkin itself when he wrote: 'A slender stone vase…', 'A tree, pierced right through by a bronze arrow'?

933

Rise with the birds

London's bird-lovers have taken to International Dawn Chorus Day with enthusiasm since it was initiated for the UK (in Birmingham) back in 1984. It's now a truly international affair, with sightings reported from as far afield as Antarctica and the Caribbean.

There are two approaches to the event, neither of which need cost a brass razoo. Those who can already tell a tweet from a twitter often go it alone in their local park or back garden, then feed their findings back to the official website. Meanwhile, sociable coves and the blissfully ignorant can set the alarm early on the designated day – the first Sunday in May – and head out to one of London's organised events. The prime birdwatching location in London (the WWT Wetland Centre in Barnes) is, unfortunately, out of our price range, notwithstanding the group breakfast, but many local reserves – notably Tower Hamlets Cemetery Park and Roundshaw Downs Local Nature Reserve – are enthusiastic participants, offering free tours. You'll probably have to be up at 4am… but you can always go back to bed afterwards.
www.idcd.info.

934

Play in Coram's Fields

You have to be accompanied by a child to gain entry to Coram's Fields in Bloomsbury. Set up in 1936 as London's first public children's playground, the seven sprawling acres of playgrounds and park are exclusively for the use of children living in or visiting London. There are massive lawns for free play and family picnics, sports pitches, a paddling pool, sandpits, a flying fox and other slides, a pets' corner (sheep, goats, ducks and hens), a sensory play area designed for children with disabilities and a café.
Coram's Fields *93 Guilford Street, WC1N 1DN (7837 6138, www.coramsfields.org).*

935

Listen to the best songs about London

Have a look at *Time Out*'s list of the 100 Best London Songs and see if you agree. In at number one we have 'Waterloo Sunset' (The Kinks, 1967), followed by 'London Calling' (The Clash, 1979), 'West End Girls' (Pet Shop Boys, 1984) and 'Streets of London' (Ralph McTell, 1969) – but there are plenty of lesser-known gems among the top 100 too.
www.timeout.com/london/music/the-100-best-london-songs.

936

Stand at the pagan heart of the City

Set low in the wall opposite Cannon Street station is a glass case protected by an ornate wrought-iron grille. It contains the bare stump of a stone that once stood tall, a pagan menhir at the centre of the Roman city, from which all measurements in the land were once taken. It is said that if the stone ever leaves London, the city will fall.

A few of my favourite things
938-944

Lisa Comfort,
Author,
Sew Over It Vintage

I grew up in the countryside, so I am a fan of big open spaces. At the weekend I love going to Walthamstow Marshes. It has amazing wildlife and in the summer they bring cows down to graze. It's also great for blackberry picking. We often walk all the way to Victoria Park along the canal towpath; I love looking at all the river boats – in another life, I would live on one. It feels like London has a different pace of life by the canal. My favourite garden centre, Growing Concerns (2 Wick Lane, E3 2NA, 8985 3222, www.growingconcerns.org), is here too. The staff are really knowledgeable and very friendly – I can't go in without picking up a new pot plant.

On Sundays, we often mosey down to Chatsworth Road Market (www.chatsworth roade5.co.uk, open noon-4pm). There are some amazing food stalls. My current favourite is Deeney's (www.deeneys.com), who make the most amazing Scottish toasties – try the 'Ham-ish'. We usually pair this with a fruit and veg smoothie from a neighbouring stall. There are also plenty of non-food stalls; I've picked up some lovely second-hand pieces for our home at good prices. Chatsworth is definitely a market for locals, and it's not full of tourists like the other east London markets, Broadway and Columbia Road.

Maeve's Kitchen (181 Lower Clapton Road, E5 8EQ, 8533 1057, www.maeveskitchen. com) is a super local restaurant. It's just perfect for autumn and winter as the menu specialises in stews and broths. It's inexpensive too. The decor is cosy and warm, and they have a wonderful counter covered in hand-painted tiles.

The Russet café (17 Amhurst Terrace, E8 2BT, 3095 9731, http://eatworkart.com/ the-russet), beside Hackney Downs park, is also a favourite – especially for weekend brunch. Dogs are welcome, which is a big plus for us.

My preferred spot for a glass of wine is L'Entrepôt (230 Dalston Lane, E8 1LA, 7249 1176, http://lentrepot.co.uk), tucked next to Hackney Downs train station. They offer over 30 different wines by the glass, and in summer you can sit outside and watch the world drift by. The food is pretty tasty too.

I'm keen on a good pub quiz, especially the one on Tuesdays at the Clapton Hart (231 Lower Clapton Road, E5 8EG, 8985 8124, http://claptonhart.com). My favourite part is the 'foil sculpture round'. It mixes it up a little and gives me the chance to feel I can offer some skills to my team.

The Hackney Mosaic Project (07530 696560, www.hackney-mosaic.co.uk) is run from the pavilion in the middle of Hackney Downs park. It is free to join, and there are drop-in sessions when you can help them create beautiful mosaics, which are then put up around the area.

937
Check out a classy convenience store

It's official. Britain's best corner shop is in E17 (though it isn't actually on a corner). The Walthamstow Village Stores Spar was named Britain's Best Convenience Store at the Convenience Retail Awards a couple of years ago. And this is no ordinary Spar.

You can pick up a pizza made fresh by its Italian chef; home-made bread; or some own-brand artisanal jam (the bacon jam is famous – and has now been joined by a chorizo version). Post-pub munchies shopping never tasted so good. Bottles can be topped up at a refillable wine station, operated by Borough Wines. There's also a Hackney branch (64-66 Brooksby's Walk, E9 6DA, 8986 6242), which also boasts a branch of Rebel Rebel florist.
Village Store *28-30 Orford Road, E17 9AJ (8521 8187, www.eat17.co.uk).*

945 *Let off steam at Kempton*

Kempton Steam Museum is home to the world's largest triple-expansion steam engines, two of them – each is the size of a small block of flats. Built in the late 1920s, these remarkable machines pumped 19 million gallons of water per day to north London, working 24 hours a day, seven days a week. One of the Worthington-Simpson Triples, named 'Sir William Prescott', has been restored to working order. It's an amazing sight, but equally spectacular is the guided tour of the other engine, 'Lady Bessie': it takes you through the ram and turbine floors, past the fascinating (and rare) mercury arc rectifiers and to the top of the engine. And if that weren't enough, the museum has its own, working narrow-gauge steam train to enjoy. Truly one of west London's best kept secrets.

The museum is 'in steam' on a few weekends in September and October; the railway is open most Sundays between March and November – best to check the website before you visit.
Kempton Steam Museum *Snakey Lane, Feltham, Middx TW13 7ND (01932 765 328, www.kempton steam.org). £7.*

Art for art's sake

Mindful of our £10 budget, **Robin Saikia** *takes a tour round the West End's finest – and most expensive – galleries.*

Spending time visiting the lush lairs of London's leading art dealers, either for private views (easy to gatecrash) or simply in search of warmth and edification, is a time-honoured pursuit of the cash-strapped Londoner. It may require a steely frame of mind to ignore the sometimes withering glances of the starchy front-of-house concierges in Bond Street, but the effort is well repaid, because London's leading commercial galleries and auction houses routinely exhibit works of art that are as good as – if not better than – the art on show in the national collections. The West End (for our purposes, both sides of Piccadilly) remains the core of the art world, and the following itinerary is easily walkable and manageable within a day (two, if you're taking your time).

Choose a busy auction house as your first port of call – they're slightly less daunting than an intimate and dimly lit Old Master gallery. Saunter purposefully into Sotheby's (34-35 Old Bond Street, W1S 2RT, 7923 5000, www. sothebys.com) or Christie's (8 King Street, SW1Y 6QT, 7839 9060, www.christies.com)

and disarm the resident ice maiden by asking her what's 'on view' – it could be next week's sale of Old Master paintings or next month's sale of oriental art. Unless you resemble a Texan oil magnate or a Russian oligarch, refrain from making loud and disparaging remarks about the prices or quality of the goods on offer. Instead, muse your way thoughtfully around the exhibits, pausing to inspect the occasional lot. If there is, say, a marvellous piece of Fabergé locked in a cabinet, you may ask to see it or handle it. Don't drop it or steal it.

One of the grandest, most civilised and most welcoming galleries in London is Philip Mould (18-19 Pall Mall, SW1Y 5LU, 7499 6818, www.philipmould.com). Mould specialises in museum-quality portraits of important people from the Tudor period to the present day, and a visit here might include a fire-damaged Charles II; Elizabeth I in the first flush of youth; Bonnie Prince Charlie's brother, Cardinal Henry; and a sensitive early portrait of Henry VIII, yet to become the harsh, unbending tyrant of later years.

Philip Mould

On the other side of Piccadilly, in St James's, is the Portland Gallery (3 Bennet Street, SW1 1RP, 7493 1888, www.portlandgallery.com), representing the unimpeachable face of British contemporary art. Here, the pictures and sculpture are unlikely to frighten, unnerve or annoy you; instead, a visit should prove an appropriate antidote, should one be needed, to the hurly-burly of the YBA scene – and a cost-effective alternative to tea in Fortnum & Mason. Expect masterly London scenes by Nick Botting, glimmering and glittering visions of Venice by Alexander Creswell, sexually charged couples by Jack Vettriano, and meditative seascapes by Sophie Macpherson.

Nearby is Chris Beetles (8 & 10 Ryder Street, SW1Y 6QB, 7839 7551, www.chrisbeetles.com), a leading specialist in British watercolours and illustrators. There is always entertaining work to be seen here: a drawing of a steely and self-assured Kenneth Clark by Ronald Searle, for instance; genially mad contraptions by Heath Robinson; pop-eyed cats playing golf by Louis Wain; dashing Italian views by Brabazon, and Winnie the Pooh as Roman emperor by EH Shepard. In recent years, Beetles has shown photography too: some elegant work by Snowden (Jack Nicholson, David Bowie, the Queen, Anthony Blunt) and Terry O'Neill (Frank Sinatra, Robert Redford, Pierce Brosnan, Bowie again, Bridget Bardot and a strikingly provocative Marianne Faithfull).

Arguably the best dealer in Dutch Old Masters in the world is Johnny van Haeften (13 Duke Street, SW1Y 6DB, 7930 3062, www.johnnyvan haeften.com). Here, you can enjoy Brueghel's skating peasants; drink-crazed boors or desperate alchemists by Teniers; or a magnificent tulip by Bosschaert. Next door is Derek Johns (12 Duke Street, SW1Y 6BN, 7839 7671, www.derekjohns.co.uk) who deals in important Italian, Spanish and French Old Masters – there is a fair chance of seeing work by Canaletto, Guardi, Francesco Zanin, Tiepolo, Goya, Murillo and Ingres.

Finally, on the other side of Piccadilly again, there are about two dozen galleries in Cork Street, a location that has successfully managed to preserve its reputation as a cradle for contemporary art. Favourites include the Mayor Gallery (21 Cork Street, W1S 3LZ, 7734 3558, www.mayorgallery.com) and Waddington Custot Galleries (11 Cork Street, W1S 3LT, 7851 2200, www.waddingtoncustot.com). At the Mayor, you can see the latest multi-million pound art phenomenon – contemporary Chinese art by painters such as Chang Xugong and Chen Weimin. A visit to the unassailably cosmopolitan Waddington's should give you a firm grounding in most of the things that really matter in the art world on either side of the Atlantic: Picasso, Moore, Robert Indiana, Barry Flanagan (refer knowingly to his 'hares', for under no circumstances are they rabbits), Josef Albers (yes, very like Rothko) and many more.

Chris Beetles

955 Have a drink in a car park

Forget the West End – for a truly sky-high cocktail experience in London, head to the top of a multi-storey car park in Peckham. The slightly ramshackle bar and barbecue is open from July to September. Cross your fingers for good weather, but if it starts to rain you can huddle under a large red canopy.

Frank's Café *Level 10, Peckham multi-storey car park, 95A Rye Lane, SE15 4ST (07582 884574, www.frankscafe.org.uk)*

956 Horse around with the Guards

For a glimpse of the capital's military splendour, trot over to the Household Cavalry Museum to see how this regiment has protected the royal family for nearly 350 years. The museum houses a wealth of artefacts, from silver kettledrums given to the regiment in 1831, to displays explaining its role during recent conflicts. You'll also get a fascinating behind-the-scenes peek at the 18th-century stables, where the horses are still fed, watered and groomed for parade, as well as a chance to try on the regimental uniform.

To see the troopers in action, don't miss the daily Changing the Queen's Life Guard: the New Guard rides from Hyde Park Barracks at 10.28am to Horse Guards Parade (earlier on Sundays) to replace the Old Guard at 11am. The Dismounting Ceremony, which takes place in the courtyard of the Horse Guards building is also definitely worth seeing. It began in 1894, when Queen Victoria discovered the entire guard gambling and drinking while on duty. She punished them with an inspection to be carried out at 4pm daily.

Household Cavalry Museum *Horse Guards, Whitehall, SW1A 2AX (7930 3070, www. householdcavalrymuseum.co.uk). £7.*

957 Take in the calm of Chiswick House & Gardens

For a glimpse of earthly paradise amid west London's urban bustle, head to graceful Chiswick House and its beautiful gardens. This is the birthplace of the English Landscape movement, which bulldozed formal gardens in favour of sweeping elegance. The magnificent neo-Palladian villa was conceived as a kind of giant cabinet to display its owner's art and book collection; and the garden's grand vistas and hidden pathways (looking particularly splendid after a £12 million restoration project) influenced designs as far afield as New York's Central Park. Lord Burlington, who completed the villa in 1729, entertained such luminaries as Handel, Alexander Pope and Jonathan Swift, while, in the Swinging Sixties, the Beatles filmed promos for *Paperback Writer* and *Rain* here. Why not join them?

Chiswick House *Burlington Lane, W4 2RP (8995 0508, www.chgt.org.uk). £6.30.*

958

Be dazzled by the Waddeson Bequest

The new gallery at the British Museum (Great Russell Street, WC1B 3DG, 7323 8299, www.britishmuseum.org), Room 2a, is something special. The bare facts are rather mundane: Baron Ferdinand Rothschild MP (1839-98), a wealthy man and avid gatherer of religious artefacts and objets d'art, gave his collection to the British Museum, of which he had been a trustee since 1896. He had been assembling this *Kunstkammer* – Renaissance-style 'art chamber' – throughout his life, adding to items originally gathered in Frankfurt by his father, Baron Anselm von Rothschild (1803-74), to beautify the New Smoking Room of his Buckinghamshire home, Waddeson Manor. Finally put on display in 2015, the Waddeson Bequest is a revelation.

If you're expecting gold and precious jewels, you won't be disappointed. Yet that is only part of the story. It is really the benefactor-collector's taste that is on display.

Just to the left of the entrance, for example, is the Holy Thorn Reliquary, a gaudy little container for a thorn from Christ's crown, decorated with rubies, sapphires and pearls, dating from 1400. A wooden St George, the size of a hobbit and with a face as smooth as that of a doll, stands with his foot on a tiny dragon's throat, the saint's valour profoundly undermined by the meagre stature of his foe, in a way that the German designers of this altar guard surely did not anticipate. Nearby, you'll find a precious tooth-and earpick set from about 1600, and a pretty little spatula-shaped knife, enamelled and decorated with agates. The latter was a tool for circumcision, probably faked in mid 19th-century Aachen to meet a sudden European fashion for collecting items associated with Jewish social life and ritual.

Much of the work on display in this gallery is simply exquisite. There is a series of fragile-looking and intricately finished cups made from single nautilus shells, as well as vessels made of rock crystal or amber that are so perfectly lit as to seem to glow from within.

The display even introduced us to a whole new genre of craftsmanship: microsculpture. From about 1500, supreme artists from the northern Netherlands began to carve devotional stories in boxwood, but in such close and tiny detail that it is easy to walk past. Look carefully, though, and you'll see multitudes of minute people, each of them rendered in realistic detail.

For us, the real highlight of the collection is modestly tucked to the right of the entrance, in a case with its back to the entrance wall. The Lycurgus Cup is made of glass with specks of gold and silver in it, a mixture that changes colour depending on how light shines through it.

The engraved cage design of the cup is impressive: it shows Lycurgus, king of Thrace, being strangled by magical vines after foolishly attacking Dionysus, the god of wine. But the curators have designed the display so that the cup changes in less than a minute from the opaque greeny white of an old man's cataract – snot green, if you wanted to be rude – to an intense and passionate translucent ruby and black, the red fire growing in the belly of the cup much as it must have done when the vessel was raised aloft at feasts. Even in its sombre case, this simple display raised gasps of awe from the selfie-stick wielders who usually drift past the museum's masterpieces with barely a pause for breath.

959-961

Download some apps

Three of our favourites are Citymapper (free), a great London journey planner, smoothly integrating multi-modal transport – tube, rail, bus and bike – with estimated times; StreetMuseum (free), a brilliant Museum of London app offering archive shots geo-located to where you're standing, with informative captions; and Toiluxe (69p), which tells you where the nearest public loo is in central London.

962-963
Check out London's mosques

There's no mistaking the London Central Mosque in Regent's Park, with its golden dome and stout 140-foot minaret. The main prayer hall is as grand as one might expect – lush red carpets, mosaics and an impressive chandelier – but this centre for British Muslims also houses a library, offices, an events venue and a bookshop. Its history goes back to World War II, when Churchill's War Cabinet put aside £100,000 for the site, though the mosque was actually built in the 1970s.

Up to 50,000 Muslims visit during the two main Islamic festivals, Eid al-Fitr and Eid al-Adha; and at lunchtime on Fridays (the main day of worship), the place is usually overflowing. Visitors are allowed in any time the mosque is open, though women must cover their heads (headscarves are available from the bookshop) and both sexes must cover their legs to below the knee. Guided tours are also available if you call ahead.

Also impressive is the towering complex of the East London Mosque in Whitechapel – one of the biggest mosques in Britain. Building work began in the 1980s and it has continued to grow steadily since; the most recent addition is the London Muslim Centre. If you'd just like to visit the building, ring ahead first.

London Central Mosque & Islamic Cultural Centre *146 Park Road, NW8 7RG (7724 3363, www.iccuk.org).*

East London Mosque & London Muslim Centre *46-92 Whitechapel Road, E1 1JX (7650 3000, www.eastlondonmosque.org.uk).*

964-968
Knit for nowt

Knitting is a fun yet (potentially) frugal pastime, and one that's easy to turn into a social event, whether you're a complete beginner or simply enjoy knitting in a convivial environment. The new generation of modish yarn shops are friendly and inclusive in a way that seems to be typical of the craft. All the ones we list here offer advice, drop-in sessions and a sense of community (as well as classes, though these usually break the £10 barrier); they also tend to be run by self-confessed knitting fanatics.

I Knit London in Waterloo describes itself as 'a shop and a sanctuary', and the same ethos is true of east London's Prick Your Finger, Crouch End's Nest and Islington's Loop. South London florist and café You Don't Bring Me Flowers is also getting in on the act, running an informal knit club on Tuesday afternoons. Have a look at www.castoff.info or www.knitchicks.co.uk for an idea of the number and variety of events out there.

I Knit London *106 Lower Marsh, SE1 7AB (7621 1338, www.iknit.org.uk).*

Loop *15 Camden Passage, N1 8EA (7288 1160, www.loopknitting.com).*

Nest *102 Weston Park, N8 9PP (8340 8852, www.nestknitting.com).*

Prick Your Finger *260 Globe Road, E2 0JD (8981 2560, www.prickyourfinger.com).*

You Don't Bring Me Flowers *15 Staplehurst Road, SE13 5ND (8297 2333, www.youdontbringme flowers.co.uk).*

969-970

Collect bits of old London Bridge

The medieval, 19-arch London Bridge – once cluttered with houses, shops and heads on sticks – was finally demolished in 1831, but you can still catch a glimpse of a few of its ancient fixtures and fittings. Most incredible of all of them is the royal coat of arms that adorns the front of the King's Arms pub in Newcomen Street, off Borough High Street. It was salvaged from the stone gateway that stood at the southern end of the old bridge until 1760, and shows the arms of George III.

From 1762 comes a collection of stone alcoves, which were installed at regular intervals on the bridge to prevent pedestrians being trampled under hoof by the traffic when the last of the teetering buildings were cleared from the bridge. Needless to say, they were quickly pressed into alternative service by dossers, beggars, footpads, thimble-riggers and their dog-eyes, street hawkers and tuppenny molls. Two of them survive in Hackney's Victoria Park, and you'll find another closer to its original home in the grounds of Guy's Hospital.

971

Volunteer at a vineyard

Calling all oenophiles – you don't need to cross the M25, let alone the Channel, to discover some grape action. Forty Hall Vineyard is a ten-acre organic vineyard that's part of Forty Hall Farm in suburban Enfield, on the edge of north London. A social enterprise scheme that provides work for people with learning difficulties, the vineyard also relies on volunteers in every aspect of the work, from planting the vines to harvesting the grapes and general maintenance – and, of course, tasting the latest vintage. It's still early days: the inaugural harvest was in 2013, and the first sparkling wine arrived in autumn 2015, so you'll be aiding the early growth of the enterprise – London's first commercial vineyard since the Middle Ages.
www.fortyhallvineyard.org.uk.

972

Reconnoitre the City's less familiar Wrens

St Paul's Cathedral may be Sir Christopher Wren's most famous creation, but the architect was notably prolific and there are many other fine churches in the vicinity that can be visited for free. If you start on the west side of Ludgate Circus and look up to St Paul's, the black spire in front of the dome is St Martin within Ludgate, while St Bride's is hidden behind you. The latter's steeple is the tallest of any Wren church and was supposedly the model for the classic tiered wedding cake. Veer left when you reach the cathedral and on your left you'll see Temple Bar, another Wren creation. It originally stood at the western end of Fleet Street to mark the boundary between the Cities of London and Westminster, but now marks the entrance to Paternoster Square. Cross the square, emerging on to Newgate Street, and Christ Church is opposite. Almost destroyed during World War II, the ruined nave is today a lovely rose garden. Head east to Gresham Street for the Wren motherlode: first, St Anne & St Agnes, with its leafy churchyard; then, a glimpse of the tower of St Alban, Wood Street; next you pass St Lawrence Jewry, the church of the Corporation of London; and finally, when Gresham Street becomes Lothbury, St Margaret Lothbury. This has one of the loveliest interiors of any Wren church, and the impressive wood screen is by Wren himself.

Over at Bank tube station, take the Mansion House exit and turn left for St Stephen Walbrook, Wren's most grandiose church, a mass of creamy stone with a soaring dome, fabulously bulbous pulpit and a slightly incongruous modern altar by Henry Moore. Near Cannon Street station, on Abchurch Lane, you'll find St Mary Abchurch, a real gem with a shallow, painted dome and a beautiful carved reredos by Grinling Gibbons. It was shattered into 2,000 pieces by a wartime bomb but painstakingly pieced together again afterwards.

973 *Bob on Apple Day*

Despite sounding more like an ancient pagan ritual, or perhaps a corruption of the Christian harvest festival, this celebration of apples, orchards and locally grown food actually only dates from 1990 (though bobbing for apples has been around for much longer). There are events all over the country, including in London, with Borough Market (7407 1002, www.borough market.org.uk) a great place to dunk, bob, eat and drink this quintessentially English fruit, in all its many varieties. It takes place around the nearest Sunday to 21 October. *www.commonground.org.uk.*

974-983 *Follow some vintage advice*

In search of cheap thrills from an earlier era, Derek Hammond plunders some old London guidebooks.

The *London Spy* was London's first-ever guidebook, published in 1703 to shout up the pleasures of dog-tossing, gaming and baiting lunatics in Bedlam. But it isn't just the long-disappeared aspects of Dickensian/Swinging/Thatcher's London that stand out when you pick up an old guide for pennies from a second-hand bookshop – there's also a surprisingly broad swathe of places, possibilities and things to do that remain strangely constant – and affordable.

Pop in to the Anchor, Bankside

'What more would you have than a tankard of ale where the greatest of all Englishmen used to have his?' demands HE Popham in his brilliantly swashbuckling *Guide to London Taverns* (Claude Stacey, 1927). 'If you prefer a West End hotel, with gold-laced flunkeys to bow you in, and a drink that costs five shillings a glass, for goodness sake leave us here and take yourself westward in the first cab that you can find, or swim upriver if you prefer it. We don't care. We are for a game of darts with our riverside friends in the taproom.' Shakespeare may be no more likely to turn up now than he was 90-odd years ago, but, on the plus side, the Anchor (34 Park Street, SE1 9EF, 7407 1577, www.taylor-walker.co.uk) has added a smart drinking area right by the river.

Gaze at a 'Roman' curio

'At 5 Strand Lane is an antiquarian's mystery,' teases Harold F Hutchinson, author of London Transport's *Visitor's London* (1954), 'and no reputable authority will vouch for its latinity. But it is an interesting relic.' It remains a thrill to dodge down this dingy alley off the Strand and shade your eyes in order to see into this spring-fed plunge bath – still in working order, and handling around 2,000 gallons of fresh spring water a day. 'The oval lead overflow pipe is considered to be genuinely Roman,' Harold stuck his neck out, 'but the bricks are more probably Tudor.'

Buy your own hanky on Petticoat Lane

'Thousands pack into Petticoat Lane between the sweatshops and bomb sites on Sunday morning, and it is the nearest thing London can offer to an Oriental bazaar.' So reckoned VS Pritchett in 1962, when Harvest published *London Perceived*. 'They used to say that you could walk through this market and see your own handkerchief on sale on a stall by the time you got to the end. I was brought up on scandals of a similar kind sold at the dog market in Bethnal Green: you met your own dear Airedale painted black and offered as a retriever.'

Get into ironwork at Leadenhall

'Leadenhall Market is solid and reassuring, and it asserts the Victorians' belief in the virtues of cast iron. The entire market with its adjoining alleys is of the greatest interest to the London virtuoso…' Londonologists don't come any more cultish than the great writer/sketcher Geoffrey Fletcher. *The London Nobody Knows* (Hutchinson, 1962) was his debut outing and subsequently made into a documentary film starring James Mason. Leadenhall Market (www.leadenhallmarket.co.uk) features in both: 'The ironwork is highly elaborated with ornament and the griffins which support the City's coat of arms… discreetly sober. One of the most attractive buildings is the Lamb Tavern, with its large hanging lamps and engraved glass. All is Victorian here, apart from the human element and the delivery vans.'

Let's all go down the Strand… on-the-Green

'A picturesque stretch of tree-lined riverside walk with Georgian houses, a boatyard and a couple of pubs. The City Barge was granted a charter for 500 years by Queen Elizabeth I, and the river entrance has to be sealed up with clay and boarding during high tides.'

Brilliantly grumpy American tourist Betty James went for a stroll down Strand-on-the-Green in Chiswick the very year the Beatles filmed scenes from *Help!* in the City Barge pub. Her *London on £1 a Day* (Batsford, 1965) is truly evocative of the times – and timeless. 'The Bull's Head has an underground tunnel to an island known as Oliver's Eyot. It is said that this tunnel was used by Oliver Cromwell and his Roundheads, which is decidedly peculiar because, as everybody knows, they didn't drink.'

Actually, there are three more-than-decent riverside pubs on Strand-on-the-Green: the City Barge (www.citybargechiswick.com), Bulls Head (ww.chefandbrewer.com) and the Bell & Crown (www.bell-and-crown.co.uk) – and it's the last that has come to the fore in claiming the tunnel myth today. Oliver's Island is now a haven for herons and cormorants.

Be very scared... at a cult leader's spooky Gothic house

'At 12 Langford Place, sheer horror: a Francis Bacon shriek in these affluent, uncomplicated suburbs at the end of Abbey Road. It looks like a normal St John's Wood villa pickled in embalming fluid by some mad doctor...' That's how Ian Nairn described the Victorian charlatan John Hugh Smyth-Pigott's pad in his witty, opinionated architectural bible, *Nairn's London*. The book was published by Penguin in 1967, but he could have written this particular entry yesterday.

Take a perfect London photo

Len Deighton's *London Dossier* is the essential guide for clawing back the mood of London in 1967. Len's own chunks are masterly, but the book also benefits from the multiple perspectives of specialist buddies roped in to write odd chapters – such as Adrian Flowers on photography: 'Some foreigners are most struck by the effect of twilight,' he wrote. 'Certainly some of London's special moments are at this time, as the artificial lights slowly take over... All along the Embankment is good for night shooting, especially the Victoria Embankment and the promenade between Westminster and Lambeth Bridges on the south side.'

Tune in, drop out

Nicholas Saunders was an anarcho-hippy self-publisher with plenty of vital information to pass on about drugs, dole, sex and squats in his psychedelic-coloured *Alternative London*, from 1972. 'There are millions of things you can do in London,' he wrote, 'like yelling at people in Speaker's Corner, climbing every tree in every park, flying kites just about anywhere, but it's best in the middle of Oxford Street or outside Buckingham Palace... See the second half of any play for free, simply by walking in at the interval... Drop in for free entertainment when the light is on over Big Ben: the entrance is the arch in the car park: you can leave your car where it says "Peers only"...' Saunders went on to found Neal's Yard wholefood empire and later wrote another underground classic, *Ecstasy and the Dance Culture* (1995).

Go window-shopping at an auctioneer's

The high-tension atmosphere of auction houses is great fun to drop in on, whether you're bidding on outlandish art yourself – or just watching others sweat it out. 'But they have their own set of rules,' warned Martin Lightfoot in his *Visitor's Guide to London Shopping* (Martlet, 1982), 'and it is well to know roughly how they work before venturing into them. If you watch an auction you will often find it difficult to see who is actually bidding, one reason for this being that the auctioneer may have recorded bids by people not actually present, and is therefore pushing up the bidding by taking a slightly higher bid "off the wall", as they say. There are horror stories of someone sneezing or scratching his ear and finding himself with a £20,000 lot. These stories are complete myths.'

Visit the birthplace of indie

Richard Jobson was the singer in punk band the Skids before he drifted into TV, and so to novels and directing films: no wonder he dealt in muso mythology with a lasting quality. 'The most independent record shop in Britain, Rough Trade was the place where the alternative music scene, born off the back of punk, really matured,' he wrote in the *Insider's Guide to London* (Virgin, 1993). 'Covered with posters from seminal punk and postpunk releases and gigs, the Rough Trade shop is the meeting place for people interested in new music. Now that CDs seem to have taken over completely, it's one of the few places you can get new releases on vinyl.'

984-993

Buy brilliant British beer at London's finest real ale pubs...

We know, we know: it's hard to spend less than £4 on a pint in central London these days, but at least at the following places your money will buy you a great British gourmet treat.

Greenwich Union

This flagship pub of Alistair Hook's laudable Meantime Brewery makes the most of the training and recipes its founder gleaned at age-old institutions in Germany. Meantime produces London Stout, Pale Ale (London and India versions), Porter, Lager, Pilsner, Wheat beer and Yakima Red, plus chocolate and raspberry varieties, all on draught and at reasonable prices.
56 Royal Hill, SE10 8RT (8692 6258, www.greenwichunion.com).

Jerusalem Tavern

Located in an alley behind Farringdon station, this creaking and cosily tatty little pub serves the sought-after ales of Suffolk's St Peter's Brewery. Almost hidden between timber divides, the bar is backed by barrels, their names and ABVs chalked on a board: Suffolk Gold, Organic and even a Whisky Beer. A rag-tag and decidedly loyal crowd muses over the *Evening Standard* crossword or tucks into their moreish roast pork and apple sauce sandwich.
55 Britton Street, EC1M 5UQ (7490 4281, www.stpetersbrewery.co.uk).

Lamb

Founded in 1729, this Young's outpost in Holborn found fame as a theatrical haunt when the A-list included Sir Henry Irving and assorted music hall stars; they're commemorated in old photos and surrounded by well-worn seats, much polished wood and a few vintage knick-knacks. Punters range from discerning students to Gray's Inn barristers, supping from half a dozen pumps – expect real ale from Young's plus a guest beer (perhaps St Austell Tribute).

94 Lamb's Conduit Street, WC1N 3LZ (7405 0713, www.youngs.co.uk/pubs/lamb).

Market Porter

Few market bars stock this range of beers. In an invariably cramped main bar area – there's more room in the back, but the bustle can be off-putting – Borough Market traders and sundry other regulars gather around the likes of Okell's Maclir, Vale Brewery Best, Acorn Brewery Kashmir, Harveys Best and Lund's Bitter. There are choices from Meantime Brewery too – in all, it adds up to around 40 ales a week.

9 Stoney Street, SE1 9AA (7407 2495, www.markettaverns.co.uk).

Pembury Tavern

Drinking in this vast, overlit Hackney bar room feels like rattling round a youth hostel canteen, but the 16 handpumps – mostly fine real ale from Cambridge's Milton Brewery (Pegasus, Sparta, Justinian and their stout Nero on our last visit) – are a delight. Bar billiards and a red-baize pool table on one side give way to bookshelves and board games on the other. Beer festivals take place in February, July and November.

90 Amhurst Road, E8 1JH (8986 8597, www.individualpubs.co.uk/pembury).

Royal Oak

The Royal Oak seems wonderfully trapped in time, complete with its unused hatch for offsales. Serving the great works of Lewes brewery Harveys, the ales – including Mild, Pale, Old, Best and Armada – are nicely priced, and a felt-tipped menu offers classics such as rabbit casserole and lancashire hotpot. Music hall stars Harry Ray and Flanagan & Allen, celebrated in framed handbills, would have tucked into the same.

44 Tabard Street, SE1 4JU (7357 7173, www.harveys.org.uk).

Sultan

In the backstreets of south Wimbledon lies an ale-drinking nirvana, named after an 1830s racehorse. A much-loved, if rather antiseptic locals' boozer, the Sultan is the only London pub owned by Wiltshire's Hop Back Brewery; on the weekly beer club evenings, chattering middle-aged locals enjoy the delights of GFB, Entire Stout and Summer Lightning. Carryouts are also available.

78 Norman Road, SW19 1BT (8542 4532, www.hopback.co.uk).

Wenlock Arms

From the outside, the Wenlock doesn't look like much. To be honest, it doesn't look like much inside either, but God forbid it should ever tear out its carpet or gastro-up its menu of salt-beef bagels and pork pies. On any given night, you might find yourself sitting next to a table of beer-bellied ale-hunters going through the excellent and ever-changing range of beers, and, of course, the eccentric, ever-talkative regulars.

26 Wenlock Road, N1 7TA (7608 3406, http://wenlockarms.com).

White Horse

This stupendously popular west London stalwart does what it does best exceptionally well: it serves a fantastic, even mind-boggling, array of beers. There are over 200 (count 'em) available at any one time, including 30 on draught, eight of them cask ales (the likes of Harveys Sussex Best, Adnams Broadside and rotating guests). And there's always a cask mild, stout and porter on offer, as well as regular beer festivals.

1-3 Parsons Green, SW6 4UL (7736 2115, www.whitehorsesw6.com).

Ye Olde Mitre

Its secluded location requires you to slink down an alleyway just off Hatton Garden, and as you do so you're transported to a parallel pub universe where the clientele are friendly and the staff (in pristine black and white uniforms) briskly efficient. A Monday-to-Friday joint, it opens for just one weekend a year – happily, that's to coincide with the British Beer Festival. Ales are certainly the speciality – Deuchars and Adnams are regulars, with frequently changing guest beers beside them – but the proprietors don't turn their noses up at wine either. Historic, but never dusty.

1 Ely Court (Ely Place side of 8 Hatton Garden), EC1N 6SJ (7405 4751, http://yeoldemitreholborn.co.uk).

994
...or direct from a brewery

Go direct to the brewer for your ale: the Griffin Brewery (Chiswick Lane South, W4 2QB, 8996 2085, www.fullers.co.uk/brewery/brewery-shop) sells the full Fuller's range.

995
Check out the MPs' secret tunnel

In the grand baroque lobby of the St Ermin's Hotel in Westminster, it's easy to overlook the small door given unusual prominence halfway up the grand staircase. Down a tight spiral staircase lies a vaulted 12-foot tunnel – now definitively blocked – which once carried MPs to and from the Houses of Parliament, some 650 yards distant. The Division Bell still sounds in the hotel when it's time for members to return to work and cast their vote.

996
Spot secret creatures at the Natural History Museum

The 70 million specimens housed in the Natural History Museum's galleries – from immense pickled squids to tiny lichens pressed by Charles Darwin – are, of course, mind-boggling: but when did you last look at the actual building (designed by Alfred Waterhouse)? Monkeys scamper up arches in the central hall, huge columns resemble fossilised trees, and outside there are even more statues of animals and plants (the extinct above the east wing, the living to the west). In a final flourish, beautiful paintings of gilded plants – many of them chosen for their economic value to the Empire – look down from the high, broken-arched ceiling.

Natural History Museum *Cromwell Road, SW7 5BD (7942 5000, www.nhm.ac.uk).*

997
Hear a free steel band concert

Do yourself a favour and avoid Notting Hill Carnival crowds by heading instead to the incredible steel drumming of the National Panorama Championship. Every year on the Saturday of Carnival (which is always on the August Bank Holiday weekend), an enthusiastic crowd converges to watch the cream of UK steelpan talent battling it out to be named national champions. In recent years the contest has been held at Emslie Horniman's Pleasance off Ladbroke Grove.

998
Be welcomed into a government office

Want to see London government in action? The 25 London Assembly members call the mayor to account ten times a year at People's Question Time – and anyone can watch: check www.london.gov.uk/get-involved to find out what's next up for discussion. Even if the hurly-burly of live politics doesn't appeal, Lord Foster's motorbike helmet of a building might. The first two floors of City Hall are, subject to a security search on entering, open to the public 8.30am-6pm Monday-Thursday, 8.30am-5.30pm Friday, as well as at some weekends. You can walk up the spiral ramp to visit the temporary exhibitions and view the Assembly Chamber, or descend to the café and – best of all – the London Photomat (on the lower ground floor). This is a walk-on aerial photo of the whole of Greater London, at sufficiently high resolution for you to be able to identify your own house. London's Living Room, located on the top floor and offering fabulous views, is also occasionally open too.

City Hall *Queen's Walk, SE1 2AA (7983 4000, www.london.gov.uk/city-hall).*

999

Explore Somerset House

Start from the river side of the building and head downstairs from the Embankment Galleries. You'll find a free exhibition on the history of Somerset House, complete with ceremonial Thames barge and the strains of Handel's *Water Music*. Next, explore the Studio and Terrace Rooms, which hold intriguing temporary exhibitions. Done? Then it's time to make an investment: cough up £6 to get into the Embankment Galleries themselves, where changing exhibitions highlight the connections between art, architecture and design under inviting titles such as 'Wouldn't it be nice…: Wishful thinking in art and design'.

Or cross the brilliant fountain court – lingering among the choreographed water jets in summer or laughing at the tumbling ice-skaters in winter – and pay £7 (children are free) to head into the Courtauld Gallery (7848 2526, www.courtauld.ac.uk/gallery). This is one of the country's best collections of paintings – diverse and compelling, yet on a more manageable scale than, say, the National Gallery. Sensational Old Masters, Impressionists and post-Impressionists are displayed in atmospherically creaky rooms, alongside prints, drawings and sculpture. Key works here include Cranach's *Adam and Eve*, Manet's *Bar at the Folies-Bergère*, Van Gogh's *Self-Portrait with Bandaged Ear* and Gauguin's *Nevermore*.

Snack options include a big branch of Fernandez & Wells, Tom's Deli and Pennethorne's café/bar; in warm weather, there are outdoor tables and chairs ranged around the courtyard. **Somerset House** *The Strand, WC2R 1LA (7845 4600, www.somersethouse.org.uk).*

1000 *Get to the top…*

… of the Monument (Monument Street, EC3R 8AH, 7626 2717, www.themonument.info). The recipient of an impressive £4.5 million refurbishment, Sir Christopher Wren and Robert Hooke's memorial to the Great Fire of London is the world's tallest free-standing column and, unlike other high points in the city (such as the London Eye or St Paul's Cathedral, to name just a couple) it'll only cost you four quid to get to the top. Scaling the internal spiral staircase, with its 311 steps, may make you a little tired and dizzy, but what the hell – you'll have London at your feet.

A-Z index

Note: number refers to page, not list entry.

I

Thematic index

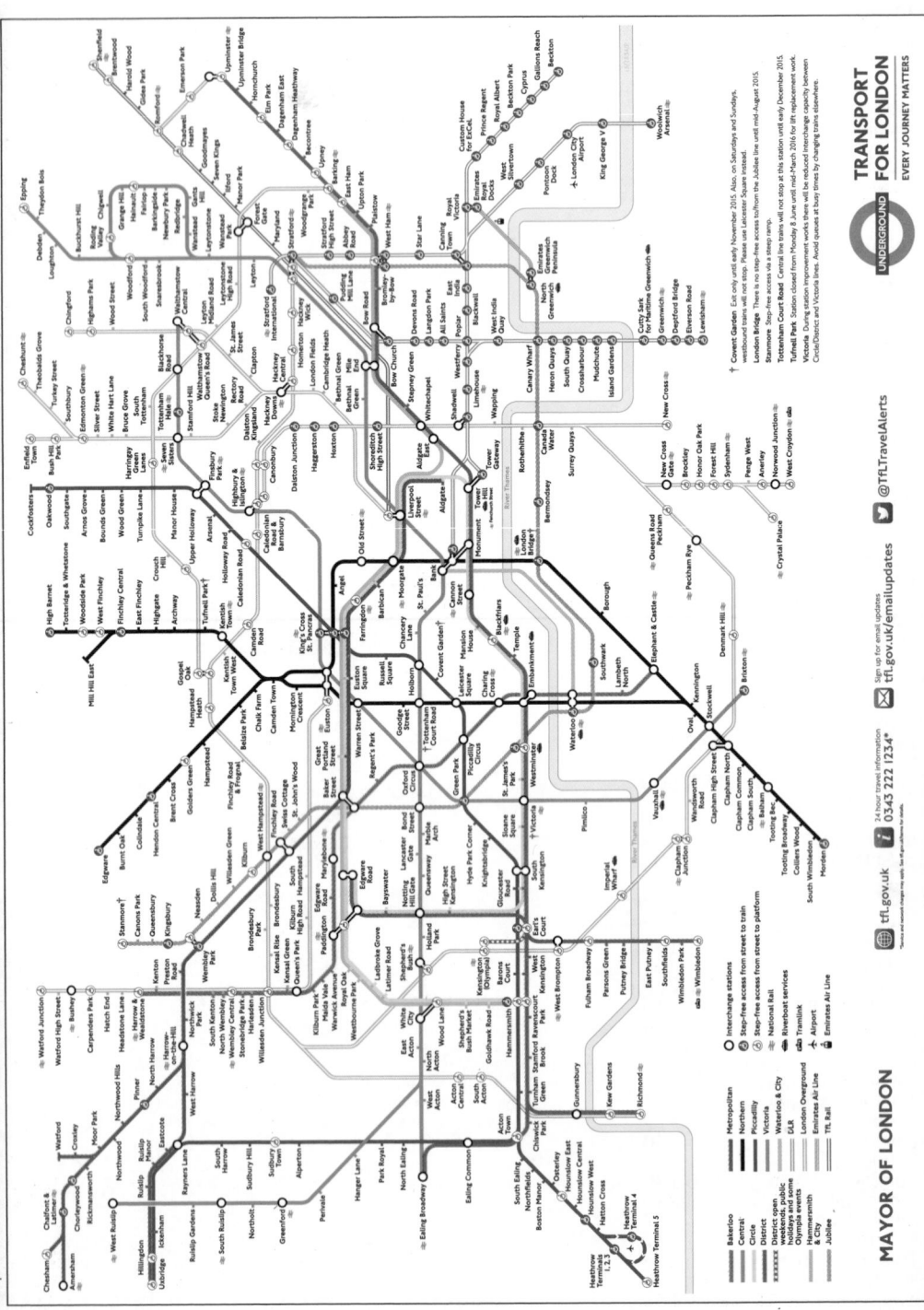